The new environmental age

MAX NICHOLSON

The new environmental age

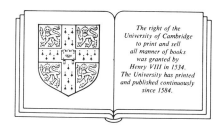

The right of the
University of Cambridge
to print and sell
all manner of books
was granted by
Henry VIII in 1534.
The University has printed
and published continuously
since 1584.

CAMBRIDGE UNIVERSITY PRESS
Cambridge
New York   New Rochelle
Melbourne   Sydney

Published by the Press Syndicate of the University of Cambridge
The Pitt Building, Trumpington Street, Cambridge CB2 1RP
32 East 57th Street, New York. NY 10022, USA
10 Stamford Road, Oakleigh, Melbourne 3166, Australia

© Cambridge University Press 1987

First published 1987
First paperback edition 1989

Printed in Great Britain at Billing & Sons Ltd, Worcester

British Library cataloguing-in-publication data

Nicholson, Max
The new environmental age.

1. Environmental protection – History   2. Environmental protection –
Political aspects
1. Title
333.7'2'09   TD1702

Library of Congress cataloguing-in-publication data

Nicholson, Max.
The new environmental age.

Includes index.
1. Nature conservation.   2. Nature conservation – History.   3. Environmental
protection.   4. Environmental protection – History.   I. Title.
QH75.N53 1987   333.7'2   86–33431

ISBN 0 521 33522 1 hard covers
ISBN 0 521 37992 X paperback

SE

CONTENTS

ILLUSTRATIONS

FOREWORD

Max Nicholson was one of the environmental revolutionaries of the early post war years. His appropriately named book *The Environmental Revolution* had a significant impact, and I am sure that it influenced many people in their thinking about the very grave threats to the natural environment.

I believe that this new book will be equally valuable. It is quite true that there is a much greater popular understanding of the dangers we are creating for ourselves by ignoring the well-being of the whole natural system. Mankind cannot exist in isolation from the rest of the living world. It is his life-support system and he damages it at his dire peril. Those of us alive at the present time may feel that there is no serious urgency because what we see of the natural world looks more or less alright. I feel that it is wholly immoral to disregard our obligations to future generations.

Carl Jung, writing in *Psychology and Religion* said:

> Western man has no need of more superiority over nature. Whether outside or inside. He has both in almost devilish perfection. What he lacks is conscious recognition of his inferiority to the nature around and within him. He must learn that he may not do exactly as he wills. If he does not learn this, his own nature will destroy him.

It is one thing to be conscious of the damage we are doing; it is quite another matter to come to understand how to repair the damage already done and how to limit further damage in the future. I believe that the value of this book is that it explains what needs to be done if future generations are to have any natural environment to inherit or, indeed, whether they will have any hope of survival.

However, I must add that Max Nicholson has always held strong views and opinions and these have not invariably been accepted without question. This in no way detracts from the value of this book, which I hope will stimulate the reader to think about these issues and to come to his own conclusions.

1986

PREFACE

During the past quarter of a century, environmental conservation has rocketed from obscurity to a position of world influence. Its network of observers watches the remotest forests, the most inaccessible ocean waters, and the best-guarded establishments from which pollution of any sort may come. Its researches present embarrassing challenges to experimenters with questionable technology. Its films, television and radio programs, and reports bring weekly into many millions of homes authentic pictures of the natural world and its manmade problems. Where necessary it organises public events, task forces and even confrontational operations. Its interventions must be taken seriously by any interests, public or private, no matter how powerful, which impinge on the environment. It is, however, an active participant in working agreements, the drafting of national laws and regulations, of management plans and international conventions, in funding and project launching, as well as in a wide range of everyday operations on behalf of wildlife and the quality of the human environment. It is, in fact, very much a part of the action of the modern world, and has become so during the past twenty-five years, with growing support from many quarters.

Yet, however well known are its activities and its immediate aims, the movement is by no means well understood, even by many of its members. The term environment itself, in its current sense, is still a novelty, and is steadily broadening its meaning. Fresh perceptions, awareness of hitherto unrecognised dangers, and of indirect and intangible threats and linkages lead to constant adjustments in ideas, strategies and tactical objectives, partly because some previous ones have been more or less achieved. Its numerous, varied and sometimes mercurial groups go forward loosely in unison by means of lively and continuous two-way communication, lateral rather than from top to bottom. There is no politburo, no hierarchy, no generalissimo, no rite of initiation. It advances rapidly on a broad front, with occasional setbacks, always adapting to fresh challenges as soon as each earlier one has been met.

In 1970 I sought in *The Environmental Revolution* (Hodder & Stoughton and McGraw-Hill) to provide a basic account of the development and achievement of the environmental movement up to that time. It still, I think, stands as a balanced and comprehensive factual treatment, needing no correction within its limits. It does, however, now need to be updated to cover the many major events and developments that have occurred since it was written. The widening meanwhile of the movement's scope, and the deepening and broadening of its perspective and awareness, now call for a more strategic and philosophical treatment, putting the movement into its new context. It has, with some reluctance, concluded that conservation is not just about saving whales and tigers and rainforests, and preventing pollution and waste, but is inescapably concerned with the future conduct, welfare, happiness and indeed survival of mankind on this planet. Our fast expanding knowledge of animal behaviour and ecology is being matched by our learning more about human mental and physical capabilities and requirements, and about human ecology. Indeed the two react upon and stimulate one another.

We begin to see how the one-sided and distorted picture which we had of the biosphere and its functioning becomes corrected and helps us towards an illuminating picture of man as an ecological and evolutionary being, no longer turning his back on the biosphere but vigorously and creatively harmonising himself with it. The muddy rut in which traditional thinking and institutions are stuck suddenly becomes surmountable. We discern that in order to harmonise with nature man must learn without further delay to harmonise with himself, not necessarily by recourse to mystical and ethical means, but by adopting the resources of a science of man.

Environmentalists, accustomed to changing widespread beliefs, attitudes and habits, are apt to become impatient with their fellows who are ostensibly improving the human condition, because all the time they see it worsen. This book, accordingly, touches on the possible spin-offs from successful environmental approaches and techniques to the improvement of the human condition elsewhere. Although the environmental movement shows no sign of growing tired or stale, it could do with a fresh look at itself and its mission. It can no longer assume that either mankind or the environment are fixed quantities – both take on fresh forms and appearances as we quickly learn more about both of them, and as we pursue the fruitful interaction between them which the movement has set in train.

In this book, therefore, we are concerned to trace how human evolution has largely occurred in response to environmental challenges, and how, by rediscovering those challenges, we can stimulate a fresh evolutionary impetus which may do much more than simply make human survival possible. It may indeed be the key to relieving some of the conflicts, tensions and frustrations that environmental blindness has brought us.

It may also show us how to fill the psychological gap arising from the decay of revealed religion and belief in the supernatural. Environmentalism is already helping powerfully to create a sense of one world, not only through respect for one earth but through the global commons which we are being forced to care for by common effort. It is stretching out our horizons in time as well as in space, and helping to correct the short-sightedness as well as the narrow-mindedness that are a reproach to our civilisation. It latches on to the rapid advances in knowledge of the workings of the human brain, especially in the relation of perception to interpretation and in the use of models and idea-systems.

The achievement of the movement in discovering and putting together a picture of the functioning of the biosphere, and the threats to it, has been accompanied by vigorous and diverse corrective action. It has involved major feats of organisation and management from which much more can be learnt, in improving conditions in this mismanaged world. Again, by studying interactions, as the movement is beginning to, some of the disadvantages of excessive specialisation, sectionalism and centralisation can be corrected. By reminding ourselves of the varied types of leadership and inputs which have come together in the movement we can learn more about the prevention and avoidance of some of the crippling maladies that so often overtake worthy large-scale efforts. We can also see how to hold in focus a range of different targets and fields of activity, while adapting our methods and resources to the necessary remedial actions. We have to be aware critically of the context and climate and the external relationships within which we must function.

Human evolution is manifested in successive cultures and civilisations that are described in history. Historians, however, have their blind spots, and are only beginning to grasp the role which environment plays. The point has been well made by Professor Robert S. Gottfried in his highly original history of *The Black Death: Natural and Human Disaster in Medieval Europe* (Hale, 1983) in which he concludes, 'Civilizations are the result of complex combinations of institutional, cultural, material and environmental characteristics. Where the underpinnings are removed the civilizations collapse'. Where now are the underpinnings of our current civilisation?

I would not have written this book if it did not seem to me to be needed to fill a gap, despite the many excellent works with which it in parts overlaps.

Although so far as possible factual, it is mainly concerned to present a fresh perspective, arising from recent events and debates, and it has therefore had to pass lightly over many detailed aspects which are more fully dealt with elsewhere in the current literature.

Literature, in any case, is no substitute for direct experience, and in judging the right perspective I have been guided less by what I have read than by what I have learnt directly during my involvement throughout the recent growth of the environmental conservation movement. I have been privileged to share the thoughts and advice of many of its gifted leaders, and to be able to recall what they had in mind, and the events which they shaped. I was at Brunnen in 1946 when the International Union was first planned, I sat on the official committee which planned the Nature Conservancy in Great Britain, I briefed the parliamentary draftsman for the 1949 Act which brought statutory nature conservation into existence, and as a charter Member and then for 14 years Director-General of the Nature Conservancy I was concerned in the main national and international decision-making of the movement. I chaired the organising committee for the World Wildlife Fund in 1961, and travelled worldwide as Convenor of the Conservation Section of the International Biological Programme.

I thus had a ringside seat, or was even in the ring myself, during the formative stages of the modern environmental movement, not only in Europe but in each of the other continents. What I have said may be questioned but it cannot be dismissed as uninformed. Its reasoning about the future is at least based upon experience of the results of doing just that in the past, where hindsight now offers its sobering help. Indeed, many of my earlier forecasts are on the record for anyone who cares to check, and the fact does not embarrass me. I think looking forward is necessary, and the art can be learnt with not much more difficulty than some others which are successfully practised. Inability to forecast where they will soon be is often a problem simply for those who do not know where they are now.

August 1986   Max Nicholson

PREFACE TO THE PAPERBACK EDITION

As *The New Environmental Age* was designed not only to bring its story up to date but to indicate trends which might be expected to develop, it seems right to comment briefly on happenings and changing outlooks since it was written in 1986. None of these call for revisions in its series of findings and messages, but some provide a new context in the array of environmental problems and in their perception.

Continuing expansion of data gathering and processing in this field, and of the wider communications revolution, have reinforced the degree and nature of public awareness of ecological and conservation problems, and the importance of their contribution to land use and land management, diet and health, and patterns of urban and industrial development. These have been brought into focus by the (Brundtland) World Commission's Report on *Our Common Future* and in the somewhat surprisingly positive and concrete British government response to it in July 1988 entitled *Our Common Future; A Perspective by the United Kingdom on the Report of the World Commission on Environment and Development*. Whether all these promising items will really be reflected in official action is in the lap of the gods; if so a significant step will have been made into the New Environmental Age. The rather modest attention accorded by world religions, especially the Christian Churches, to their Assisi undertakings of 1986 is not a good augury, and the spectacular recent sequence of natural disasters, partly attributable to human follies, is perhaps a more powerful influence towards better ways. Renewed public concern about pollution and the disposal of toxic wastes, leading for example to the enforced acceptance by the Italian government of poisons which it had sought to dump first in Nigeria and then in Britain, is an example of the hard way to learn, which politicians still tend to choose. The name of the *Karin B* now passes into history to join the *Torrey Canyon* and the *Rainbow Warrior* among ships not to be forgotten. The catastrophic floods,

famine and disease in Bangladesh and the Sudan are at last plainly linked
with the reckless deforestation of their catchment areas, and organisations
concerned with relief of poverty in Africa are learning, better late than
never, to recognise the importance of the concept embodied in the title of my
late friend Edward Graham's memorable book, *Natural Principles of Land Use*,
as relevant today as when it was published in 1944.

Political setbacks have also overtaken the military industrial establishment, with the first feeble steps towards disarmament, and the farm lobbies,
with the impossibility of sustaining their inflated subsidies and the consequential misuse of the land. As parts of the 'developed world' begin to run
out of airspace for mass tourism and of road space for vehicles in and around
their cities the spread of destabilisation of unsustainable policies and institutions is proceeding fast enough to be apparent now even in so short a period
as a couple of years.

I wish I could point also to conspicuous advances in the capacity of
conservationists to handle the vast problems which face them. It is true that
the IUCN's Assembly in Costa Rica in February 1988 was the largest and
most confident ever held, and was notable, for example, in leading to a close
alliance of conservationists with the United Nations and international
population and family planning organisations. The continuing vitality of
ecology is also indicated by the growth of interest in biodiversity as a positive
focus to balance the inevitably negative emphasis of the campaign to save
endangered species and habitats. One eminent reviewer of *The New Environmental Age* has taken me to task for my gloomy assessment of the effectiveness of the International Biological Programme, and I am glad to be so
authoritatively assured that in ways beyond my purview it achieved more
than I have credited it with, although I did express my view that 'in spite of
everything it did succeed internationally in vindicating and consolidating
the scientific base for conservation, and in dragging ecology into the
mainstream of biology . . .' Spokesmen for the Greens have also criticised me
for my unfavourable attitude towards their efforts to introduce conservation
into party politics. May I make it clear that their efforts so far have had most
useful results, and are worthy of credit; my fears are simply that in the
unlikely event of their progressing beyond political nuisance value they will
harm the movement and discredit themselves.

Finally, I have encountered some criticism for not being sufficiently
explicit about the future of the movement. Ready as I am to stretch my neck
out I am not unaware that prophecy has been defined as the most gratuitous
form of error, and I would claim that I have struck about the right balance in
indicating what environmentalists would in my view be wise to do and to
avoid doing in the near future. At all events, reviewing two years later the

way the situation is taking shape I see no reason to offer corrections or apologies, and I trust that environmentalists will not find that they have been led astray as things unfold further.

1

The context of the struggle

If we seek to understand what environmental conservation means, to-day and for the future, we must know something of its roots in the past. That involves history, but nearly all historians have until lately failed to grasp the extent to which its course has been influenced both by human interactions with the environment and by current attitudes, myths and limitations of knowledge about it. Even such a vast environmental catastrophe as the Black Death of the mid fourteenth century, which decimated the population and transformed the history of Europe, has normally been treated in blind ignorance of its environmental aspects. Underlying these, however, and conditioning the course of history, is human evolution, and the development and use of human capabilities.

The emergence and employment of these capabilities has determined the origins and unfolding of the vast and varied tasks of damage limitation that we call environmental conservation. This introductory chapter needs accordingly to outline, inevitably superficially, relevant knowledge which bears upon the treatment of conservation issues in later chapters. It ranges from evolutionary processes and stages, through changing perceptions and motivations, demands, cultural and social conditions, practices and technology, to the resulting ideas, beliefs and institutions which have had impacts on the natural environment.

Natural environment is itself fast becoming a historical concept, as over ever widening parts of the earth it is being replaced by a humanly created semi-natural or even wholly unnatural substitute. Our growing knowledge of ecology must more and more be applied indirectly, to reconstructing past situations or to making the best of new ones in which natural processes are inhibited, distorted or prevented from functioning, at least temporarily, by human influences. Conservation therefore becomes a kind of bastard applied ecology, seeking to avoid disaster by bringing together natural and human elements to function in balance in a blended, new, global ecosystem.

A poet in a wiser generation wrote that 'the proper study of mankind is man'. Conservationists, concerned to defend nature, are now driven by bitter experience to give more and more attention to that good advice. Here, then, is a brief outline of what appear from a conservation standpoint to be some most significant points in human evolution, as they have affected and will affect the biosphere.

Human evolution has over many millennia transformed the descendants of certain large forest apes into remarkably sophisticated beings, capable of doing much good to one another, and perhaps even more harm, as well as to their fellow creatures and to the small planet on which they live. Fortunately, during recent decades the unravelling of the human evolution-ary story has made rapid progress, and has even attracted fairly wide public interest. Unfortunately, however, its implications for the guidance of correct human conduct at the present critical stage of evolution have hardly begun to be appreciated. Unfortunately again, in these circumstances it falls to conservationists to begin remedying the lack.

Early man, as a tropical food-gatherer and hunter, emerging in very small numbers from the edge of the dense forest to the open savanna and grasslands, had to use his latent capacities to turn to account for his survival their varied plant, animal and mineral resources. In doing so, he reached an expertise and acquired skills far surpassing those of most people now living. In particular he identified, and learnt to exploit, the properties of an impressive proportion of the food and medicinal plants on which we rely to this day. He learnt to cope with the rhythms and changes of climate, and to colonise widely contrasting habitats.

Already, while living in the trees, his ancestors had acquired some highly valuable adaptations, such as agility and mobility, quick responses, sharp vision (rather than relying, like most ground mammals more on smell) and skill in signalling a variety of messages by sight and sound. He adapted to reproducing his kind with only one or two offspring at a time, spaced out and cared for long enough to be able to learn much from accumulated experience, and to get to know one another well enough for spontaneous co-operation.

When forests gave place to open plains during the Miocene, man began to take advantage of his comparatively long legs and keen vision to walk upright over distances and thus to break away from the sedentary and confined incurious habits of his ape cousins, exploring avidly what lay on the other side of the hill. This helped to make him the intensely inquisitive animal that he now is, and to tax his slowly expanding brain with questions and with the wish to communicate and discuss them. Evolution of hand and foot thus had to be matched by the distinctively human expansion of brain capacity, to a scale more than $2\frac{1}{2}$ times greater than that of his progenitors who first left the forest, already endowed with exceptionally large brains compared with other mammals.

Our human world has thus been shaped by the interplay between a variety of rewarding but demanding habitat features and a remarkable physical and mental adaptability enabling us to respond to and eventually to understand and to some extent to control them. As time has passed those in charge of human destinies have come to underrate or even to ignore the fundamental role of the environment and grossly to exaggerate their power of surviving without caring for it. Conservationists now have the task of quickly making good this default in the proper study of mankind, and of spreading awareness of the indispensable preconditions of man's tenure of the earth.

Although we have as yet unfortunately no means of knowing how the expansion of brain capacity is distributed between parts of it responsible for visual interpretation, speech, interpretive functions generally, and co-ordination, we can make some inferences from the evolutionary changes that actually occurred. Among the most conspicuous, were those in capacity for communication, collective as well as individual memory, tool-making and techniques, questioning and the search for plausible explanations, together with skills in social relations and the establishment of accepted values and rules of conduct. In stressing the cardinal importance of social evolution we may overlook the extent to which it had to be stimulated by physical challenge, coming essentially from coping with the natural environment as well as with humans. Physically the adoption of walking erect had left man's strong arms free to serve his special endowment as a load-carrier and eventually as a manually skilled tool-maker and tool-user, with a capacity to work for long stretches at a visualised task.

Taking to the plains had probably coincided with a change in diet from a mainly herbivorous to an opportunist omnivorous pattern, based on widespread food-gathering. Eventually the economies in the energy budget obtainable from trapping or hunting large animals which could be tracked and overcome by hunting groups gave rise to emphasis on leadership, teamwork and forethought, swiftness, endurance and reliable immediate communication, as well as to close attention to the habits and habitat of the game species. Modern management studies have shown that the more closely organisation in business can approximate to such a primitive hunting group the more likely it is to succeed.

A change towards food obtained not incessantly in small amounts but at longish intervals in large quantities called for replacement of continual transient camping and moving on by finding a safe settled and accessible base for females and young, possibly in a cave near water. Settlement brought more intimate, year-round knowledge of the local environment and its resources, and suggested ways of using them to better advantage. These must have included methods of storage, making tools of horn or rough stone or wood from local sources, and learning how to make and control fires for cooking, hunting and eventually for fashioning artefacts, culminating in the smelting of ores for metal. More sedentary living enabled suitable animals to be domesticated and plants subjected to primitive cultivation. This in turn called for division of labour and elaboration of speech in succession to sign language, which occurred in such a way that modern babies have come to possess an innate capability for it. The need to communicate must have emerged with overwhelming emotional force, as a condition for satisfying curiosity and facilitating understanding and co-operation.

One of the most remarkable features of early human evolution was its long apparent confinement to parts of tropical and sub-tropical Africa, and the suddenness and speed with which apparently quite small pioneering groups then launched out into the colonisation of Europe, Asia and eventually the Americas, adapting themselves to widely different climates and environments, and acquiring distinctive physical characteristics. It is

Warm arid regions can generate winds strong enough to form deserts and to spread their sand and dust over neighbouring fertile tracts, as this view of a dust-storm in Tunisia shows. Not only primitive but even modern technology is powerless here.

tempting to speculate that such far-reaching initiatives within a relatively short time must have been triggered off by drastic climatic change, such as we know occurred when the previously habitable Saharan region became an immense desert. Whatever the cause, these still-primitive pioneers were faced with fresh challenges and opportunities as they explored their new environments. It can hardly have been an accident that these explorations were soon followed by the appearance of the first traces of recognisable cultures almost simultaneously in different regions, at a period currently dated at some 30 000 years ago. In remarkably short order these primitive cultures were succeeded by more sophisticated patterns, and then by unmistakable early civilisations.

Substantial pressures must have been felt to bring about this accelerated evolution, and these must have included: climatic change, with severe droughts, floods, and stormy and cold spells; confrontation with new environments; exhaustion of some long-exploited animal and plant re-sources, such as accessible game and readily workable timber; and in some regions expansion of human population and collisions between locally organised tribes. The occupation of so much new land must have stimulated much more making and use of tools, and more explicit and hierarchical exercise of authority and direction. These must have called early for some kind of religious sanction, crystallising in sacred groves, springs and mountains; superstitions must have arisen naturally among primitive peoples. Their reverent acceptance could readily be built upon by emergent priestly castes. Wonder at the gifts of nature and dismay at its occasional arbitrary and punishing catastrophes must have created widespread attitudes and beliefs favourable to the establishment of religions.

As priestly teachers and castes emerged, however, and as primitive societies became more concerned with a favourable outcome for their diverse organised activities, the temptation must have grown to relegate the environment to a peripheral status, and to shift towards a man-centred histrionically presented focus. Nature became regarded as designed, perhaps by some supernatural being, for the enjoyment and sustenance of man, whose superior arts could and should improve upon its crude wild state. That the earth might actually be harmed and impoverished by man's unwise stewardship was to be perceived only much later. Nevertheless the awe and reverence felt for nature was long paid tribute by the practice of hermits and holy men retiring to the wilderness for meditation and spiritual inspiration, far from the contagion of the rest of humanity. It is perhaps significant that much of the earliest known art, apparently having religious overtones, tends to depict animals rather than mankind, which captured art only at later stages, just as gods were gradually stripped of their animal features, and were portrayed with human forms and personalities.

While the emergence of priestly and kingly cults and their interdependence cannot, in the present state of knowledge, be traced back to its origins, it is obvious that both must have needed to show results in what would now be called advancing standards of living. This meant a bias towards encouragement of the tool-making, technological capability of man, and a progressive subordination of aspects closest to the natural environment. A vast historical accident was decisive here. The overflow of human population from tropical Africa, and its growing concentration in higher latitudes of north-east Africa and south-west Asia, was faced with the

Early man was inspired to portray, originally on rock faces, scenes of special significance both to his livelihood and to his sense of wonder about surrounding nature, particularly the wildlife, about which he learnt by hunting and trapping. Art was born in this way, and the intensity of the feelings involved may still be faintly reflected in concern for wildlife conservation. This picture from about 3 500 BC show hunting scenes from caves in the Sahara, the canoe implying a much wetter climate than todays.

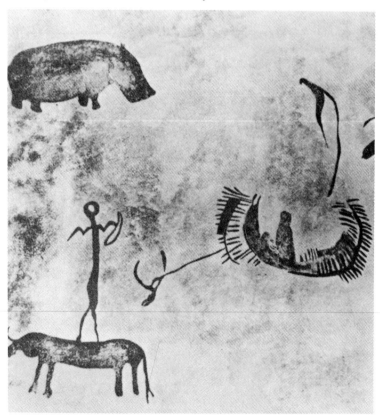

problem that, despite warm climates, soil fertility, level plains and valleys, and a diversity of plants suitable for cultivation, the other essential, water, was missing, at least in the shape of regular, ample rainfall.

A challenge was offered by the presence of such mighty rivers as the Nile, Tigris and Euphrates, and the Indus, to tap their water flows for widespread irrigation. In contrast to the scattered and unorganised peasant farmers of the regions of rainfall agriculture, those who were compelled to take this new path had to band together in large collective enterprises. The success of such enterprises depended upon accurate survey and calculation, keeping records, measurement, intelligence and communication, funding based on some form of taxation, and other specialist services. The manager, the administrator and the expert had arrived. Almost before they knew it these naive moisture-seeking farmers had saddled themselves and their posterity with layers of expertise, bureaucracy, and, riding on the backs of all, a tenacious and often tyrannical ruling class.

A great investment was called for in making canals and dykes, anticipating and controlling floods, and in regulating the orderly apportion-

Early exploitation of the great river valleys of south and east Asia depended upon rapid elaboration of technology for management of water and for transporting timber, metals and other materials. The organisation and learning required soon converted settled agriculture into urbanism, but such impressive examples of hydraulic civilisation as Mohenji-daru in the Indus Valley, whose public baths are seen here, lasted rather briefly (*c.* 2400 to *c.* 1750 BC) before being brought to an end, probably partly through external invasion and partly through environmental factors such as cumulatively increasing salinity arising from irrigation. The collision between human ambitions and sustaining natural resources had begun.

ment of water where and when it was needed. This work was done not by any public or private agency but by the forced labour of the same farmers who were to do the cultivation, mowing and harvesting. The problems of planning and managing these complex operations by the necessary executives and clerks called for the back-up of more academic groups, who were stimulated to develop astronomy for monitoring the calendar dates, as well as algebra, geometry and refinements of mathematics.

Thus, in addition to the substantial environmental impacts on parts of the valleys of the Nile and a number of Asian rivers, these gifted innovators provided mankind with a large part of the cultural, technical and economic skills that were required to launch all subsequent human assaults on the biosphere, as well as countless sound and beneficial uses of it. The hydraulic civilisations themselves, although triumphantly successful for a period, especially in their heyday between c. 3000 and 300 B.C., proved vulnerable in the long run. This was partly because of environmental weaknesses such as the spread of salinity through the soil, but also because their success generated unprecedentedly high population densities, leading to mass urbanisation and to political instability or conquest from outside. The cultural and political progress which they initiated became in part arrested at a fairly early stage, although it in some respects foreshadowed elements in modern Western civilisation.

The technical, political and military spin-offs quickly spread beyond the homelands of hydraulic civilisation, with varying degrees of acceptance and application. Perhaps the most universal and enduring was the demonstration that large numbers of hard-working people could be so organised, and large natural resources could be so exploited with their aid, as to maintain ruling groups enjoying highly privileged lifestyles and the capacity to exert pressure, if they so desired by military force, on their rivals. There could have been alternative means of developing and allocating the use of natural resources; it is an accident of history and prehistory that this power has been placed in the hands of small self-centred groups of powermongers derived either from *ancien régimes* or from modern usurpers of their status.

During the first half of the twentieth century such groups engaged in frenzied competition for 'a place in the sun', for *lebensraum* and similar goals. It took two vastly destructive world wars to expose not only the wickedness but the mistakenness of the idea that such advantages were necessary. Ironically ex-Nazi Germany and ex-Imperialist Japan now demonstrate that they can become world leaders without them. Nevertheless they manage to become dominant in a new world economy recklessly exploiting and wasting the natural resources of many of the ex-colonial and equivalent states.

Politically this world economy is matched by the grossly wasteful military competition of the two superpowers, the USA and USSR, with their respective allies, and by their arming of small states to make futile and destructive local wars. Both the economic and the political pretensions of the second half of the century are in the course of being discredited no less than those of its first half.

The pretensions of the 'great powers' and their successor 'superpowers' in contesting for an ever larger share of world resources and an ever more formidable array of high technology, military and civil, are ending in stalemate, and in a global power vacuum. Even the ever-greater capacity for overkill of the world military-industrial establishment begins to embarrass its masters; they can no longer produce any credible scenario for its worthwhile and effective use, or justify its spiralling costs, its accelerating obsolescence matching its breathless technological advances, and the daunting ineffectuality of recent efforts to use it decisively in conflict.

Such trends should have assisted the diplomatic efforts of the United Nations agencies, had they been better and more resolutely led, less fearful of outdated sovereign government prejudices, and less at the mercy of ill-informed and often unrepresentative Third World pressure groups. Multi-national business enterprises have cashed in to some extent, but their short and conventional perspectives have prevented them from exerting strategic influence. *The Environmental Revolution* was subtitled A Guide for the New Masters of the World, but the world has no masters now – only a blind deadlock between confused and defensive faceless interests, inhibited by such impersonal forces as the communications revolution, the almost worldwide population explosion, runaway urbanisation in the Third World, the disarray of the world economy and its inability to fulfil hopes of income and employment, and the bankruptcy of political programs.

Nowhere has the propensity towards short-sighted exploitation of the natural environment, and towards riding roughshod over consumer and citizen interests, been more conspicuous than in the Third World. That propensity has been aggravated by the perpetuation and reinforcement of large, rigid, self-centred Western-based institutions, pursuing anachronistic policies and practices, increasingly at the expense of countries which had come to be dominated by Western power and influence, and possessed no counter-force sufficient to mitigate its impact on themselves. The hoped-for relief following the break-up of colonial empires and the winning of political independence by numerous former colonies did little to free the latter from economic subservience.

Lacking an adequate core of citizens with the necessary education and experience to sustain a healthy Western-style democracy, many lately emancipated Third World countries have fallen under the control of lawyer-politicians and half-trained experts, misapplying principles and practices believed to work in advanced countries. or of even less qualified military cliques, or business and other chiefs, with little to restrain their natural leanings towards corruption and self-aggrandisement. The mass of the inhabitants might well find themselves worse off than under the usually more efficient and less corrupt previous colonial administration.

Two particular scourges of the new regimes were indulgence in futile and disruptive local wars, using equipment foisted on them by the piratical armaments industries of a few advanced countries (including Britain), and the pursuit of grandiose prestige projects for dams, highways, airports and great industrial plants, which their countries did not need and could not afford.

Many of these enterprises were paid for either by diverting Western aid from much more urgent investment in food production, education, health and other needs or in reckless overborrowing with the encouragement of overseas banks, including British, which thereby put at risk the whole international credit system when the inevitable day of reckoning dawned. Much of this wasted investment went on projects which were highly counter-productive to the health of their natural environments and to the future of their life support systems.

It was not until the ultimate folly of the great Ethiopian famine, under the aegis of a Marxist government too busy fighting civil wars to see to the feeding of its people, that fresh minds and resources under the leadership of the young pop singer Bob Geldof came to the rescue. World attention was at last directed to the culpable mismanagement of the situation by international and national agencies, both official and voluntary. These had for years ignored serious warnings about desertification, erosion, unchecked population growth far in excess of carrying capacity, and the misuse of land for export cash crops rather than for feeding home populations first.

The quarter-century after the much acclaimed bestowal of political independence on so many countries under United Nations and other auspices has seen a sorry series of crimes, blunders and misappropriations of resources. These have not been redeemed by the efforts of those supposed to be taking care of the situation, whose euphoric forecasts of the 1960s and 1970s now look to all as absurd as they were seen to be at the time by a number of conservationists who were not listened to. Many primitive people who had for long periods successfully conserved their supporting environment were taught or forced by Western experts to embark on its destruction.

Our concern here is with the interaction between man and nature, and with the blind spots about it in successive cultures, which have had progressively more devastating effects upon the biosphere. The Chinese, who were among the earliest to be alerted to the dangers, seem not entirely to have forgotten the advice to them of Mencius, a mandarin who believed in human goodness and on its dependence upon the peace of mind arising from material well-being, and would thus qualify to-day for membership of the International Institute for Environment and Development. Writing some 2300 years ago, he commented on the effects of tree-felling on a mountain, followed by browsing by cattle and goats, in these words: 'To these things is due the bare and stripped appearance of the mountain, and when people see it now they think it was never finely wooded. But is this the nature of the mountain?' Plato, a slightly earlier contemporary in Athens, had given much the same message in his *Critias*, yet it was virtually ignored by his many disciples through the ages. Most of the places that were cradles of the highest human cultures have been eroded and spoilt by blindness in this respect. Our own is headed in the same direction, on a much larger scale.

The long unheeded menace of unnecessary soil erosion – a picture taken in western Kenya in 1960, a quarter of a century before famine in Africa hit the headlines.

Every intellectual, and all members of the worlds of learning and the arts, ought to feel a deep burden of guilt for this continuing dereliction of moral duty.

With the exception of certain Oriental faiths, the religions also have defaulted. The Judaeo–Christian tradition has been especially wrong-headed in this respect, despite the occasional fine leadership of such men as St Francis of Assisi, whose example has been celebrated there by the World Wildlife Fund on the occasion of its twenty-fifth birthday in September 1986. Considering the orthodox religious view of the Creation it is astonishing that there has been so little said by the Church about man's obligations to his natural environment. This failure has been aggravated by the rigidity of church institutions and their inherent inability to listen or adapt to considerations other than those which have, often by historical accident, become permanently embedded in their doctrines.

To-day the environmental movement demonstrably has a special attraction to caring people. Perhaps if the churches showed more signs of caring in this as in other ways, a few more environmentalists might be disposed to care for them. As Christendom fades away, materialist Western civilisation, which has so long been propped up incongruously by its noble and personal mission, is placed morally and spiritually at risk. Marxism,

This is not, as at first glance it may appear, a picture of desertification in the Third World; it shows farming in one of the most fertile parts of central Italy in 1986, responding to the thoughtless pressures of the Common Agricultural Policy by destroying shelter and creating erosion.

which at one time aspired to supersede revealed religion, has practically abandoned the attempt, its even more man-centred message being discredited in terms of upholding personal liberties and beliefs, and of its unshakable commitment towards sterile statism. Other traditional religions, despite some shining merits, are manifestly incapable of fulfilling the needs of modern Westernised man.

In the absence of a now unlikely Christian revival, mankind is faced with learning to continue human evolution without any religious basis, or alternatively of devising something new, using what viable strands from the past may be acceptable and reconcilable with the New Environmental Age. (Julian Huxley in 1961 assembled in *The Humanist Frame* contributions on various aspects of the problem from some 26 authors, including myself; those interested might do well to consider producing an equally comprehensive updated version.)

During recent stages of human evolution, a dilemma has arisen between the lively unpredictable course of imagination, reflection and abstract thought and the accumulated social patterns governing everyday living. The latter form a rich framework of beliefs, values, assumptions and rules or guidelines of conduct shared with others of the community and serving to give life meaning and a sense of belonging. Unfortunately they must from their nature be rooted in the past, and thus conflict with current thoughts and aspirations, contributing to a generation gap and, in traditionalist or authoritarian regimes, to feelings of alienation and dissidence. The difficulty is aggravated when institutions of long standing, often run or dominated by people wedded to obsolescent ideas and values, have an influential role in supporting or policing matters of understanding or belief, where they may attach universality or eternal validity to formulations which others regard as outdated or one sided. This is Mr Gorbachev's problem.

Unfortunately we live in a period of unprecedented rapid change in so much that affects our beliefs and actions, faced by an array of powerful and self-assured institutions whose interests and convictions may be much at variance with the views of many who have to deal with them. This widespread institutional block hinders the processes of adaptation to change in many aspects of life, and often inhibits or discourages it. Institutions which feel themselves threatened by new pressures tend to respond defensively or negatively and, for example, to dismiss unpalatable suggestions as the workings of an 'environmental lobby' brought into existence simply by their own unreadiness to listen and to adapt. Some of them are dead but they won't lie down.

The environment of environmentalism, or the context of conservation, has accordingly to be viewed against the very broad background of human evolution and development which goes on proceeding apace, despite our almost universal inattention to it. Instant global communications, the easier sharing of knowledge and the replacement of divisive and emotionally exclusive attitudes by a preference for openmindedness and integration are part of the movement towards One World with which the environmental movement is strongly linked. Current research on the brain and on its mechanisms for perception and interpretation of the world we live in are highly relevant here. They are, however, filtering through only slowly to correct false conventional ideas about 'human nature', and about the validity of our judgments and store of knowledge. Artificial barriers erected in the past between man and nature, leading to abuses of the biosphere and of natural resources, are consequently more difficult to remove.

It may be urged by some that all human activities can be viewed against the background of evolution, so what is so special about environmental conservation that it merits special treatment in this way? The answer has already been given, that the natural environment has played, over many millennia, a key role in human evolution, and unless it soon comes to do so again the prospects for further human evolution are poor. Insofar as other activities can make a case for being looked at against an evolutionary background, they are most welcome to do so. As will be shown in Chapter 6, other world movements have much to gain by working in concert with environmental conservation.

Longer and broader perspectives are much needed, and it is to be hoped that this book will do something to encourage them. The implications of living in harmony with the biosphere and its life support systems are fully consistent with the objectives of the other great global movements for peace and disarmament, for family planning and reduction of population growth and for development and remedying of mass poverty. They are also consistent with the aspirations of growing numbers, especially among the young, towards a more decent and reasonable way of living, recognising that the earth can with good housekeeping provide enough for everyone's need, although not enough for everyone's greed.

Whether we like it or not change is in full swing and more change is coming. Whether that change will give our children and grandchildren a better or worse world to live in depends to no small extent on how we act now.

Environmental conservationists need to conduct their activities in the light of some such background as has been lightly and superficially sketched in this chapter. In order to bring it into practical focus for this purpose I conclude with a list of points which seem relevant.

1. Logically it is essential to complement the now well-developed picture of man's impacts on the global natural environment with a corresponding comprehensive picture of man's own development and activities as a tenant of the earth.

2. It appears that only during about the past 30 000 years has man acquired the necessary capabilities and developed the necessary human biomass to bring about significant changes in the biosphere, and only in much more recent years have these changes become widespread, drastic and in some cases irreversible.

3. The forces that have caused these changes, and the instruments used in them are fairly clear, but their motivation and the priorities and choices adopted have only recently been studied; for example, through the use of mandatory Environmental Impact Assessments. Even now there is little study of environmental impact causation, and of the implications of minimising environmental impacts without unacceptable repercussions on social and economic objectives which are sufficiently important to be weighed in the balance.

4. It can, however, be assumed safely that the majority of recent harmful environmental impacts could have been avoided, without inflicting unacceptable deprivations or losses, if to-day's knowledge and public concern could have been enlisted at an early enough stage to find less damaging and objectionable paths to the desired goals. Such measures would, moreover, have greatly reduced losses of natural resources, damage to ecosystems and harm to the quality of life, for which all future generations will have to bear the sacrifices imposed on them by us.

5. Although certain interests have already more or less fully corrected their propensity to inflict environmental damage, and others are effectively caught up in controls enforced through laws and regulations, there are still many that continue to develop projects and to follow practices highly injurious to the environment. It is therefore necessary for conservationists to study why, how and where these continuing threats originate, and how they can be checked, either by finding acceptable alternative approaches or by control.

6. Already, as is shown in the following chapter, a number of effective steps have been taken in this direction. However, with the exception of the World Conservation Strategy and its national action programs, most of these have been *ad hoc* and reactive. There

is still a need for more positive and profound initiatives to anticipate and avert further schemes and actions that ought not now to be conceived or promoted in the light of modern environmental knowledge.

7. Such a prescription cannot be pursued by the environmental movement in isolation. It calls for much lateral exploration of the related fields from which environmental problems arise, and for the conclusion of a series of broad, constructive alliances with hitherto adversarial interests, as has been done in the United Kingdom with farmers through the Farming and Wildlife Advisory Groups, and their back-up by the National Farmers' Union, the Country Landowners Association and the Ministry of Agriculture, Fisheries and Food.

8. Practical and specific measures on these lines will not, however, suffice unless they are backed by a much broader and deeper transformation in attitudes, beliefs and life-styles. Such a transformation is visibly in progress, but it is slow to gather pace, and above all to enlist the support of such backward and vitally necessary institutional partners as education, the churches, the business world, political parties and many leisure pursuits. A vigorous educational drive will be needed to persuade these retrograde bodies to face their responsibilities to the future. Fortunately the response of the younger generation, which is crucial, is no longer in serious doubt, but the adverse attitudes are deeply entrenched and well funded, and re-education will be a lengthy and difficult task.

9. In the light of the above points, the environmental movement will need to broaden and to deepen its efforts over the coming decade, along lines which have already been foreshadowed and to some extent adopted by some of its supporters. Its ultimate goal must be to see a world in which its values and aims are so completely integrated in a revitalised and reoriented civilisation that its mission will have been successfully discharged.

The implications of these nine points will be discussed in the remaining chapters.

2

The early years of environmental conservation

Conservation is not embarked upon by anyone without good reason, and the reason is usually to avert a threat of loss or serious damage to some valued feature of the environment, which may be a property, a habitat, a species, a concentration of rare animals or plants or a landscape or natural monument. It follows that conservation is most often reactive to other activities, and these are commonly man's activities. It also follows that the full development of environmental conservation occurs only as a sequel to a long series of threats and impacts which may no longer realistically be dealt with *ad hoc*, and which call for some properly organised counter-mechanism. In fact, it is only over the past three or four decades that conservationists have been compelled to move over from a piecemeal approach to a global network of specialised bodies working to a coherent long-term strategy.

In *The Environmental Revolution* (1970) I traced at some length the history of this build-up, both internationally and in Britain and the United States, in more detail. That account will not be repeated here, but will be complemented by a review tracing the successive and cumulative *needs* to which the environmental movement has sought to respond, and the relations of these to evolution, which has been outlined in the foregoing chapter. It will therefore be looking at the movement as it were from the outside, and not, as in *The Environmental Revolution*, in terms of its inner development. Such an approach would hardly have been appropriate, even if it had been possible at an earlier stage, but it becomes relevant now that the movement is called upon to relate more closely and constructively to the worlds of politics, economics, social affairs, science and technology, and the arts. It will thus afford a basis for the review in Chapter 6 of the present and prospective interactions of environmental conservation with the wider world.

To a modern conservationist, the general case for environmental conservation is so obvious that he often fails to appreciate how sophisticated, how secondary and how recent is its role in human affairs. For primitive people, the primary concern is to locate and acquire from their environment the substances needed for food, clothing and shelter. The availability of these items is as likely to be affected by flood, drought, frost, tempest and other natural forces as by the usually modest toll levied by the human beings. Against such forces, they have no defence. That moves them towards religion, and the adoption of prayer and propitiatory ceremonies addressed to the gods, who they suppose must be in control of such phenomena. In its origins, therefore, religion is in effect a substitute for measures of conservation, which may have some bearing on the persistent failure of most religious leaders to recognise and assist in more practical corrective action against the abuse and destruction of what they claim to see as God's creation.

Primitive people, however, do possess a keen perception of the natural world around them, and of its health or decay. They watch with close attention the succession of the seasons, the ecological succession of vegetation, and the differences between good years and bad years, which were long remembered and recalled by word of mouth even before the appearance of writing. A surprising number of them have drawn the necessary conclusions to establish rituals, or practices such as terracing of hillside fields, which must rank as a dawning of conservation.

A more frequent early reaction to shortages and decreases of resources was simply to shift to new unoccupied areas and start over again, as is still done to this day by nomad tribes, mining enterprises and all sorts of people from industrial managers to pensioners, who become dissatisfied with their surroundings and see opportunities of improving their lot elsewhere. Pastoralists keeping too many livestock on overgrazed areas are among the most persistent followers of this migratory pattern, which in many cases has the conservation benefit of resting the land and permitting its vegetation to recover, and in some cases has become a regular pattern of seasonal movement or transhumance.

Shortages, whether naturally or humanly caused, have to be met by some appropriate adjustment. First, however, they need to be perceived in ways that enable such adjustment to follow, and conservation is one of the most recent, coming long after shifting elsewhere or prayer to some supernatural force supposedly able to produce a quick fix. Indeed conservation may often have been a spin-off of these approaches, through rationalisation of shifting sites such as slash-and-burn tropical forest agriculture, or transhumance, or ceremonies and rituals which may have subconsciously influenced their participants towards attitudes more consistent with sustainable yields.

Even to-day the needs and prescriptions for conservation often go unrecognised for long periods. Leading agricultural scientists long argued against any causal relation between early applications of toxic agricultural chemicals on the land and the mass mortality of wildlife. American conservationists allowed the peregrine or duckhawk to be exterminated and the osprey gravely reduced in the eastern United States before diagnosing its chemical causes, despite the publication of Rachel Carson's *Silent Spring* (1962), and action already set in hand in Britain. Even where new research is not needed there is a wide predisposition to seek explanations first in natural developments.

Man is a hunter, and it was probably in following the fortunes of the hunt for game beasts that the highly motivated and communicative hunting groups were led to see some connection between the scale, timing and quarry composition of their kills and the trend of quarry numbers in subsequent seasons. Indeed the racking of brains and the conduct of discussions on these matters may well have influenced the evolution of brainpower, memory and communication, since the hunting groups would have included many of the leaders of their day, whose genes counted disproportionately in successive generations at a time when the total population was quite small.

Few people are induced to think harder or to tax their ingenuity more

Pastoralists have for millennia ignored the limits of carrying capacity and thus damaged or even destroyed their basic natural resource, as in this picture from Mali.

than those who have spent a tiring and frustrating day in the open trying to catch something that they have failed to track down or to bring to bay. It seems not unreasonable to suppose that in the course of such fireside inquests some prescient and dissatisfied hunter may have come out with ideas in which lay the seed of conservation. Could it, perhaps, be that last year's catches had not been so fortunate after all, if they had exceeded the reproductive capacities of the quarry? Could the quarry perhaps be assisted to reproduce better in their season by not disturbing or not felling that part of the forest at that time?

Be that as it may, it is a matter of historical record, as recounted in Chapter 6 of *The Environmental Revolution*, that early kings in the Middle East set aside game reserves and parks for hunting, and also began to conserve and even to introduce trees and plants found to be of value. These actions, of course, came long after the prehistoric hunters of Lascaux, Altamira and other sites, in Africa as well as in Europe, had painted on the walls of caves evidences of their deep emotional attachment to the animals forming their quarry. The intensity of the interest in and identification with wildlife before the dawn of civilisation is evidence of the depths to which it was imprinted on the human consciousness. This strongly suggests a profound psychological base for the modern concern with conservation of nature, which has grown faster and spread more widely than can otherwise readily be accounted for.

Other early activities which had implications for conservation were fishing, gardening, medicine based on herb collecting, and the tending of landscape. All these were of special interest to kings and others near the top of early hierarchies, and thus acquired a social status that some of them have never since lost. They were also of special interest to the scientifically minded, and to those who had to care for the provisioning and variety of diet of courts and other establishments. (Just picture the officer in charge of commissariat having to report an empty larder.) The construction and tending of fishponds and vineyards, so assiduously continued by monks through the Middle Ages, formed some common ground between conservation and farming, and played no small part in the development of healthier living and European trade.

In all these activities, however, the conservation element was implicit rather than overt or primary, and must have been seen in narrow and immediate terms, rather than as an important underlying principle. The same must have been true of early livestock domestication and farming, which involved the seeking out of suitable animals and plants no longer for immediate food-gathering and consumption but for propagation and genetic improvement.

The success of these initiatives in so many areas, and over so short an evolutionary period, is evidence of advanced powers of perception and skills in what we would now see as applied ecology. Indeed it is arguable that in no period before this century must mankind have been more keenly and successfully preoccupied with the natural environment and its resources. The echoes of that enthusiasm and dedication of skills may still resound faintly among us. Conservationists are among the most up-to-date groups in our culture, but they may also be among the most atavistic.

These reminders and reflections on the origins of the environmental movement suggest some apparently inconsistent and conflicting conclusions. On the one hand, early man was highly dependent on the sustained yield, within a compact area, of a range of natural products that he did not know initially how to cultivate or breed, nor had he any means of perceiving their response to his cropping. The latter was fortunately at a light level, and was much less of a constraint than other factors such as weather and soil fertility. On the other hand curiosity and expanding requirements made him an explorer, and to some extent a student, of his natural environment, although largely with the intention of learning fresh ways of exploiting it. At that time, however, its exploitation required much working with nature and involved little drastic damage or enduring destruction.

Almost throughout prehistoric times, therefore, man was on a course broadly compatible with the survival of the biosphere, and even with its full health. Throughout those times also evolutionary pressures were tending to align him more closely with the biosphere and to qualify him to understand it better. Unfortunately the culmination of this process led him onto quite different paths, involving much more and worse exploitation of natural resources, combined with a fast declining interest in and knowledge of the natural environment and a capacity to exploit it on an ever more damaging scale.

As this process ran on inexorably, to the point when in our own time it began to threaten even man's survival, an urgent need arose for what was newly conceived as scientific conservation, but in essence constituted a return to the path of living with nature which had been abandoned only a few thousand years earlier – a brief interval in the entire story of mankind, and probably too brief to have obliterated much valuable previous inheritance of tuning in to ecology.

It is in this quest of how to revive man's earliest senses of wonder and responsibility towards nature in terms of modern ecology and of the framework of the modern world that we now have to proceed. It was a particular misfortune that the switch by most of mankind's leaders, away from the natural environment had to precede their main activities in developing, within the various cultures, a series of customs, religious doctrines, laws, institutions and codes of procedure and practice that largely ignored environmental conservation. They left mankind with very few relevant and influential guidelines, and very many which were mischievous and damaging to it. The legacy for our time is therefore one of learning plenty and unlearning even more.

It has lately been fashionable in some leading circles to speak of 'the environmental lobby' and to regard its message as extraneous, and as inseparable from confrontation. In the long term nothing could be farther from the truth. The necessity for a sharply separated environmental conservation movement has only been created by the shameful deviation of recent economists, business leaders and politicians from their plain and ultimately inescapable duty to include provision for conservation and sustainable use among their essential management objectives. As that comes to be recognised and acted upon, the pressure-group aspects of the movement will naturally subside, and even eventually disappear. The positive, ecologically far-seeing aspects will no doubt continue and go on developing, at least until the unforeseeably distant day when politicians and business men have learnt to live with time horizons comparable with those of ecologists.

In seeking out the origins of conservation, we find fewer examples of its separation from mainstream development, and even fewer of confrontation, than recent experience might lead us to expect. Game reserves, close seasons and other such practices were not imposed upon early hunters but were invented and practised by them spontaneously. Irrigation for agriculture, especially within the early hydraulic civilisations, was fundamentally a form of water conservation, on a scale relatively greater as a public works program than almost anything since in those regions. Unfortunately, as with many modern projects for large dams and reservoirs, the planners were too blinkered in terms of catching the water and putting it to immediate use, and accordingly failed to take into account repercussions and side-effects that were environmentally counter-productive, such as salinisation and siltation.

Prevention of hillslope erosion by terracing, and the trapping of flash floods by making bunds and impoundments, are other examples of primitive conservation measures which have proved highly successful. It is no accident that so much pioneer work in modern environmental conservation has been done in the Netherlands, whose people have long since learnt the hard way that their survival depended on effective works to conserve their farmlands and settlements from incursion by the sea.

More locally, the Swiss also have long since learnt the vital importance of conserving forest cover on their mountainsides in order to safeguard themselves against avalanches. These precautions fitted well with the continuing need for timber and firewood, which led to the communal management of local forests – a conservation system that continues successfully to this day, involving not only the adult inhabitants but the

One of the most ancient and effective practices for soil conservation in various parts of the world has been the terracing of cultivated slopes to catch runoff water and prevent it from creating gully or sheet erosion down hillsides. Its necessity is now being relearned the hard way, as this picture taken in Burkina Faso shows.

schoolchildren as well, thus helping to reinforce the firm base which the environmental conservation movement has long enjoyed in Switzerland.

In feudal England such conservation as was practised originated either with the Crown, in such areas as the royal forests under their special legal protection, or for specially protected species such as swans and other birds valued as game. Before small firearms became efficient, falconry was a main method of securing edible birds for the table, and, as the quarry was mobile and vulnerable to interference, laws for protection of certain birds were passed from the early sixteenth century onwards.

Wars at sea and the demands on timber for charcoal and making gunpowder created more serious national problems, leading in the seventeenth century to a campaign for planting in particular more oaks, initiated by John Evelyn's *Sylva* (1664), and for restricting by law the destruction of standing trees (see Chapter 7, p. 154). This early conservation legislation was inspired mainly by the need to safeguard raw materials for the navy's wooden ships, but it was resented, particularly by the ironmasters, just as much as later legislation attributed to the 'environmental lobby'. In forcing them to switch from charcoal to coal for smelting pig-iron, the move was instrumental in bringing about the Industrial Revolution.

Coal-burning in open fires in cities was one of the earliest sources of intolerable pollution. Exposure to soot-laden fogs remained a curse, particularly for Londoners, until after the middle of the twentieth century, when the Clean Air Acts took advantage both of political feeling after the heavy mortality of December 1952 and of the growing availability of electric power and gas, which made possible the phasing out of appliances burning raw coal, both domestically and in industry. Although there was a kind of lobby in existence by this time, its campaign had not availed until these two decisive events came to its support.

It is interesting to observe that the outstanding eighteenth-century naturalist William Curtis was compelled by soot pollution to shift his pioneer botanic garden first from Bermondsey to Lambeth in south London and then across the Thames to a site by the Fulham Road, but he seemed to accept this as a fact of life for which there was no remedy.

Yet, in retrospect, the eighteenth century may be seen as a turning-point on the way to modern conservation. It began in England with a revulsion against the geometrical landscape architecture that had reached its culmination at Louis XIV's Versailles and, with a swing of taste, partly aesthetic but partly also philosophical and political, towards natural patterns of landscape, which were felt to be more congenial to the freer and less authoritarian spirit of the age. At the same time the power of the monarchy was crippled. With virtual control over parliament and the church, the aristocratic landowners could devote themselves to improving their estates, partly as well-managed, mixed-use, money-making enterprises, and partly to yield returns in sports such as fox-hunting, in the creation of pleasing 'natural' landscapes, and in social prestige.

Spending so much time on their country estates these aristocrats and squires became clients for talented landscape designers such as Capability Brown and his successors. They combined innovative agriculture and livestock improvement with remunerative silviculture and other varied enterprises, all of which were harmonised with what we would now regard as conservation management of entire estates. Except for the gentle persuasion of a few imaginative friends such as Alexander Pope the poet and Joseph Addison the essayist, they embarked on this widespread campaign of conservation without any external call or pressure; it just came naturally, and blended spontaneously with their income-earning enterprises.

Aided by their power, wealth and progressive techniques, they did more than any other generations to create the picturesque English countryside. Unlike some of their successors who are with us 200 years later, they maintained and planted hedgerows and spinneys rather than clearing them away. Not infrequently they obtained Inclosure Acts which tended to benefit them at the expense of their poorer neighbours, whose loss was posterity's gain in terms of environmental quality. But already, by the opening of the nineteenth century the new temptations of exploiting mining and manufacturing opportunities led a number of their heirs to become accessories to the rape of much fine countryside, especially in the industrial north and Midlands.

Nurtured in the eighteenth century, the Romantic Movement in painting, poetry and literature developed into Victorian times a powerful influence towards kinship with nature, initially mainly in terms of scenery but gradually embracing also what we have now learnt to call wildlife. A great schism was, however, opening between this artistic and intellectual trend and the rough vigorous upsurge of industrial and commercial development, uncompromising in its materialism and in its pursuit of expansion and progress. Almost throughout the nineteenth century and the first half or more of the twentieth, these forces were in the ascendant, and the tender plant of caring for nature had to be cosseted among the more perceptive minority.

Some aid came from Queen Victoria's discovery of, and passion for, the Scottish Highlands, which gave prestige and wide publicity to wild country. Much also came from the impact of Darwin and his followers after the mid-century, whose preaching of evolution inevitably turned minds towards the biosphere, although too late and too marginally to check the spread of man-centred attitudes and beliefs. More romantic writers such as Thoreau and Emerson in America or W.H. Hudson and Richard Jefferies in England, and painters such as J.J. Audubon and Edwin Landseer kept nature in the forefront, without being able to reverse the materialist tide. Culturally they won admiration, but in real life they were the losers. Not entirely, however, since the seeds they sowed proved to be an important source of growth when at last the climate began to change towards environmental conservation.

Already, during the final third of the nineteenth century a few decisive steps were taken actually to organise practical conservation. In the United States, ever since 1681, when William Penn had provided for Pennsylvania 'to leave an acre of trees for every five acres cleared', there had been occasional voices calling for constraints upon 'rude and thoughtless wood-choppers' and for the setting aside of wilderness areas safe from exploitation. The first political response, however, occurred in crowded urban areas, where the risks to health and public order of corralling so many recent immigrants and others in overcrowded tenements without access to open space and fresh air became too menacing to be ignored.

By a miraculous chance the highly talented Frederic Law Olmsted, who was creating Central Park in New York, became free during 1863–5 to go out to California and initiate there what is now Yosemite National Park. It was visited at the outset by a group led by Speaker Colfax of the US Congress

In the creation of Yellowstone National Park, the superb adjoining Grand Teton range was omitted, but it won equal status much later and had a place in the Yellowstone Centenary of 1972, when this view was taken.

and the concept of a series of National Parks was born, although by historical accident Yellowstone, created by Act of Congress in 1872 takes first place. Even then it took another 44 years before the National Parks Service was constituted, and the original recommendation that Yellowstone should become a natural outdoor laboratory for the study of earth and life sciences has remained a dead letter.

Having recovered from the Civil War, the United States at this period gave rise to a vigorous movement for conservation – a word which was first used there in its modern sense (by a forester) almost simultaneously with the creation of Yellowstone. An impressive intellectual basis for it had been provided in 1864 by George Perkins Marsh in a book that, when revised some ten years later, was sensibly retitled *The Earth as Modified by Human Action*. By 1885 a start had already been made with what was much later to become the federal Fish and Wildlife Service – which competes with the almost simultaneous Hungarian State Centre for Research in Economic Ornithology for the honour of being the modern world's earliest official conservation agency.

This period, however, coincided with such mass slaughter of wildlife as was soon to lead to the extinction of the enormously abundant passenger pigeon and the vanishing of the vast herds of bison, which had up to then dominated the prairies of the United States. True to its reactive model the infant American conservation movement responded by creating the nucleus of the later powerful National Audubon Society, while a young hunter, Theodore Roosevelt, formed the Boone and Crockett Club, and the veteran John Muir, who had saved the Big Trees of California, launched the crusading Sierra Club. These were prototypes that were to gain immensely in importance during Theodore Roosevelt's term as President of the United States (see Chapter 7, pp. 156–8).

From a global standpoint these pioneering American contributions were later badly compromised by the side-tracking of the movement into a political role too esoteric and too involved in the complexities of the United States constitution to be suitable for wider application, even if the Americans themselves had not come to regard it as a purely domestic game, comparable with baseball. It thus happened that the rest of the world benefitted remarkably little from this excellent American pioneering, and had to set to work to re-invent the wheel.

The idea of the National Park proved adaptable in widely varying circumstances, as in New Zealand where a Maori chief's concern about the future of his tribe's mountainous holy places led to the device of handing them over to Queen Victoria and entrusting their care to the guardians of the Tongariro National Park, created for the purpose in 1894. Having thus acquired a model the New Zealanders proceeded to create other National Parks, starting with Egmont in 1900 and Fjordland in 1904. These, like their American prototypes, were mainly scenic and wilderness areas, in contrast to the contemporary South African models which were primarily wildlife reserves, such as the Sabie Game Reserve (1898 – now the Kruger National Park) and the Umfolozi Game Reserve established in 1897 in Natal, together with two others.

The spread of National Parks came later, but their early invention and successful establishment provided the conservation movement with an inspiring and widely popular model, vindicating the positive rather than the merely reactive approach. Their pioneers contributed greatly to the build-up of global interest and support for environmental conservation. Their easiest opportunities, however, occurred in thinly populated regions with plenty of wild, preferably mountainous scenery. More developed countries, especially in Europe, were mostly confined to contenting themselves with much more modest and less pristine terrain, although there were some partial exceptions such as the Swiss National Park in the Engadine, established during the second wave, in 1914.

In contrast to the American National Parks, the somewhat younger African network often displays spectacular wildlife rather than scenery as is shown in this view of the Kruger National Park, which dates from 1898.

By historical accident, the first moves toward international conservation were made in the late nineteenth century in Central Europe, partly as a by-product of the intense rivalry between Hungarians and Austrians in their joint Hapsburg empire, and partly through exaggerated fears on the part of German farmers that their crops were unduly exposed to pest damage through the massive slaughter of the insectivorous birds on migration through southern Europe. In the then political situation the Hungarians saw an opportunity to assert their international status. Having established a pioneer state centre for research in economic ornithology they pressed hard for an International Ornithological Congress. To their chagrin, however, this was eventually convened in Vienna, in pursuance of a resolution that had been passed there 16 years earlier by a meeting of German farmers and foresters requesting concerted international action for the protection of animals useful to agriculture and forestry. Although badly bungled and almost abortive, this meeting proved historic in putting conservation on the international agenda, and in providing it with a firm base in ornithology.

Through the persistence of the Hungarians, and the personal interest of Crown Prince Rudolf, himself an enthusiastic ornithologist, a second and this time effective congress was held in Budapest in 1891 under the presidency of Professor V. Fatio. (Rudolf had meanwhile died at Mayerling in a shooting incident which continues to intrigue many who are unaware of his much more lasting and significant role in assisting the launch of international conservation.) By this means also, conservation became founded, however shakily, on a scientific base in Europe. That eventually gave it a solidity and a status which has proved more enduring and authoritative than the power bases of other comparable international movements.

The vigour of the new initiative was demonstrated by a meeting in Paris in 1895 to discuss a French draft, followed in 1900 by a Third International Ornithological Congress, also in Paris, and by the signature in 1902 of an International Convention for the Protection of Birds Useful to Agriculture, signed by twelve European countries, not including the United Kingdom. In retrospect we can see this as the prototype for an eventual long series of international conservation measures, many of which have proved much more effectual.

Before the outbreak of the First World War in 1914 put a halt to progress, several other promising initiatives were taken, including measures against the slaughter of Antarctic penguins, agreed upon at the Fourth Congress in London in 1905, and the creation, at its successor in Berlin in 1910, of a standing fourteen-nation International Committee for Bird Preservation. This included the Americans, and no doubt encouraged them soon after the war to launch in London in 1922 the still flourishing International Committee for Bird Preservation (ICBP).

Meanwhile, at the Eighth International Zoological Congress at Graz in 1910, Dr Paul Sarasin of Basel had secured a resolution to 'establish an international or world commission for the protection of nature . . . it would have as its mission to extend protection of nature to the whole world from the north pole to the south pole, covering both continents and seas.' Although the Swiss Federal Government pursued the matter on behalf of the elected committee, drawn from Europe, America and Asia, inevitable delays deferred until November 1913 the meeting, at Basel, of an International Conference for the Protection of Nature. It unanimously resolved to establish in Basel a Consultative Commission for the International Protection of Nature, to form a clearing-house for international nature protection. This promised to compensate for the refusal of the succeeding American administration to fulfil President Theodore Roosevelt's intention, arising from the Conference of Governors in 1908, to convene an international conference on conservation. Unfortunately it was stopped short by the outbreak of war in 1914, and later efforts to revive it proved abortive.

As a spin-off, however, from the Roosevelt initiatives and from his friendship with the British Foreign Secretary, Sir Edward Grey, a North American Migratory Birds Treaty was signed in 1916, calling for major legislative and administrative back-up in both Canada and the United States, massively co-ordinated through the annual North American Wildlife Conferences and their associated special meetings. Equipped not only with money and manpower but with extensive research and monitoring facilities, vehicles, boats and aircraft, this operational and management network has, for almost seventy years, set an example of conservation in action, designed to meet not only the needs of a great army of shooters but of bird-watchers, scientists and many others. Mexico also joined in 1937.

In America, much more than in Europe, conservation concern began early to be focussed on the care of natural resources. An 'Arbor Day' to encourage tree-planting had been launched in 1872, and in 1873 Congress followed William Penn's example of almost two centuries earlier with a Timber Culture Act, which required settlers to plant with trees one-quarter of the plots allotted to them; however, this proved ineffective for want of public interest. Influential publicists could obtain new laws, and in concrete instances such as the safeguarding of Niagara Falls they could get action, but the mass of recent immigrants, townspeople and provincial farmers proved a formidable obstacle. Their inertia and short-sightedness called for vast and sustained efforts of education and propaganda. These, in turn, led to an earlier and greater build-up in America of conservation member societies, such as the National Audubon (1902) and the National Wildlife Federation (1930), and a strong but only partially successful drive for the teaching of conservation in schools.

One eventually important extension of conservation was achieved by President Theodore Roosevelt in 1907, when he established the Inland Waterways Commission with a remit to 'consider the relation of the streams to the use of the great permanent natural resources and their conservation for making and maintenance of prosperous homes.' Under his Presidency also this principle of unified river basin management was complemented by the development, with much more political muscle, of a strong professional United States Forest Service, which was able successfully to withstand a number of the land-greedy speculators and developers (see Chapter 7, pp. 156–8). By 1914, therefore, conservation was much more of a force in the United States than anywhere else, largely because the counter-pressures against which it had to struggle were also much more overt and politically powerful.

In Europe, the challenges calling for a conservation response had developed on quite different lines. Traditional and settled systems of land ownership in Britain were managed mainly with respect for the environment, and disputes were largely localised on such issues as enclosure of common land, and, later on, public access and rights of way. Threats to these, especially on the urban fringe gave rise in 1865 to the first nationally organised pioneer of the 'conservation lobby' the Commons, Open Spaces and Footpaths Preservation Society, which provided expert and legal advice and co-ordination for voluntary efforts at points of conflict.

This was a reaction to the encroachments triggered off by the General Inclosure Act of 1845, and more generally to the environmental degradation that became increasingly felt as the latter stages of the Industrial Revolution gained fresh impact from the nationwide spread of railways. It coincided, however, with a surge of interest in nature, stimulated partly by Darwin's disproof of the separateness of man, partly by a more positive interest in life and its quality as against crude materialism, through the influence of John Ruskin and others, and partly by the wider spread of good pictures of scenery, birds, and plants, which excited many imaginations.

The Selborne Society, the British Ornithologists' Union and other natural history and bird protection societies gave evidence of the growth and crystallisation of fresh interests. Some of these had scientific leanings, while others were aesthetic or ethical and even sentimental, and others focussed on saving threatened parts of the national heritage. In contrast to simultaneous trends in America none, however, showed special concern for natural resources of scenery as such, although influential individuals such as William Wordsworth in the Lake District had expressed deep concern for it.

In continental Europe, the disbandment of the *ancien régime* through the French Revolution put the control of land use in new hands, and was instrumental in creating a large horde of *chasseurs*, having little or no link with the land or its wildlife, who have to this day formed a major obstacle against comprehensive conservation of the natural environment, most of all in a number of Mediterranean countries. Art, especially painting, turned away from nature, and in effect (despite protestations to the contrary) became an ally of industrial materialism in promoting a man-centred universe.

In the British Empire, however, many administrators and other expatriates with good opportunities for travel and leisure pursuits keenly pursued interests in wildlife and the natural environment, and were able to lay strong foundations for their further development in India, in a number of African countries and in south-east Asia, where the founder of Singapore, Sir Stamford Raffles, was a gifted precursor of the movement.

Having thus attempted cursorily to pick out significant factors, from the earliest times until around 1920, which appear in retrospect to have had relevance to the emergence of environmental conservation, it seems fitting at this stage to bring the threads together before proceeding to describe the unfolding of the New Environmental Age.

Contrary to the false perspective that has been prevalent recently, the record shows that throughout most of human evolution the co-operative interaction between man and nature has been a paramount influence, holding man in no doubt that he must rely on the bounty of nature and on his skills in using it for subsistence and survival. Only comparatively lately in his story has man developed capacities for unilaterally modifying natural processes and resources, sufficiently to have to consider whether the results were wholly in his interest, and if not how he should modify his own conduct towards them.

For example, excessive hunting bags and indiscriminate felling or burning of forest led to obvious inconveniences, but in primitive times these were met either by minor changes of practice or by shifting elsewhere, or were psychologically compensated for by rituals of a religious nature. With the onset of more positive interventions such as domestication of livestock, cultivation of crops and then diversion of water for irrigation, there was scope for more adverse repercussions. Responsibility for handling these remained, however, in the hands of the interveners themselves, who could and sometimes did incorporate specific conservation practices in their operations, for instance by terracing hillside cultivations against erosion.

More complex organisation of states and economies, together with the growth of cities, often separated decision-making from continuous exposure to its impacts on the environment, and also tended to place it in the hands of persons particularly liable to overlook or dismiss them. While many land managers and others continued to exercise respect and restraint, the number and adverse consequences of irresponsible actions evoked first comment and later intervention from other quarters. For a long time these were mainly ignored or brushed off, except where matters of life and death were involved, as in the medieval measures adopted in Switzerland against interference with tree cover significant to the prevention of avalanches.

With such minor exceptions, we have to wait until the seventeenth and eighteenth centuries to find signs of a modern approach. Then nature ceases to be a hostile, brutish or simply exploitable background to human life and begins to arouse interest in its own right, first encouraging essays in imitating it in gardens and parks and soon attracting open admiration of its scenery and its wonders, eventually leading to nature-worship.

Modern environmental conservation, unlike that which came naturally to our remote ancestors, needs an ethical and moral base and a range of sophisticated perceptions and appreciations. Fortunately these were vigorously developed, both in Europe and North America, before the Industrial Revolution and its accompaniments lent urgency to the practical problems. Unfortunately, however, the power-base rapidly established by economics and technocracy soon became sufficiently dominant and blinkered to ignore and brush aside for several generations the parallel interest in the natural environment, which could make headway against it only gradually by learning to fight it piecemeal on many fronts.

Among these some were merely reactive, such as the protection of wildlife against persecution or excessive exploitation, the commercialisation of heritage sites, and the wanton waste of natural resources. Others were constructive, such as the identification and permanent reservation of outstanding areas as National Parks. It was only, however, at the end of the first quarter of the twentieth century that a start was made towards seeing and treating the various aspects of conservation as a whole, and towards building up the necessary knowledge, support and organisation to ensure that it would be taken seriously in the public arena.

How this culminating process was conducted, to the point of bringing into existence a New Environmental Age, is the subject of the next chapter, while others following it will describe its relations to the spread of knowledge and the growth of ideas, and the means by which the necessary organisation and resources were built up.

3

Environmental conservation comes of age

One definition of conservation equates it simply with applied ecology, and it was the somewhat tardy emergence of ecology as a scientific discipline during the early decades of the twentieth century that enabled conservation in this sense to develop. There had, however, been alternative concepts of conservation, ranging from the ethical and sentimental to the enhancement of quality of living, and right through to the most hard-boiled American view personified by Chief Forester Gifford Pinchot, which made it out as a comprehensive and well-planned management of natural resources of every character, based on sound ethical and economic grounds, but regarding failure to obtain a sustained yield as an unacceptable waste. 'Conservation is wise use' thus came into conflict with the ideas that conservation may often mean refraining from use, or even withdrawal from use.

During the period covered by this chapter, roughly the half-century from 1920, a free-for-all was accordingly conducted between those who disclaimed any serious role for conservation of any sort, those who espoused conservation in almost religious terms as meriting priority over any practical use of resources that was held to conflict with it, and those in between, some of whom leant towards conservation as simply a qualifying factor on economic development like Pinchot. Others, for scientific and pragmatic reasons sought compromises which would restrain economic and social development from embarking on types of land use incompatible with ecological and other values. These last placed special value on those methods and uses consistent with sustainability of yield in the biosphere. While champions of the first two groups have often hogged the limelight, the more serious dialogue has increasingly been between upholders of the second rival pair. The analysis of such ideological differences must, however, await the next chapter, this one being concerned rather with the unfolding of the events as they were played out.

34

With hindsight we can now begin to understand the highly complicated nature of the crisis during the mid twentieth century that forced the emergence of the environmental conservation movement. Earlier widely accepted obligations to keep the land in good heart, to care for trees in the interests of future timber supplies, and to build cities to last and to be livable had become neglected as new and more destructive technologies and more massive and irresponsible patterns of organisation spread. More power was shifted into the hands of men more and more ignorant of the environment, and readier to overexploit it to the limit. Whatever environmentalists may have thought was totally disregarded by decision-makers in business and in government.

The record of the central part of the twentieth century is of a gradual awakening to the full horror of this situation: the laborious and painful exploration of ways of coping first with some of the nastiest particular threats and abuses, and the arousal of public opinion, then with the mustering of its forces to fight and defeat environmental abuses and to campaign for the renewal of a lively sense of obligation and appreciation for environmental quality and diversity.

By reviewing what took place in the light of the origins and characteristics of the challenges and the problems encountered in analysing and meeting

Galinga volcano in Virunga (formerly Albert) National Park, Zaïre, which combines great scenery with wildlife interest and a record of scientific research.

them, we can now arrive at a better grasp of the broader underlying misconceptions, institutional faults, imbalances and follies which generated, and which still proliferate, activities inconsistent with the continuing health of our global environment.

Among the sectors in which the evolution of conservation is clearest and best documented over more than a century the National Parks rank as preeminent. After the early successes mentioned in the previous chapter, and others created in Australia, Canada and Mexico, there were initiatives on similar lines in Argentina, and Sweden, while societies with more modest aims were formed in the Netherlands, Germany, France and Great Britain. Spain set up two National Parks in 1918, followed by Italy in 1922–3 and Iceland in 1928, but in Europe history and land use confined most efforts to smaller nature parks, nature reserves and wildlife refuges.

Africa led the way in formulating an internationally accepted and reasonably adequate definition of the requirements for a National Park, enshrined in the London Convention of 1933. Africa also produced the outstanding example, in the Albert National Park of the then Belgian Congo, of the use of such a park as a base for a major scientific research program. By 1972 it was possible to list 167 National Parks and Equivalent Reserves in Africa, of which 111 included grass and woodland savannas, 73 lowland and gallery forests, while only 49 had alpine and montane habitats and only 5 included desert.

Japan began designating National Parks in 1931. In 1960 the International Union for the Conservation of Nature set up an International Commission for National Parks, having persuaded the Economic and Social Council of the United Nations at its session in Mexico City the previous year to endorse their value and to request help in compiling, on strict criteria, a comprehensive world list. This great task was duly performed by the International Commission (of which I was a member), and within a decade the total recognised came to 1204, of which 286 were in the United States.

By this time insistence on full evidence of the legal status and effective management of the areas had, to a large extent, countered the previously widespread tendency to declare National Parks for prestige purposes but to neglect to take effective care of them or to prevent encroachments upon them. Also, by means of World Conferences on National Parks held at Seattle in 1962 and at Yellowstone in 1972, much was done to raise the status and morale of the isolated Directors, and to assure them of technical and material support, which proved most valuable to them both practically and politically, in helping them to defend their charges and in encouraging governments to avoid the opprobrium of becoming listed as defaulters on their published international obligations.

By means of this world network of National Parks, many millions of interested visitors won some insight into the realities and values of conservation, while official and unofficial circles internationally became accustomed to the responsibilities involved and to the prestige accruing from fulfilling them. Important contributions were also made to scientific research and education, and to the promotion of tourism on lines satisfactory both to tourists and to the environment. Above all, the National Parks confuted persistent suggestions that conservation was dedicated solely to confrontation, restrictions on progress and interference with legitimate activities. On the contrary, it showed conservation as constructive, rewarding, attractive and even fun.

Under international rules, a National Park is acceptable only if it enjoys enduring legal protection that is adequately maintained by the central authority, and if it is of adequate size and open to visitors. There are many other areas, not fulfilling the United Nations criteria, that have been selected for protection on other grounds. Some of these have been so designated by governments, like the so-called National Parks in England and Wales, despite the fact that their integrity can be and is violated with official

Although not qualifying for international recognition, the British Snowdonia National Park affords a major recreational resource and outstanding scenery, as shown in this view with Snowdon in the background.

permission for new highways, defence and other inconsistent uses, quite apart from continuance of agriculture, forestry and human settlement.

Oddly enough, Great Britain contains many other areas which *are* accorded the necessary parliamentary protection, especially the inalienable lands of the National Trust and the National Nature Reserves of the Nature Conservancy Council. The latter call for some description here as they are so far the main examples in the world of the important conservation principle of permanently safeguarding the best surviving sites for each of the main ecosystems and habitats characteristic of a country.

In Britain, after an abortive attempt before the First World War to use the National Trust as an agency for managing such nature reserves, a special Society for the Promotion of Nature Reserves was formed by Charles Rothschild, and it duly prepared and submitted to the government a carefully selected list of sites whose scientific interest qualified them for special reservation. Unfortunately no action was taken until the Second World War gave occasion to revise and amplify the list, which this time was adopted (after further revision) by the official Wild Life Conservation Special Committee (England and Wales), of which I was a member, in its Report (Cmd 7122 of 1947) to the Minister of Town and Country Planning, on *Conservation of Nature in England and Wales.*

That Report was a landmark in several ways, most notably because it was quickly implemented by the establishment, as an official Research Council, of the Nature Conservancy, enjoying both charter and statutory powers. Of that more will be said in Chapter 5; it is relevant here to explain that the National Nature Reserves which it created were embodied in a comprehensive series of critically examined key sites throughout Great Britain, graded by national or international importance and by ecological type, such as coastlands, woodlands, lowland grasslands, heath and scrub, open waters, peatlands and upland grasslands and heaths. These were fully described and evaluated in the monumental two-volume *Nature Conservation Review* of 1977, which has been accepted as a final authority by numerous official inquiries and in parliamentary debates. It has thus rendered superfluous the often biassed and partial statements of the case on which arguments for conservation of particular sites had previously to be based and decided.

While this British national list was still in preparation an opportunity occurred to tackle the problem globally, within the International Biological Programme (IBP) of the International Council of Scientific Unions. IBP arose from a desire among leading biologists to match the prowess of International Geophysical Year, 1957–8. Early scrutiny showed that the studies first favoured, such as genetics and molecular biology, lacked the essential characteristics of differing widely in their manifestations in different parts of the world. That characteristic was strongest in ecology, which was then among the least advanced and worst supported branches of biology, and was indeed virtually unrepresented in many national Academies of Science. Far from being able to emulate the prestige and ample resources of International Geophysical Year the IBP attracted only limited and uncertain support among biologists generally, and was grossly underfunded and neglected by the scientific world.

As Convener of the Conservation (CT) section, I made great efforts, over the eight years 1963–71, to galvanise and assist the somewhat patchy national groups, in face of the frequent apathy or even opposition of their leading biological colleagues. As the late Professor C.H. Waddington observed in his frank description of the origin of IBP in the first volume of its results (*The Evolution of IBP*, 1975):

> The general idea among biologists at large seemed to be that ecology dealt with a blow-by-blow account of a day in the life of a cockroach, woodlouse or sparrow; and the notion that it could study such questions as what does the ecosystem do with the incident solar energy, tended to be greeted with blank stares of incomprehension.

To this I added, in my Introduction to volume 24 on *The IBP Survey of Conservation Sites; An Experimental Study* (Cambridge University Press, 1980)

> Waddington's idea that ecology should be looked on as a matter of energy throughput and processing was strange and largely unwelcome to biologists.
>
> Not for another four years did it really take roots and flourish on both sides of the Atlantic. Although within the perspective and programme of the British Nature Conservancy it integrated fairly easily with ecology applied in conservation, that kinship was not readily recognised elsewhere in the worlds either of biology or of conservation. The idea of massively expanding ecological research, to complement the ethical and social forces dedicated to conservation of nature along less scientific lines, proved even more difficult to put over than that of biological productivity. By far the greater part of the institutions and manpower deployed throughout the world on conservation were indifferent, or even suspicious and mildly hostile, towards the injection of ecological principles, methods and monitoring into their empirical arts.

In no other activity during my whole life have I suffered so much frustration and disillusionment as in the IBP, and even now, after the issue of nearly forty major volumes of results, the significance and value of the effort is little appreciated within biological and conservation circles, let alone elsewhere. As all is so fully on the record it would not be appropriate to treat the subject more lengthily here, except to state my view that in spite of everything it did succeed internationally in vindicating and consolidating the scientific base for conservation, and in dragging ecology into the mainstream of biology, with however much kicking and screaming on both sides.

While these events were in train to embody environmental conservation both in the governmental and scientific establishments and in the international comity, much else was also advancing within the field of voluntary bodies or, as they came to be called in international jargon the NGOs or non-governmental organisations. In few other spheres were so many NGOs so active, so effective and so well respected, despite the sneers in some business and other circles about 'the environmental lobby'. It must be clear from what has already been said that the lobbying aspect, forced upon the movement by the ignorance and stupidity of those who coined this pejorative term was secondary, and incidental, to a vast positive contribution. The network of thousands of properly acquired and well-managed conservation areas was on the map, and would steadily expand as evidence that the movement means business and has come to stay. Some of the more seminal aspects of the work of the voluntary societies and trusts must now be outlined.

In the late nineteenth and early twentieth centuries a substantial part was played by women in launching the prototypes of the present Royal Society for the Protection of Birds, the National Trust and the Selborne Society. The atmosphere was social rather than impersonal, and the dominant qualities were concern and missionary enthusiasm rather than expertise and field experience. From these beginnings it proved not too difficult to arouse public sympathy with the objects, and to construct a base which might not have been so readily created in other ways. The appeal to women was opportune, because at that time there was a boom in the sale of plumage which could be shown to be obtained for feminine adornment at the cost of slaughtering parent birds at nesting colonies – a sure means of arousing the right emotional response. It also attracted support for the tentative and limited initiatives that had already been taken on the scientific plane by some leaders of the British Ornithologists' Union and in terms of bird protection against wanton shooting at the Yorkshire seabird colony on Flamborough Head, resulting in the Act for the Preservation of Seabirds of 1869.

This early feminist bias – no man was admitted during the first year of the Society for the Protection of Birds, which consisted only of more than 5000 women – had an unfortunate outcome in sharply dividing the growing bird protection movement from the development of its natural scientific base in the then all-male British Ornithologists' Union and similar bodies. Only with the spread of the new habit of acquiring bird sanctuaries and equivalent nature and recreational reserves did the need for professional management begin to bridge the gap between sentiment and informed judgment.

The rapid progress of natural history and incipient conservation groups towards the turn of the century was promoted in part by some outstanding writers such as W.H. Hudson – a leading light in the Society for the

W. H. Hudson, one of the most inspiring and influential pioneers of conservation and an early leader of the Royal Society for the Protection of Birds, whose familiar logo is shown inset.

Protection of Birds (see Chapter 7, pp. 159–60) – and Richard Jefferies, and by the spectacular popularity of bird photography, largely through the daring and skilful pioneer field-work of the Kearton brothers. It was also a period of exceptionally hard winters, in which Victorian humanitarianism was readily attracted to feeding the birds in distress, while the popularisation, first of bicycles and later of motor vehicles, conferred a new mobility and led to a seeking out of new interests in the countryside.

In the earlier and middle nineteenth century, naturalist interests had been mainly devoted to the more static plants, invertebrates and geology, but with the new tools, including field glasses, birds steadily came to the fore. Being so elusive and lively, they attracted some more alert and enterprising characters, who were later to provide a disproportionate share of the pioneers and leaders of conservation. It is interesting to recall that one of the first of these new bird-watchers, using a penny-farthing without waiting for the modern bicycle, was Alfred Harmsworth, later vastly successful as founder of the *Daily Mail*, which some thirty years later still gave centre-page prominence to bird articles (often contributed by me, and helping nicely to support my early ornithological and other studies).

It is questionable whether, in the absence of such new tides as the emancipation of women, the growth of mobility and the availability of low-price cameras and optical equipment, the surge of interest in outdoor natural history and the environment would have occurred in Britain so early, so rapidly and with such enduring results. It also no doubt benefitted from more and better higher education and a wider and better range of books and periodicals, including the monthly *British Birds*, which from its foundation in 1907 successfully built up a keenly committed readership of active co-operative field ornithologists, forming the base on which large organisations could be developed.

At this time a trend became noticeable: the budding off from the often mainly social sharing of enthusiasms and concerns, characteristic of the late nineteenth century, of more serious and elite types of group aiming at a systematic output of scientifically respectable results. Outstanding among these were the ecological pioneers led by A.G. Tansley, who surveyed and evaluated the types of British vegetation and ranged more widely abroad in their phyto-sociological excursions, in the years leading up to the foundation of the British Ecological Society in 1913.

Equally elite socially, if not scientifically, were the founders in 1903 of the influential Society for the Preservation of the Wild Fauna of the Empire (or the Flora and Fauna Preservation Society as it is now more simply styled). They included: the then Duke of Bedford, who was already active saving the remnants of Père David's deer; Ray Lankester, Director of the Natural

History Museum; Sir Edward Grey; Sir Harry Johnston, discoverer of the okapi; and others of distinction. President Theodore Roosevelt of the United States was among the vice-presidents. Some had been concerned in a pioneer seven-nation Convention for the Preservation of Animals, Birds and Fish in Africa, which had been signed in London in 1900, and were troubled over a threat to an important game reserve in the Sudan.

As the British Empire then comprised about a quarter of the earth's land surface, and as interest in big game and their conservation was centred in Britain, it seemed reasonable then for such a group to regard itself as a global centre, and historically its foundation represented the start of organised international wildlife conservation. From the outset it has been based at the Zoological Society of London, and it has had close links with most of the international organisations that have since become established in this field, while long retaining a special interest in Africa.

By 1914, therefore, it was possible to trace a wide variety of small but flourishing initiatives, often unrelated, which were moving beyond the realm of learned discussion groups, or pursuers of outdoor enthusiasms or simply good causes, and were beginning to add up to a discernible if loose and complex movement. They were most prolific and are best documented in Britain, but similar trends were apparent in a number of other countries, and even internationally. Their total membership and muscle remained small, and they were often treated by the public and the media as a joke, but in retrospect it is evident that many of the foundations of the environmental conservation movement of to-day had already been laid.

That was just as well, since the environment was about to be faced with a range of challenges much greater, more numerous and more hazardous than anything that had previously been seen. A sample of these, and of the kinds of response made to them, will now be described briefly, but treatment of the underlying new thinking and strategy and the build-up of the necessary institutional structure, programs and legislation will be reserved for the two following chapters.

In the inter-war period, problems of persecution of wildlife by shooting, egg-collecting and trapping still held the forefront of concern. It was feared in the Scandinavian countries that a number of their treasured breeding species of ducks, geese and swans would be decimated by excessive shooting in their winter quarters. In 1925 Professor Einar Lönnberg of Sweden drew attention to the great decrease of the Anatidae in Europe, and through the support of Dr Percy Lowe an international conference on wildfowl was held in London in 1927. Immediate results were disappointing, but reports of the disastrous declines and consequent clampdown on shooting in the United States a decade later led to an awakening awareness. A series of well-judged initiatives gradually checked and reversed the decline and eventually resulted in European stocks increasing and spreading to an extent undreamt of, except by Lowe himself, sixty years ago.

This highly visible recovery on an international scale not only benefitted the species concerned but also the wildfowlers, who could thus continue their sport without severe restriction, and were consequently persuaded by a few courageous leaders to switch from an adversarial to a co-operative attitude towards conservationists. That was eventually symbolised by my election as a Vice-President of the Wildfowlers Association of Great Britain and Ireland (now the British Association for Shooting and Conservation). Co-operation has led to a settled confidence in the future, contrasting with the insecurity and bitterness characteristic especially of the early 1950s.

A valuable by-product has been a National Shooting Survey by the Association during 1979–84, which showed that, of some 866 000 British shotgun certificate holders, only around 160 000 were active in shooting ducks, either inland or on the coast, accounting for a total annual kill in Great Britain of just under a million ducks, of which some two-thirds were mallard. While the bag looks heavy in relation to estimated wintering stocks it has proved consistent with maintenance or even increase of populations, while the larger geese and swans have increased to an almost embarrassing extent. These results, which have been matched in North America by different methods, have had widespread effects in increasing the confidence of conservationists, and confidence in them by many others, including not only followers of field sports but landowners, agriculturalists, and even governments, which have become increasingly involved.

Another main activity of the International Council for Bird Preservation (ICBP; the senior international conservation agency, founded in London in 1922) has been the prevention of oil pollution at sea. While legislation against oil pollution in territorial waters of the United Kingdom dates from 1922 things got much worse after the Second World War. It was then wrongly contended that the evil was due to the gradual breaking up of ships sunk during the war, but some of us were sceptical. At the ICBP meeting in Uppsala, Sweden, in 1950 arrangements were made to collect samples from beaches in Britain; I then obtained the Government Chemist's agreement to analyse the specimens as to their type and probable origin. Once this became known to the major oil companies they perceived the advisability of co-operating, which they did by means of a large-scale sampling program.

It was soon clear that irresponsible release of oil by tankers and other vessels was a main cause, and this was unremittingly pursued by Phyllis Barclay-Smith, who formed a Co-ordinating Advisory Committee on Oil Pollution in 1952, and worked so effectively that in 1954 representatives of

32 nations met in London, at the invitation of the United Kingdom Government, to promote an International Convention for the Prevention of Pollution of the Sea by Oil. This, despite its sweeping title, was of limited application and only received the necessary ten ratifications to bring it into

The impact of the Torrey Canyon oilspill off Cornwall: (a) attempting to clean a neighbouring beach and (b) a few of the oiled guillemots, victims of pollution.

(a)

(b)

force during 1958. Even then the vital United States participation was delayed by the obstruction of shipping interests, until the deadlock was broken by James Callaghan MP, the Chairman of the Advisory Committee, on a later visit to Washington DC in company with Phyllis and myself.

The saga of irresponsible leakage of oil at sea, and irresponsible navigation leading to such unforgettable shipwrecks as that of the Torrey Canyon on the Isles of Scilly in March 1967, has continued, through the default of the International Maritime Organisation, the shipping interests and their governments, almost up to the present day. In ending it, the environmental movement received only puny and spasmodic support from other interests equally affected, such as tourism and the seaside resorts, yachting and the guardians of amenity. Nevertheless, aided by the dramatic catastrophes so liberally provided by shipping, the powerful and stubborn marine polluters were finally and very publicly brought to book. Their humiliating defeat helped to persuade others of the same kidney to come into line sooner rather than later. The message got home that it does not pay to be too obstinate in environmental matters.

A third worldwide confrontation, which helped decisively to confirm the new authority and power of the environmental movement, was the struggle over spraying of toxic chemicals on the land. Their use on a large scale and with drastic consequences began only towards the end of World War II, but already in 1949 the First International Technical Conference for the Protection of Nature (at Lake Success, New York) strongly and accurately warned against them and emphasised the necessity for avoiding 'the blind use of DDT – in time'.

The blind, however, led by the US Department of Agriculture, persisted on this tack. Their spokesman proudly assured the Fifth Technical Meeting at Copenhagen in 1954 that 'Since 1945, Americans have used 300 million pounds of insecticides annually to fight their insect enemies', largely in indiscriminate and wasteful ways. Despite the devastating effects, it needed the national shock of Rachel Carson's *Silent Spring*, some eight years later, to awaken the American public to the menace. (It is a healthy reminder of the importance of the prompt and effective media coverage lately developed for the environment that a topic of this importance then needed some thirteen years from the time it was first spelt out at Lake Success before it finally hit the headlines.)

Even after *Silent Spring* effective action in North America followed feebly and at snail's pace, while in Britain it had already been set in hand before Ms Carson's book was published. The first relatively secondary encounter between British conservationists and the spreaders of toxic chemicals over the environment began as early as 1952, when the Nature Conservancy reported to Parliament in measured and sober tones about the dangers of a new technique – the use of chemical sprays – for the control of roadside vegetation. Although still in its infancy – as indeed was the Conservancy itself – this technique was thought sufficiently significant to merit a small research program. County Councils contemplating its use were invited to consult the Conservancy and to enable data on its results to be obtained. It thus emerged that the efficiency of the method for the permanent control of abundant roadside weeds was limited, but it was unfortunately more successful in eradicating certain interesting and attractive wildflowers. It could also hit the populations of many insects that were already at risk through the impact of insecticides on neighbouring farms.

In response to the Conservancy's advice a somewhat reluctant Ministry of Transport and Civil Aviation issued in August 1955 a circular, in effect calling for the use of sprays to be limited to trunk and class I roads and to certain dangerous corners on class II roads. Under pressure from commercial interests and from ignorant criticism of 'untidiness', some highway authorities only fell into line when they realised that failure to do so would cost them more in high-level manpower hours than the few which they had hoped to save by spraying. This small success alerted the chemical industry to the fact that finding a profitable outlet for their products in the British environment was not going to be so easy as they had supposed, and that public relations as well as markets were involved.

Meanwhile, the Minister of Agriculture had set up a Working Party, under Sir Solly Zuckerman, on Precautionary Measures against Toxic Chemicals used in Agriculture. Its report, issued in 1955, included specific advice, suggested by its members appointed from the Nature Conservancy, to limit possible damage to wildlife. Although a keen watch was kept for evidence of such damage, none could be found in the ensuing seasons, and owing to lack of scientific funds field trials could not be conducted. Progress was however made with setting up a Wild Life Panel of the Inter-Departmental Advisory Committee, including members from the Conservancy, to assist in vetting products before they could come on the market.

While in 1959 the Conservancy was still vainly appealing for evidence, the spring of 1960 yielded a mass of reports of mysterious deaths, not only of birds such as pheasants, woodpigeons and finches, but of something like 1300 foxes. That flushed out the hitherto standoffish Masters of Foxhounds, and ensured their vigorous and valued co-operation. The appearance of a dazed fox wandering about in broad daylight in the yard of the Master of the prestigious Heythrop Hunt, and the sight of half-blind foxes eating grass, touched a tender nerve in the countryside.

The hitherto unconcerned government hastily approved the creation in

1960, at Monks Wood Experimental Station, near Huntingdon, Cambridgeshire, of a unit to investigate the effects of toxic chemicals on wildlife, with a complement that instantly made it the strongest team on earth dealing with this subject. That was just as well, since a number of leading agricultural and medical scientists who ought to have known better pooh-poohed the possibility of a connection between toxic chemicals and the deaths of wildlife. Their pompous but unfounded advice might well have stopped the necessary research, but for the promptitude with which the Association of British Manufacturers of Agricultural Chemicals saw the red light. At their annual dinner in May 1960 they had the chairman of the Conservancy as their guest and assured him of their wish to establish 'a real working partnership'.

Few research programs have had to be more rushed, and few have come up with valid results of the first importance so rapidly as that of Dr Norman Moore's new unit at Monks Wood. Action also followed quickly, both among environmental bodies and within government, and the industry lost no time in accepting the need for a comprehensive non-statutory system to regulate the use of toxic chemicals on the land through commercial channels.

Monks Wood Experimental Station (Cambridgeshire) and plots, just after construction, with woodland National Nature Reserve in the background.

The severe reduction in numbers of treasured species such as the peregrine could not be made good for several years despite the fact that this co-operative scheme was, on the whole, put into operation with efficiency and integrity by the manufacturers and distributors, and was accepted by all but a small minority of farmers. Internationally, however, the heads of Shell in London found themselves under severe attack from their Royal Dutch colleagues at having gone along with conclusions that could undermine the highly profitable export of similar toxic chemicals for indiscriminate use in the Third World.

This case was especially significant because it required scientific research of a high quality to be rapidly performed in order to convince the science-based chemical industry and government departments concerned of the validity of the conclusions which conservationists were drawing. The novelty of these made them suspect, even to leading scientists elsewhere. Had not the scientific base of ecology and conservation been already so sound, the successful agreement with the industry could not have been concluded, a long and futile argument would have ensued, and wildlife would have continued to die.

A very different confrontation on the land, directly between farmers and conservationists, was to build up in England later during the 1970s, coming to a head in the early 1980s, during the passage into law of the Wildlife and Countryside Act. Its origins extended back more than half a century to the depression of the 1920s and 1930s, during which such birds of derelict farmland as the woodlark and stone-curlew had flourished, together with rabbits and ragwort. The poet Hilaire Belloc had then lamented, in *Halnaker Mill*, that there was 'never a ploughman under the sun'.

Some of us had seen the way to recovery in Agricultural Marketing Boards, and in the intensive development of agricultural research as a lifeline to a new science-based agriculture – causes to which I devoted some time at Political and Economic Planning (PEP) during the 1930s, and which did indeed enable advantage to be taken of the sudden transformation of the agricultural scene through the necessities of World War II. After that war ended, the Attlee administration had to face fears that agriculture would once more be abandoned. As the Minister of Agriculture was not then in the Cabinet, I was marginally drawn in, as head of the Office of the Lord President, who had to sponsor the great Agriculture Act of 1947, which has ever since remained the keystone of United Kingdom agricultural policy.

Under these far-sighted provisions, farming prospered as never before, and the National Farmers' Union, in close concert with the Ministry, developed into what was widely regarded as the strongest political lobby in Britain. Entry into the European Community, with its peculiar brand of agricultural policy complicated, without for a time on balance worsening, the British farmers' situation. Far from being content to achieve national self-sufficiency in cereals and other favoured crops, and lacking the capability and drive to build up large export markets or to compete successfully with various temperate-zone imports, British farmers were content to press on with the creation of unsaleable surpluses, won by ever increasing mechanisation and reliance on costly applications of chemical fertilisers and of pesticides and herbicides. These, although no longer environmentally bringing instant disaster, were still injurious in various ways.

The misfortune of Dutch Elm Disease, permitted to spread through the negligence of the Forestry Commission over infected timber imports, put a spotlight on the rural landscape at a most inconvenient time for the farmers, who were already brutally ripping out treasured hedgerows in several regions, and were making ever more drastic use of the heavy equipment, which they were buying largely out of public subsidies, or on borrowed money, or both. It was clear to all, except the lending banks and to many of the farmers, that they were heading for financial trouble in a big way.

Unluckily, irritated by mounting criticism from environmental conservationists, agricultural leaders in league with the Ministry chose this moment to become embroiled in massive public confrontation with the environmental movement, both in its amenity and in its conservation aspects. No more foolish course could have been imagined by farming's worst enemies. Just at the time when agricultural leaders needed to win all possible friends, and to concentrate on a difficult and far-reaching change of direction away from the creation of impossibly expensive crop surpluses and towards a more varied and balanced rural economy, they chose to nail their colours to the mast of their good ship 'unlimited expansion at any cost', which they did not perceive was already beginning to sink. Their war with the environmentalists cost them their good standing with the public, and accordingly with the taxpayer.

Even after the Wildlife and Countryside Act became law, a number of farmers and their associates persisted in a campaign to undermine parts of it, and on Sedgemoor they even staged an event at which the Chairman of the Nature Conservancy Council was hanged in effigy. Being involved as President of the Royal Society for the Protection of Birds, I and some of my colleagues met the Presidents of the National Farmers' Union and the Country Landowners Association and asked them bluntly whether we were to proceed on the basis of trying to make the Act work, or whether we were going to let it become unworkable and shape up for a further battle for a new one. This was an issue to which we had to have a plain answer, and if the answer was 'make it work' then we must be able to rely fully on the goodwill and resolution of the entire farming and landowning community to do all that was necessary, including the disciplining, however strictly it might be required, of members or staff who stepped out of line. While we would not have shrunk from a confrontation we were greatly relieved by the response that our point was taken, and that there could be no question of anything except working together to fulfil Parliament's expressed requirements. Subsequent events have shown that the farmers and landowners have been as good as their word, and that, with the aid of their much increased support to the Farming and Wildlife Advisory Group and its county branches, a degree of positive co-operation has developed which would have been almost unthinkable as lately as 1980.

It is interesting to compare the stories just outlined, of environmental relations respectively with the wildfowlers, the interests in oil at sea, the agricultural chemicals manufacturers and the farming community. In all four cases initial confrontation was followed by extensive surveys and research on the issues at stake led by the conservationists. In the case of the wildfowlers the ensuing dialogue started on bitter terms but could readily be focussed on localised tangible situations and on open clashes of interest that were in practice largely reconcilable, once the emotional cross-currents could be identified and neutralised.

With oil at sea, the trouble was not between the main interests of conservationists and the oil and shipping industries, but rather with the initial lack of concern and awareness, and subsequently with the frequent sheer inability of their leaders to police and implement the necessary remedial measures over the wide oceans, and often even in ports. The global and indirect problems involved led to negotiations being extended over more than three decades before a tolerable result was attained, against less than one decade with the more compact and approachable British wildfowlers.

In the case of toxic chemicals on the land, the British industry concerned was also science-based and ready to listen, and its channels for influencing applications in the field were better, especially in terms of two-way communications. Agreements were negotiated quickly and smoothly and only a few years passed before monitoring of the worst affected wildlife populations showed that the measures were working, not only to halt further damage but to permit substantial recovery from past destruction. Elsewhere, however, no such good fortune was experienced. In the United States in particular, the clear message went long unheeded and even derided, while in the Third World products and dosages demonstrated to be unnecessary and destructive continued to be applied for commercial gain.

In the cases just described, although the aims and results of the conservation initiatives were related primarily to wildlife interests, others, including human beings, benefitted as well. There are, however, many cases in which this situation is reversed, and action is taken primarily for the interests of people. In the case of water pollution there were risks of unpleasantness, illness and even death if steps were not taken to restrain irresponsible discharge of effluents or other contamination with toxic substances. The lessons had to be learnt the hard way, making sanitation and pure water supply historically among the earliest steps towards conservation.

Fish populations harvested commercially or for sport are also susceptible, and concern for the stocks has led to some notable interventions, such as that of the Anglers Co-operative Society, who, under brilliant legal advice, successfully invoked the Common Law of England against industrialists who were spoiling their catch. Bird-watchers, in contrast, are usually less concerned about polluted waters, otherwise than with oil or the leaden weights and nylon lines of the anglers; indeed sewage farms and polluted tidal flats such as Seal Sands at Teesmouth have proved especially attractive to bird life.

Much the same applies to most air pollution, which may be feared as a risk to health or disliked as odorous, or as interfering with visibility, or depositing dirty or objectionable materials. More recently, even interferences with climate have been added to the list. While humanly caused fog can interfere with bird navigation, and plants can be killed by sooty and other deposits, in measures against both water and air pollution most of the running has been made by environmental health interests and others commonly seen as peripheral to the modern environmental conservation movement.

Yet similar types of survey, research and monitoring are called for, and in cases where those responsible do not readily respond to complaints it becomes necessary to use pressure groups that resemble and may even overlap with those of mainstream conservation. The same applies to threats to close, or convert to other uses, open spaces prized for recreation and amenity, which also commonly have features of natural or even of scientific interest.

Civil, and to a less extent military, aviation has been unfortunate in that its demands for rural landtake and sometimes for much consequential industrial and residential development have been accompanied by a growing volume, intensity and spread of unpleasant noise, to which many people are keenly sensitive. Airlines, airport authorities and aircraft manufacturers have accordingly found themselves exposed to environmental pressures that have built up the more strongly because they were so long belittled or ignored. In the case of *Concorde* these pressures were severe enough to fetter intended operational patterns and routes. The siting and extension of airports in Europe and Japan, for example, has come up against formidable and at times insuperable environmental objections. In such cases recourse has sometimes been made to the new device of Environmental Impact Assessment, which is discussed in Chapter 5, p. 101.

In all the examples so far given, except for oil pollution of the sea, environmental conservation was concerned with a clear localised target, and the connection of cause and effect was obvious and unarguable. Even for oil at sea, although the offender was difficult to track down with certainty, the presence of an oil patch was indisputable, and so was the legal responsibility of a shipowner whose vessel could be proved to have offended.

In time, however, the tracing of crimes against the environment became less direct and less clear. In the early case of whaling it was difficult to monitor non-compliance with quotas, and the carefree attitude towards conservation of leading whaling countries led some conservationists to conclude that nothing short of physical interference with the operation in circumstances of worldwide publicity would suffice to restore order. This daunting task was undertaken by Greenpeace, who courageously and with great skill and persistence made arrangements to harass the whale harassers, and gradually to convince them that their cruel and piratical enterprise was not worth the candle.

Meanwhile Sir Peter Scott and others were no less persistent and skilful on the International Whaling Commission in using research data progressively

Whale-watching – the civilised replacement for whaling – off the coast of New England, USA.

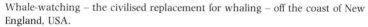

to extend the scope of protection. For some time it seemed that the stubbornness of the whaling interests would prevail, but their own persistence in overkill finally convinced most of them that their 'industry' had no long-term future. Unfortunately, by that time the numbers of some whale species were so alarmingly reduced that at best a recovery can be hoped for only after some decades. Nevertheless the struggle for whale conservation counts as a success story, in that by the early 1980s payments for trips to go out and watch whales at sea for the first time exceeded the returns from killing them.

Thanks to the courage of Greenpeace volunteers and the unremitting efforts of conservationists fighting the wanton destruction of these noble animals, it seems now reasonable to hope that posterity will be able to enjoy them. Meanwhile worldwide publicity has enlisted the keen sympathies of many who have never seen a whale, but will regard its rescue from extinction as an inspiring reason to support the conservation movement.

A whale is at least a visible object, even if its location may not be easy to establish in the wide ocean. The record shows that environmental conservation sooner or later succeeds in dealing with offences of a tangible character, but recently the trend has been towards much more disturbing intangible damage to the environment, either through chemicals let loose to roam through different layers of the atmosphere, or through nuclear radiation. The resulting problems are particularly disturbing because they strike so widely at the roots of global life support systems, because their agents are technically so difficult to trace and monitor, especially when they combine spontaneously with one another after release, and because of their ability to become transported rapidly over long distances and at varying altitudes by air currents, whose movements are imperfectly understood.

The recent international controversy over 'acid rain' and its suspected capacity for killing forests illustrates the problems of tracing and mitigating the effects of large discharges of toxic chemicals released high into the atmosphere and then carried across national boundaries. Suspected consequences in the deaths of fish, trees and other forms of life may only occur in distant regions after long lapses of time, and in circumstances where droughts, frosts, plant or animal diseases or other unrelated factors may be present to confuse the investigation. In addition, the suspected agent at the point of striking may have been transmuted by processes on the way from the suspected agent at the suspected point of origin, perhaps hundreds of kilometres distant. Even when it is generally agreed that the recipients of such ecological damage have a case for compensation and for the prevention of the nuisance, tracing the cause may defeat existing scientific capabilities. At best there may be a probability that it is due to some industrial practice that could be credibly modified only at great cost, and with no certainty that the damage imputed to it would be remedied.

This apparently almost insoluble problem is the outcome of many years of one-track approaches to the control of pollution, due largely to the habit of tackling each situation reactively on the basis of specific and often localised complaints. Just as the movement itself has evolved from a series of isolated groups to a network with a co-ordinated strategy, so pollution control must now shift from *ex post facto* interventions to comprehensive safeguarding of the total atmosphere. Prevention of death is not enough; support of healthy life everywhere is the essential.

Hitherto, the assumption has been that it is in order to release into the air, water or soil any unwanted substance or vapour unless it has been shown to be so toxic or damaging in itself as to call for legal regulation or prohibition. That assumption is inadequate for three reasons.

1. It assumes that those responsible for regulation can invariably and promptly ascertain which substances possibly to be released are harmful and in what way and at what range.

Such pictures as this are widely claimed to illustrate the horrors of acid rain, which undoubtedly exist but are most difficult to trace conclusively in relation to forests, although easier for lakes and rivers. Release of a wide range of toxic chemicals into the atmosphere, where they become subtly blended and transported over long distances, is an environmental hazard which should be stopped, but the task of tracing cause and effect between distant points subject to immensely diverse influences is one for the rash.

2. It cannot take account of the toxic or injurious combinations that can be formed spontaneously in the atmosphere, unknown to those who released or authorised the original possibly individually harmless components, or may arise from processes occurring long after release.

3. It rests on the pernicious economic doctrine of externalities, rather than on the English Common Law principle that no one has a right to extrude into commons such as watercourses or the atmosphere anything that may impair the rightful enjoyment of these by neighbours. The preservation of common values should be the responsibility of all, and they should put it at risk entirely at their own peril, without expecting the community to provide safeguards against their malfeasance.

This line of thought led, at the Third General Assembly of the IBP at Varna, Bulgaria in 1968, to proposals for the regular and comprehensive monitoring of changes in the environment, complementing existing meteorological and other recording. It was proposed that baseline stations at carefully chosen sites not only might enable trends to be traced generally but might also be linked with in-depth ecological studies leading to better understanding of the factors involved. After being closely examined by the International Council for Scientific Unions' newly created Scientific Committee on Problems of the Environment (SCOPE), the project was reported to the UN Conference on the Human Environment in 1972 at Stockholm, and has since become part of the standing United Nations Environment Programme (UNEP), which resulted from Stockholm.

As recently as 1970, a number of scientists had serious doubts as to whether such global monitoring could be carried out at acceptable cost and would provide data which would be meaningful for the purpose. Yet to-day, politicians, administrators, and business men take it for granted that such a service is instantly available worldwide, without giving a thought to how it came to be provided.

The way has thus been opened to a positive and comprehensive international commitment to the health of the biosphere. Recordings of relevant factors are checked at enough stations to give reliable early warning of excesses or deviations from regularly reconsidered levels of readings judged consistent with that requirement in the relevant sector, including the stratosphere and the ocean depths.

On this basis it becomes possible to prepare a regular full and accurate report on the *State of the World*, as is indeed being excellently done annually by the Worldwatch Institute of Washington, DC. Its regular *Reports on Progress towards a Sustainable Society* provide up-to-date facts on many subjects which it is accordingly unnecessary to spell out in such a book as this, where they would quickly become outdated.* For example, the 1985 *Report* shows that combustion of fossil fuels in power plants, factories and automobiles emitted into the atmosphere in 1950 some 1.6 billion tons of carbon and that this had more than tripled by 1979, but was reduced in the ensuing three years by more than 5%, following the reversal of the increase in oil consumption. More remarkably, limited conservation measures and switches have yielded since 1979 a 10% fall in world carbon emissions per $1000 of gross product.

The many obvious and large opportunities for energy conservation that are still neglected, especially in the United Kingdom, could incidentally greatly reduce risks of climatic deterioration through the 'greenhouse effect' of increasing carbon dioxide, and also the grave damage due to 'acid rain'. If, by the year 2000, American cars were as efficient as Japanese, assuming saturation in car ownership, 5% of world oil use would be saved. In aluminium production a doubling or tripling of the recycling rate is feasible, and could cut energy requirements by 90%. Japan manages to be a world leader in industry with an energy consumption per head well under half that of the United States, and a commercial energy consumption only one-fifth as high. Japanese improvements in energy efficiency in every major industry have typically paid for themselves within two years, yielding savings of up to 38%. Swedish homes, in a worse climate, use 30–50% less heat than American homes. Vast expenditure on housing subsidies in the United Kingdom could have been saved, if the authorities and the building industry had paid attention to modern practices in energy conservation, the subject of a belated and inadequate government campaign in 1985.

These few examples, out of many which could be given, show that standards of living, especially in the United Kingdom, are not being safeguarded but are being heavily reduced by failure to listen to messages that conservationists have grown bored of repeating year after year to politicians, managers and economists who will not listen. Conservation is not a fringe luxury; it is bound up with essential improvements, with which civilisation will have to dispense as reckless exploitation of non-renewable resources has to shrink.

Those in government and industry who have so long imposed such losses and wastes on their hapless citizens and consumers had better do their clear duty in achieving economies in resource use which can be and are achieved

---

* After this chapter was written, the World Resources Institute and the International Institute for Environment and Development have also launched jointly a major factual and statistical *Review of World Resources 1986: An Assessment of the Resource Base that Supports the Global Economy* (1986). A major Environmental Data Compendium is also to be published by UNEP in 1987.

by efficient producers today, and could undoubtedly be bettered if business managers gave their minds and energies to the job.

Far from being entitled to feel sorry for themselves over being criticised for pollution and avoidable hazards they should feel lucky that environmentalists with access to the figures have not launched direct attacks upon them for so badly letting down their own shareholders and consumers by failure to reach reasonable standards of efficiency. Let them not be complacent for too long.

One special industrial case remains to be briefly discussed on its own account – nuclear energy. The romantic love affair that many politicians, civil servants and business men have had with it has run for nearly forty years, and it is time to do searching sums on its cost-effectiveness and necessity – a subject which I first ventilated at the Public Inquiry into the Dungeness Power Station in December 1958.

The government at that time was convinced that a major program of nuclear power was urgent in view of its failure so to organise the coal industry that it could be relied upon to mine the necessary quantities to provide for future British energy needs. I submitted evidence to the contrary, much to the displeasure of the Central Electricity Generating Board and the government, who would no doubt have been even more displeased had they been vouchsafed the prevision to check that my view was right and their's was wrong, as the event finally showed.

I also took exception to the rush decision to construct half-a-dozen stations of an untried type at once, but I failed to foresee that, owing to massive delays and cost overruns, the economic justification for the program in terms of electricity output also would be upset. Nor did I or they foresee that, within a decade of the start of construction, oil would replace nuclear power for a critical period as the favourite energy source. The lead times for nuclear power stations are very long in the most favourable circumstances, and their subsequent useful life is short, after which their demolition and removal raise problems that make the white elephant appear a useful animal. I mention these to illustrate the difficulties of forecasting correctly whether and when investment in nuclear power will prove worth while.

Despite the above I have never adopted an outright or dogmatic attitude of opposition to nuclear power, and I made a helpful response to the Board over certain initial problems which it encountered at the original Hinkley Point and Sizewell sites. At that time it was wrongly assumed that technical work on the safe disposal of nuclear wastes would produce a generally acceptable solution, but for reasons that are not entirely clear no such solution had emerged by the time the problem of waste disposal had to be faced.

In view of the extent and very long duration of the hazard, and the secretiveness and unsatisfactory attitudes of those responsible, conservationists have become increasingly concerned, and have pressed for some clearly acceptable means to be devised and explained to them before there is yet more public investment in additional stations. Their disquiet has been increased by a series of careless accidents. Until 1986, the most notorious had been that at Three Mile Island, which had the effect of virtually suspending further nuclear power development in the United States for an indefinite period, although expansion of this nature continues in France and elsewhere.

In England, the accident record of Sellafield (previously called Windscale) has placed the nuclear industry under a dark cloud of its own making. It has become clear that, given really efficient conservation of energy and a modest development of safe renewable sources, the world could get by without expanding nuclear facilities for as many decades as it may take the nuclear scientists and engineers really to get their act into shape. It is also clear that, in the United Kingdom, erroneous budgeting and poor management during construction led to the misinvestment during the 1960s and 1970s of sums so vast that if properly redirected they might have decisively strengthened the now enfeebled national economy.

Quite apart from the follies of nuclear weapons, and the uncomfortable overlap between them and nuclear power developments, it seems now more

Using renewable energy from wind power with a 75 kW aerogenerator at Inganess Bay Salmon Farm, Orkney, Scotland, 1986.

than doubtful whether the massive switch towards nuclear development in the 1950s and 1960s was anything better than a prime example of hi-tech intoxication. At any rate the nuclear story strengthens two emerging maxims of environmental conservation experience – do not bank on future technical solutions before they are unquestionably achieved, and do not overlook the hazards of terrorism, human error or sheer negligence because where they can happen they will, sooner or later: see Murphy's Law.

The internationally damaging accident at Chernobyl in the Ukraine in April 1986, magnified in its impact by the long delay in ascertaining what was going wrong, and by the unpreparedness of the Soviet authorities to perceive and respond to the emergency, has dramatically vindicated environmental warnings that had been shrugged off as scaremongering by the nuclear power establishment. After this it became politically necessary in all countries, not excluding the USSR, to face the reality of nuclear radiation hazards arising inevitably from inevitable accidents, many of which were flushed out as having occurred without external consequences and accordingly having been hushed up. The rapidity and extent of the spread of radiation over Europe, finally reaching the United States and Japan, brought home the planetary implications of even peaceful nuclear processes, and led the Soviet government immediately to call for international co-operation over safety measures to which it had hitherto been rigidly opposed. Through a blend of heroism and good fortune neither the immediate nor the indirect casualties and damage proved, at least in the short run, as catastrophic as was at one time feared, but Chernobyl has made an enduring worldwide impression. Environmental cautions have been raised to even higher levels of credibility and respect. Above all, claims to national sovereignty as an excuse for environmental misconduct will be regarded with much more suspicion in future, and pressure for total nuclear disarmament will be intensified, not least within the ranks of the superpowers. If the shock waves of Chernobyl do not prematurely fade out they may bring results more than compensating for the injuries which it has inflicted.

Chernobyl obviously took the Kremlin by surprise, and precious time was wasted while mechanisms for scientific inquiry were improvised. In the United Kingdom, in addition to an Inspectorate for Nuclear Installations and a Health and Safety Executive with wide authority, there has existed since 1970 a standing Royal Commission on Environmental Pollution charged with advising the government 'on matters, both national and international, concerning the pollution of the environment; on the adequacy of research in this field; and the future possibilities of danger to the environment'. Its membership includes several leading scientists, Fellows of The Royal

Society, and its comprehensive Reports are taken seriously, attracting wide attention, and minimising risks of being forced to deal piecemeal with unforeseen pollution crises.

So far, in systematically going through the types of problem that have recently arisen in pursuing environmental conservation, most have been

Following the Chernobyl radioactivity disaster, vegetables showing excess radiation contamination are disposed of by a worker wearing protective clothing at Wannsee dump, Berlin, 1986.

found within developed countries. These tend to be better documented and more closely linked to the evolution of the movement. There are, however, very many and important examples also in developing countries, and a number of these arise directly out of projects for 'development', often funded from overseas, and involving the services of overseas 'experts'. Unfortunately over a long period it has been the exception rather than the rule to include among these any who are competent to perceive or deal with the numerous environmental problems which cry out for sound treatment.

The Third World is littered with the results of crass environmental blunders often perpetrated by engineers, economists and others who ought to have known better. In the words of one of the most experienced authorities, Professor Gilbert White of the United States:

> A puzzling aspect of many development projects is why they are not accompanied by more searching investigation of their ecological consequences. To what conditions can we trace the lack of attention given to fisheries studies in a hydro-electric project. The same question can be directed to irrigation projects and schistosomiasis, flood control schemes and soils, the effects of pesticides or fire control, and a host of other relationships . . . . There is good reason to think that development projects are spreading faster than efforts to anticipate their full consequences.

With such issues in mind I took the initiative, as Convener of the Conservation Section of the IBP, to assemble in Rome in 1970 representatives of the World Bank, FAO, UNDP, IUCN, the Conservation Foundation (Washington, DC) and United States and Canadian international development agencies, together with some representatives from developing countries. A conclusion of this meeting was that, in view of the recurring failures by development agencies, banks and others concerned to anticipate and take into account ecological problems that could compromise or cancel the success of development projects in the Third World, a handbook should be prepared, under the guidance of IUCN and the Conservation Foundation, to make the requirements and the means of fulfilling them readily available to decision-makers.

This was duly produced by Raymond F. Dasmann, John P. Milton and Peter H. Freeman in 1973 under the title *Ecological Principles for Economic Development*. It provided the decision-makers with just what they required, but so far as I am aware hardly any of them paid any attention to it, with the result that further large sums were expended on unwise investment and many innocent men, women and children starved. Environmental blindness prevailed, and it proved once again that where there is no vision the people perish.

One territory that fared better because it was totally undeveloped and not ripe for commercial exploitation was the Antarctic Continent. Through an unusually enlightened international initiative the twelve nations interested in Antarctica signed in 1959 an Antarctic Treaty that froze their respective claims to sovereignty and delegated a substantial responsibility for scientific research and conservation to a committee of the International Council of Scientific Unions. This was partly due to the prestige and success of the preceding International Geophysical Year. Despite recurrent alarms about the future, the peace and integrity of Antarctica has so far been successfully maintained. It is a marker and a demonstration (as yet precarious) of the values of international conservation.

Another recent multilateral international treaty of significance for conservation has been that for the control of pollution of the Mediterranean. That sea, with only 1% of the world ocean surface, was estimated in 1977 to have 50% of its floating oil and tar, fouling the beaches and fishing gear and tainting fish and molluscs, as well as damaging spawning grounds.

The position became so indefensible that eventually in 1976, on the initiative of UNEP, a Convention was concluded between the coastal states for the Protection of the Mediterranean Sea against Pollution. This was reinforced by three protocols for the Prevention of Pollution of the Mediterranean Sea by dumping from Ships and Aircraft, for Co-operation Concerning Pollution of the Mediterranean Sea by Oil etc., and for its protection against Pollution from Land-based Sources.

As a virtually landlocked sea serving as the depository of the waste products of 200 million coastal inhabitants, plus some 100 million seasonal tourists and substantial movements of badly behaved shipping, the Mediterranean clearly could not be left indefinitely to a free-for-all. It is to the credit of the coastal governments that they eventually proved willing to face the responsibilities for conservation.

At the other end of the spectrum a local reaction in India by women against the indiscriminate felling of forests by the forest authorities, in alliance with commercial timber interests, started in 1974 the successful Chipko movement, which has been widely publicised and to some extent imitated elsewhere. While preserving the local source of fuel, food, and water, this non-violent protest contributed towards relieving the exposure of valley dwellers to sudden unbridled floods that destroyed crops and dwellings far down-river. This helped to confirm the soundness of the Swiss system, under which forest management is thoroughly decentralised down to local commune level, instead of being subject to centralised decisions that can more easily ignore ecological and social considerations on the spot.

These examples given from different classes of conservation represent only a sample of the many and varied tasks that have been or are being brought to fruition in different parts of the world. They are in no way intended to form a comprehensive account, but merely to open the reader's eyes to the advanced stage and substantial scale of what is actually being done in terms of environmental conservation. They lend support to the thesis that the pioneering stages of the Environmental Revolution are now giving way to a more mature phase in which conservation is becoming widely embodied in the practice of good government and good management, with increasing public support.

Underlying the progress are strong currents of new thinking and changes of attitude, which will be reviewed in the next chapter. It is hoped thus to reinforce the account of events and developments already given by explaining some of the underlying ideas and organisations which help to underpin them. The corresponding organisations will themselves be reviewed in Chapter 5.

4

The growth of knowledge and the spread of ideas

In reviewing the age-long course of human evolution we have traced, since the dawn of civilisation, its deviation from a path of harmony with the natural environment. That deviation has at last brought awareness of its disastrous implications, which could even mean the close of the career on earth of *Homo sapiens*. Although the prophecies around 1970 of imminent environmental bankruptcy, under the title Doomsday, have been proved to be rashly premature, grave risks do persist. Indeed, the examples of Ethiopian famine and the Chernobyl nuclear disaster are warnings for all to see. Mankind, however, is showing signs of response to the challenge. Events during the past few years, although far short of being adequate, at least indicate that a turning-point is perhaps being reached, provided it is not already too late.

Most people note the progress and the setbacks without being able either to read a trend or to discern the underlying causes at work. But if the advance which we think we see is to continue, those engaged in furthering it need to know more. It involves the workings of our individual and collective minds, and without their successful performance there can be no happy ending. It is not enough simply to observe how the key science of ecology has gone ahead in elucidating the functioning of the biosphere and the problems of sustainability of yield. Nor can we be content with the rapidity of dissemination of so much relevant knowledge in so many countries, encouraging though that is, so far as it goes. Man is a learning animal, but in such times as these unlearning outdated ideas and attitudes is no less important than acquiring fresh ones.

The spread of understanding of basic environmental concepts and information has been so far very patchy. In open-minded circles, unattached to political, religious and economic dogma, it has proved rapid and widespread, but where those taints prevail, even among supposedly intelligent and educated people, there has been a high incidence of 'Don't knows' and even 'Don't want to knows'. Unfortunately these latter circles are influential in the running of some of the most powerful institutions in Britain, few of which show more than a lukewarm attitude towards environmental conservation.

In inquiring into the reasons and indeed the rationality of this resistance, we need to probe more deeply. It is now known that we delude ourselves in supposing that what we 'see' comes directly from the retina of our eyes. They merely perform the first stage of photo-reception, which would be chaotic unless it were instantly decoded and processed according to complex programs, reinterpreting it in terms of what we expect or indeed want to see. Such programs are fashioned to relate the image to something meaningful to us in terms of our capacity for understanding and our need to pick up the right signals for action. As J.Z. Young has expressed it, there are:

> sets of pathways and activities in the brain, determined partly by heredity but largely by learning, which organize the search for the meaning of the code signals in the visual pathways generated by the patterns of light on the retina. Each human individual learns to pick out from the maze of light, shadow and movement those patterns that symbolize objects of importance for him for life in his social world.

The relevance of this in relation to what we call environment appears to be three-fold. In our urbanised, verbalised and conceptualised civilisation, many people have never been exposed to the living world as it exists around them. They have had no occasion to develop the necessary internal program to 'see' it at work; to them it is no more than a backdrop or a painted veil; they suffer from total environmental blindness, of which they are blissfully unaware. Others may have become programmed to see a part of the environment dynamically, as a hunter will perceive his quarry and its immediate habitat, but they are blinkered and incapable of relating to the environment as a whole. Even those gifted with the fullest environmental vision are still inhibited, by limited knowledge and interpretive capacity, from eliminating much blurred background, which stays meaningless to them.

Those of us in the third group persist in addressing those in the first under a total misapprehension: that because they possess eyes they must see what we see and know what we are talking about. It is as if we were discussing the conspicuousness of strawberries with a colour-blind individual to whom they appear to be the same colour as their leaves. There must, however, be many whose environmental blindness simply derives from failures in their education and upbringing to activate latent capacities. In such cases remedial treatment must often have been provided by colour television and programs about nature, which will have stimulated and developed their vision and their understanding of the significance of what they are seeing, even if their everyday horizons are city streets.

Viewing and listening ratings show that many tens of thousands switch on to such programs as a regular preference, and are often tempted to go out in the field and look for such experiences at first hand. Indeed, their numbers often exceed those tuning in to, for example, politicians or speakers on economics, who find it hard to understand how they are failing to compete for public attention. While the subject is still speculative it would be well for environmentalists to bear in mind that some of our frustrations in explaining and exercising persuasion may be due to some such hidden barrier.

Even where no such barrier exists, the establishment of understanding of a new realm of awareness can be difficult. Some light on this is thrown by work done by a study group convened by Julian Huxley, of which I was a member over 30 years ago. We pursued the theme that common understanding and lines of conduct were often brought about by simple compound words expressing 'idea-systems', compressing together a wealth of meaning and associations, readily and widely understood as between one social or language group and another, and carrying a degree of acceptability enabling them to be readily recalled and brought up in conversation or in written communication. Such idea-systems were often enshrined in key words or stereotypes commanding ready assent and understanding, such as Fair Play, gentlemanly conduct, chivalry, Progress, and Democracy. In other cases they would be associated with institutions or groups of a more controversial nature, such as Communism, Capitalism, Propaganda, or Free Trade.

Our approach was focussed on understanding the role of such 'ordering concepts' in our society. While these could be examined in terms of semantics, scientific validity, social origins and associations, cultural significance, symbolism, emotional charge and much else, we were concerned with them particularly as tools of social advance or conflict, and as indicators of degrees of commitment, and intensity of concern, regarding identifiable matters on the agenda of human interaction. We were analysing whether it was possible to trace a social counterpart to biological evolution, and on that basis to promote better awareness and a capacity for constructively influencing its course.

The group envisaged itself as preparing the way for an advanced Institute of Human Relations, but although profound exploratory discussions were conducted, especially in the United States, by Julian Huxley, Jacob Bronowski and other members, nothing came of these. Perhaps some day the group's interesting and path-finding discussions will be suitably edited and published; it would be unfortunate if they were lost through being so far ahead of their time.

In conclusion, some idea of the group's contribution may be afforded by an extended quotation from a Memorandum for it by Julian Huxley dated March 1951:

> We can already define, at any rate in broad outline, certain key ideas or 'principles of order' . . . . I propose to call these '*key concepts*'. New key concepts, though they always meet with intellectual and emotional resistance when first put forward do in point of fact simplify the situation, in that they make it possible to understand it more readily, or at least to demonstrate that it is comprehensible on the basis of one or a few general principles . . . .
>
> One of the most important key concepts of the modern world has been the validity and the significance, both theoretical and practical, of the scientific method (rejection of any claim to absolute or complete knowledge; scientific doubt, limited certitude, but establishment of an increasing body of increasingly well organised and well tested 'public' knowledge . . .). The major crisis in the present ideological situation would appear to be the conflict between the ordering concepts provided by science and those provided by traditional religion or some substitute faith . . .. The present grave ideological breakdown in the West is due to the absence of overall key concepts capable of bridging the gap just mentioned, and of providing some dynamic incentive . . . . It is important to recognise that a new key concept may have a considerable practical effect . . . before it has been worked out in full detail . . . . As an example one may refer to the belief held by Bacon and the founders of the Royal Society in the immense practical importance of dispassionate enquiry into all aspects of natural knowledge. This they held to in spite of ridicule, and in spite of often not being able to show any practical results . . . . It would appear that one of the things required now is a comparable belief in the importance for human life of a real 'science of man'.

To that I will simply add from a simultaneous note of my own:

> The importance of Idea-systems may be attributed to man being a symbol-making and symbol-guided animal; to their Protean vitality and capacity for evolution and adaptation; to their power

within wide limits to reconcile irrational, rational and institutional initiatives by key minorities of high prestige and power such as priests, politicians, artists and scientists. Idea-systems might even be regarded as the 'matter' of which human society is composed, and the budding-off of new or the breakdown of old idea-systems as a process comparable to nuclear fission . . . .

The importance of key words and their wide dissemination has by no means been overlooked within the environmental movement. 'Ecology', the first of them, was coined well over a century ago to define the relationship between animals and plants and their natural environment; however, it remained generally neglected for nearly all its first hundred years. 'Environment' itself, in its main current meaning, is much more recent; among the first occasions of its use was by Professor Paul Sears at Princeton in 1955 in the pathfinding Wenner-Gren Symposium on *Man's Role in Changing the Face of the Earth*. Scientifically, the 'environment' is simply the biosphere looked at in man-centred terms. In other words it is the global biological and physical system and endowment on which man depends for his existence and wellbeing, and which he may modify with impunity only within certain limits. The invention and wide use of such a bridging word became necessary only as the widespread cases of interaction between man and nature, and their serious implications, became forced on public attention.

In the United States, largely for political reasons, 'conservation' gained national currency before the turn of the century. In Britain it emerged only in 1960 to express new public awareness that the environment needed to be treated systematically with care and respect, conservation being the term for that attitude and professional practice, on the part of environmentalists. Finally 'wildlife', as one word, was also imported from America to cover living plants and animals at large. None of these four key terms or 'buzzwords' would have been understood in most circles in Britain before 1960; now they carry with them a vast array of information, understanding, intentions, commitments and emotional awareness of the previously ignored realm to which they relate.

It is interesting to note the historical sequence of earlier key words in this area. 'Nature' seems to have come in during the Renaissance, followed during the sixteenth century by 'natural', 'naturalist' and 'natural history'. New schools of painting drew attention to enjoyable views of the countryside which were termed 'landscape', but as fashion veered towards admiring wilder terrain the word 'scenery' was coined some 200 years ago, followed a little later by 'habitat'. Each of these words charts a new stage in articulate human awareness of the environment.

As we have seen earlier, primitive man was probably intuitively aware of all this. Our contribution is to define and analyse it, in order by using modern techniques and capabilities to refresh ourselves from the same sources as our primitive forefathers. This contribution does not come from artists and intellectuals, but from ecologists and from countless quite ordinary people who have seen the light far ahead of them.

The force and pace of the environmental impact on our consciousness is attributable to the coincidence of a number of widespread and potentially universal sudden changes in our situation. Knowledge about, and concern for, our natural environment has gradually and modestly progressed to a point where it has been seized upon, partly as a means of redress for the excesses of materialist culture and its practical nuisances in pollution, waste and destruction of the living support base, and partly as a valued positive system of belief and integrated thinking. It thus makes good the near collapse of revealed religion and the disillusionment with dogmatic politics and with promises of 'progress'.

It is also related to the profound, although as yet still barely grasped, influence of our fast-growing knowledge of the workings of the brain and the mysteries of the mind, in terms of both their miraculous capabilities and their inconvenient limitations. We become preoccupied with what we perceive, how we perceive it, and how we wrestle with the resulting influx of information, and attempt to understand its significance, its usefulness and its interrelations. Revolutionary shifts are implied away from traditional impermanent intellectual and artistic material towards the analysis of environment, natural resources and the uses which man has made of them.

Two important fields of relevant interest here are model-making and lateral thinking. The brain evidently has a need and a capacity for model-making, but the process is in practice very faulty; so much so that myth-making might often be a fairer description. To make models adequate for sound thought and action calls for full access to the relevant facts, thorough training in analysing and evaluating them, and a capacity to identify and to choose correctly between alternative interpretations and options.

This would be central to a worthwhile modern system of education, but most educationists do not know and do not want to know about it. As a result their charges emerge from schools able to make only models that are distorted, partial, mistaken or simply cock-eyed, leading them from wrong premises to mistaken conclusions throughout their lives. The urgency of correcting this grave educational deficiency is heightened by the rapid computerisation of so many activities, and by the manifest unemployability of so many. The waste of human resources involved is vast.

The many successes of the environmental movement indicate that its performance in sound model-making must have been much better than average. This may be because the environment is a highly suitable subject for model-making, aided by modern ecology, and because it attracts people with probably better than average capabilities in this direction, partly for positive reasons and partly in an effort to escape from more traditional closed systems of thought. The gradual shift towards fieldwork, in informal and now even in formal education, inevitably involves ecologists and conservationists. There is much to be said for including the promotion of model-making in suitable contexts as one of the priority interests of the movement in coming years, despite disillusioning results from premature and simplistic attempts at ecological model-making.

Lateral thinking also is a developing trend helpful to environmental conservation, and signs have recently multiplied that this is being understood and acted upon. It appears that we start at a disadvantage through our dependence for the synthesis of information in the brain upon an infinity of tiny cells, with little access laterally to others, bringing potentially related information in separate streams to a much higher level. There, if anywhere, the lateral combinations have to be teased out. Awkward and time-consuming processes of cross-checking, linkages, comparisons, and tracing inconsistencies, gaps and conflicts have to be brought into play in compensation; fortunately this is an area in which the computer can help to make good our innate deficiencies. Indeed there is a convergence between the new kinds of thinking emerging in the environmental movement and the new kinds implicitly demanded for the operation of modern computers and communications.

It is by no means impossible to train the mind in this direction, especially among those such as environmentalists who do not suffer from blockages by cherished dogmas, inhibitions, prejudices or obsessions. It begins to appear that, as compared with politicians, clerics and business men, environmentalists do tend to show up better where lateral thinking is demanded. This may link with the observed fact that businesses managed by known environmentalists are also often the same as those achieving the best records in growth and profitability, which call for similar qualities.

Another marked characteristic of environmentalists, sometimes ruefully commented upon by their adversaries or rivals, is their frequent unusual degree of motivation – a quality in which key sectors of business and public administration are visibly lacking. Part of the explanation may be traceable to the images and arena of activity, going back to the scene of the instinctive drives of primitive man and his hunting groups. A keen perception of the natural environment, its dangers and opportunities was then not a sophisticated luxury but an essential for survival, which may still give echoes from our psychological depths. The confidence and sense of belonging arising from keen identification with a perceived habitat may also distinguish committed environmentalists from the alienated, apathetic, overstressed children of arbitrarily devastated and reconstructed inner cities, where a sense of not belonging and neglect leads to conflict, vandalism, criminality and even rioting. Concern for the environment has socially healthy consequences, and unconcern for it the reverse, as has been learnt and acted upon by civic leaders and business men in many great American cities, but unhappily not yet by their British counterparts.

Looking at the problem of inspiring and motivating a new environmentally oriented worldwide culture, we are faced with the contrast between the rapid and sweeping advances made by the environmental movement in some areas and its almost total lack of progress in others. Comparison with equivalent global campaigns for other good causes shows that most of them (see Chapter 6) have fared even worse, partly through faults in strategy or presentation, partly through inherent difficulties in their particular fields, but also through coming up against similar invisible barriers to receptiveness for the message. What are these barriers, which cause so much loss and suffering, and how can they be surmounted?

There is evidently no simple answer, but the direction in which we must search is in defining positive targets, in terms likely to prove acceptable to those who are currently resisting advance, and negative targets for the demolition or neutralisation of outdated attitudes, institutional policies or doctrines, and tracts of ignorance or prejudice which stand in the way. As successful advertising campaigns show, the essential need is for thorough analysis of the potential benefits and how to present them, and of the sources of resistance or competition and how to circumvent them. Empirically the environmental movement has not done badly in such respects, but the more its target areas are diversified and extended the more it will need to study and apply some of the approaches which have been lightly touched upon above.

The same goes for the other parallel movements for improving world conditions (see Chapter 6). These might add to their effectiveness and be easier to work with if they could take on board some of these conclusions. The time is past for one-track, blinkered approaches to the necessary strategies and presentations. The scientific, psychological and philosophical tools are in course of being developed. All that is needed is to learn about them and to use them. This is not a matter of propaganda or manipulating people, but rather of helping them to become aware of the potentialities which are open to each of them.

The environmental movement, at any rate, has no Pope, no Grand Master or dictator, no establishment or hierarchy and only a modest and low-profile group of leaders resolved to communicate and co-operate with one another as fully as is humanly possible. The movement does not offer affluence, power or honours, but it is wide open and it offers much else.

Part of the success of the movement has been due to its skilful division of labour between different groups with different talents and interests, serving different functions on different levels with different techniques and in different tones of voice. It is important in assessing the record and the future potential of the movement to be aware of the ecology of the ecologists, and indeed of environmental conservation as a whole.

Research and survey are fundamental, as we recognised in building up in Great Britain the official Nature Conservancy, which was originally one of the government Research Councils, before its main research functions were unwisely transferred away to the Institute of Terrestrial Ecology under the separated Natural Environment Research Council (NERC). The reconstituted Nature Conservancy Council (NCC) has, however, gradually been able to win back the essential direct research role in support of conservation, while NERC tries to focus on the more fundamental and broader aspects.

Specialised studies such as those concerning birds are provided under contract by the British Trust for Ornithology and the Wildfowl Trust, and contributions are also made by such bodies as the Game Conservancy, the Royal Society for the Protection of Birds, the Zoological Society of London, the Jersey Wild Life Preservation Trust, the Pheasant Trust, and others, with the technical back-up of the Biological Records Centre at Monks Wood. It can thus be claimed that conservation of the natural environment compares not unfavourably with agriculture and defence in the facilities which it can draw upon in Britain for providing it with all necessary scientific data and advice.

There is also provision for graduate and post-graduate training in environmental studies at Aberdeen University, University College London, the University of East Anglia, the Universities of Oxford, Sussex, Durham and elsewhere. A vocational course for wardens, interpreters and others is being launched in London, by the Trust for Urban Ecology and the Royal Society of Arts. The well-established Field Studies Council provides many, mainly briefer, courses.

As a result it can be said that the supply of trained men and women in this field is becoming fully adequate to meet recruitment needs, and sometimes more than adequate. There is capacity also for training candidates from other parts of the world, whose numbers could indeed be expanded. Perhaps the most serious gap is in training at the highest level for future top conservationists, to replace the notable band of leaders who appeared miraculously, as if from nowhere, to participate in building up the movement during the 1950s and 1960s. The recent creation of a Julian Huxley Fellowship at postgraduate level at Balliol College, Oxford, is a first step towards filling this gap.

The program of acquisition and management of Nature Reserves is also being well underpinned by research and experiments in applied ecology and techniques of conservation, notably by the NCC, both on sites managed for the purpose such as Moor House, Cumbria, and by numerous projects run directly or under contract, which are reported in special publications. These afford fairly comprehensive coverage of the field of required advice and information in practical conservation.

In 1986 this coverage was extended to urban ecology by the publication of *Promotion of Nature in Cities and Towns* by the Ecological Parks Trust (now renamed the Trust for Urban Ecology) with NCC support. This comprehensive practical guide fully describes the state of the art, for the benefit of those creating or managing city nature parks and similar projects relating to the Greening of Cities. It is being followed up by an international research seminar in London in 1987, to give cohesion to hitherto isolated studies of urban ecology in various countries.

Some ambitious habitat creation projects have been successfully undertaken, notably by the RSPB at Minsmere, Suffolk, and on a similar but even more ambitious model at Acebuche, beside the Parque Nacional de Doñana in south-west Spain, by the official agency ICONA (see p. 102) with the advice of the maker of the Minsmere network of pools and observation hides, H.E. Axell.

Considerable expertise has thus been acquired, not only in the maintenance and ecological upkeep of a wide variety of natural areas, but in recreating semi-natural conditions even from scratch, on sites where they have been lost. Although ecological research programs have been run in a number of National Parks in different countries, these have generally played only a limited part in informing and guiding management, which has often tended to concentrate more upon visitor facilities, interpretation and public control.

It is, however, now rare for sites acquired on account of their natural characteristics and wildlife to be allowed to degenerate into, for example, uninteresting scrubland, as was unhappily the case for a time with the Society for the Promotion of Nature Reserves' land at Woodwalton Fen, Cambridgeshire, towards the middle of this century. The necessary knowledge and expertise is now widely accessible to serve a variety of conservation objectives.

Recently what used to be called 'landscape architecture' or even 'landscape gardening' has taken ecology on board in a thorough manner, and may now be regarded as a form of applied ecology with design as a guiding factor. The Landscape Research Group has made valuable contributions in this part of the field, which is clearly a growth sector, enabling key principles of ecology and conservation to be persuasively demonstrated in many areas.

As recently as thirty years ago most conservation tasks were performed unpaid by amateurs, and even now the expanding core of professionals needs to be extensively reinforced by volunteers, mainly part-time but some full-time. The enrolment, induction and supervision of these volunteers is itself a major commitment, even involving national specialist bodies such as the British Trust for Conservation Volunteers, which has come far since I promoted its first field operation at Box Hill in Surrey in February 1959 (when it was known as the Conservation Corps).

The governmental Manpower Services Commission, inspired originally by some pioneer activities in Canada, has found environmental conservation a particularly appropriate field for the recruitment and giving of job experience to young people who are unemployed. This has been something of a mixed blessing to voluntary bodies, who value the extra manpower at their disposal but find it hard to manage the administrative responsibilities involved, and are troubled by the very short period allowed for training before a fresh lot of raw recruits have to be tackled. Thanks to the data and advice referred to above, these voluntary bodies have on the whole managed to develop an impressive degree of professionalism.

The decentralisation of such vigorous organisations as the County Trusts for Nature Conservation and the Farming and Wildlife Advisory Groups is providing an expanding network of well-informed and experienced advisers and promoters throughout England, and to a less extent over the entire United Kingdom. It should be noted that by far the greater part of the time and efforts of all of these is devoted to positive practical activities, contrary to the oft-repeated allegations that environmentalists do nothing but agitate and obstruct the activities of others.

Indeed, a recent Annual Report of the NCC devoted some ten pages out of seventy-seven to detailed accounts of Working with Others, of which the majority were voluntary bodies, and an equal amount of space was needed to describe Advice to Government Ministers and others, including the carrying out of legislation, while a further seven pages were required to outline the Council's active participation in International and Overseas Activities. In respect both of interaction on equal terms between official and voluntary bodies and of playing a leading initiating rather than reactive role in international developments, the British environmental conservation movement compares strikingly well with most of its world counterparts. The account here given for Britain could however, if space allowed, be impressively complemented by descriptions of comparable developments in other countries.

Since 1970 especially, there has been a remarkable development of environmental law and regulation. Indeed it is arguable that there was an excess of enthusiasm on the part of some environmentalists for putting everything on the statute book, matched by the readiness of public administrators to add to their official tasks and often by the preference of progressive industrialists to see responsibilities that they would have been content to assume made mandatory upon their less public-spirited fellows. Spurred on by public opinion and by threats of Doomsday, and concerned at the slowness of such alternative methods as education and voluntary effort, the path of environmental law was unquestioningly followed by legislatures and the Courts. This extended to pulping many trees for the printing of voluminous Environmental Impact Assessments that were often too bulky and too irrelevant to be useful.

In the United Kingdom all this was superimposed on a very detailed and comprehensive system of planning law and controls, which, since the invention in 1949 of Sites of Special Scientific Interest, had become increasingly involved in environmental conservation, and in numerous lengthy Public Inquiries, in which well-paid lawyers and largely unpaid conservationists took a prominent part.

Nature study in schools is one of the oldest elements in the complex of environmental activities, and it was responsible for the stimulation and early training of many leading pioneers. For reasons which are not entirely clear, the lively outdoor element in what is now called environmental education became frozen out of the standard curriculum, and replaced by a second-hand pattern of desk and class-room pedagogy in the hands of biology teachers. Most of these lacked either the interest or the competence to show their pupils, or even to explain to them verbally, any part of the workings of the biosphere, or of particular ecosystems.

The tendency to teach conservation as a Good Thing rather than as a subject of objective study, and the tyranny of examinations, brought about the strange result that while ecology and conservation were being eagerly absorbed in the outside world, not least by children, the decades of the 1950s to 1980s must go down in the history of environmental education as simply years which the locust has eaten. The Ministry of Education, in an official publication issued in 1960, summed up with appalling frankness the current type of advanced biological studies in schools as making a contribution to the pupil's education that 'is so small that it is doubtful whether such a subject ought to find a place in a school at all'. I quoted this in *The Environmental Revolution* in 1970, but despite all efforts little real improvement is yet visible. There are, however, some signs that, with the introduction of the new General Certificate of Secondary Education and its provisions for including fieldwork, some improvement may gradually be achieved, although not in time to enable the schools to have contributed on any worthwhile scale to the environmental revolution, which has had to go through without them.

To round off the picture of the main occupational groups involved, it is necessary to mention the land-linked professions, including surveyors, land agents, agricultural advisers, foresters and arboriculturists, public park superintendents, gardeners, civil engineers, site developers, town and country planners and the above-mentioned landscape designers. Some of these, particularly landscape designers and foresters, include a number of self-selected fellow-travellers of the environmental movement, with similar perceptions and interests. Others, notably town and country planners, without apparently sharing such predispositions and tastes, are commonly

Creation of ponds and other water bodies on unused land within and around human settlements has been facilitated by modern equipment, and also by recruitment of young volunteers to realise such conservation projects, which bring benefits not only to wildlife but in several other ways. This picture shows part of a conservation project to improve an area of scrub within the grounds of Gladstone Primary School, Barry, South Glamorgan, to provide a science study area for children aged 4 to 11. This local project was initiated by the school with grant aid from the Nature Conservancy Council, 1986.

sympathetic to environmental views and objectives, and can be of great assistance in promoting them. Agricultural advisers and civil engineers, however, appear to start from a remote base, and only become interested and understanding over a long course of persuasion and instruction.

Some of the rest, despite their involvement with site surveys and site management, seem still more distant and uninterested, even in parts of their professional concerns that might be thought to overlap with environmental conservation. On the whole, expectations of enlisting such professions as allies of the conservation movement have so far been disappointed, and indeed a number of them have proved persistently subservient to contrary or exploiting interests.

With increasing frequency, members of these and other professions have appeared as environmental consultants and have thus sometimes been influenced either directly by clients or by confrontation with critics of the projects in question, to adopt new attitudes and to take trouble to master the environmental implications. In such circumstances more progress is often made than where opinions may be expressed and attitudes maintained which are sheltered from reality by a self-contained institutional back-ground. This area of retrogressive professional overlap, like that of the educational establishment, is a source of much concern and hindrance from the standpoint of environmental conservation, and is taking much too long to resolve.

The final area calling for mention here is that of the media. These have brought big surprises. On the one hand most editors and journalists start from an opposite end of the spectrum and are little predisposed to be sympathetic to, or perceptive about, the material of conservation. On the other hand their nose for a good row soon taught them that conservationists had much to offer in terms of publicly interesting and newsworthy confrontations with major groups, on whose injured responses they could count. It has therefore been as news creators that conservationists have best succeeded in claiming media coverage, although, given the evidence of widespread reader interest, even some non-controversial environmental topics increasingly qualify for treatment. A special case is that of film, television and radio documentaries, the popularity of which has encouraged the rise of a remarkably talented and ruggedly capable group of directors, producers, advisers and others, including cameramen, sound recordists and supporting technicians, who go out into the field and come back with enthralling pictures and recordings, often of rarely encountered species or behaviour in unusual and fascinating habitats. The results of their valiant labours are in objective terms stunning, but have become taken for granted through their unfailing succession on the screen or radio.

As lately as June 1971, this view of an ugly gash in the Panama rainforest was issued by the United Nations with a 20-line explanation of the 'justified introduction' of the mineral survey project, and without a word concerning the ecological and environmental impacts, which had evidently not crossed the minds of those responsible.

No appraisal of the advance of environmental conservation should fail to pay tribute to the outstanding, and indeed decisive, contribution of this group to the rapid acceptance of the message of the movement, and indeed to the enrichment of the message itself. Series such as the BBC's *Life on Earth*, by David Attenborough, and Anglia Television's *Survival* have proved a major British contribution to the worldwide movement, without which its following would be much less enthusiastic and well informed, and also more narrowly limited. They are vividly perceived by each individual, and their message is quickly and faithfully embodied in the social conscience.

So much for the composition of the main sectors more or less professionally concerned in environmental conservation. Compared with, say, a quarter of a century earlier they are strikingly increased in numbers, in sophistication and confidence, and in their support base and consequent status in the world. The steadiness and continued buoyancy of their growth is a good augury for the future, provided that they can avoid sinking into a rut, and can continue to expand their perspectives and capabilities. The institutional aspect of this expansion will be dealt with in the following

David Attenborough, one of the leading exponents of communicating conservation through the media, in a rainforest in Ecuador.

chapter, but meanwhile it is necessary to review briefly the changing patterns of motivation and attitudes of the movement, as they are reflected in its strategy, tactics, style and tone.

In a past which is already distant in terms of development of the movement, but pretty recent as history, a heterogeneous bunch of sentimentalists, scientists, outraged citizens, nature writers, explorers, hobby naturalists, collectors, painters, photographers and others found themselves gradually driven together by circumstances, with little sense of common interest, and certainly no idea that they were marking out the way for a worldwide movement. Challenges from outside rather than their own intentions drew them inexorably into a loose community faced willy-nilly with a set of diverse targets that gradually grouped themselves into subjects for common treatment. Botanists, ornithologists, lovers of scenery, and many others tended to focus on their own particular parts of the field, coming together only as and when common interest so prescribed. (In Chapter 7, an attempt is made to illustrate this in terms of the personalities involved.)

Other divisions began to crystallise, according to degrees of expertise or vague amateurism, intensity of commitment and time available to devote to it, perception of the importance and urgency of tasks of conservation, and the style and tone favoured by people of different temperament, whether gently persuasive and educational, subtly diplomatic or openly challenging and even aggressive. All these and other divisive elements existed and had to be faced, sometimes with explosive or painful impacts on particular groups. It is one of the remarkable features of the broad church of environmental conservation that its worshippers have been quick to perceive, and tolerant in responding to, the differences between them, in these and other ways, and have freely recognised that there may be nine and ninety ways of composing their tribal lays but that every single one of them may be right. There have been enough distinct but parallel or converging bodies to cater for all tastes, and occasional grandiose and misguided projects for herding them all into one have been quietly but firmly declined.

Indeed, experience has led many conservationists to see the wisdom of the maxim *Vive la différence!* Since the Copenhagen Assembly of the International Union for the Protection of Nature (as it was then named) in 1954, it has been accepted that the main international parliament of the movement should be science led and science based, without, however, excluding supporters of other complexions, except some suspected of conflicting loyalties to incompatible interests.

As I explained to a Canadian gathering of timber interests in 1973, the conservation movement includes sharply divided elements that may, in oversimplified terms, be categorised as polarisers and integrators. The polarisers are the heirs of its pioneering missionary and campaigning stage. Partly from temperament, and partly through their reading of events, they cling tenaciously to the belief that modern culture, and above all modern industry, is incurably exploitative and destructive towards natural environment, and can only be curbed from ruining it by incessant warfare through the media, the law courts, and pressure groups operating with no holds barred.

The integrators, on the other hand, while sharing much the same historical analysis, attribute environmental damage not to unalterable selfish attitudes and interests but to defects in scientific analysis, in appraisal of costs and benefits, and above all in education and training, which can be and are being gradually remedied – especially in the ranks of many large economic agencies, both public and private.

I explained also at that meeting that, while any integrator worth his salt still stands ready to join the polarisers in an all-out assault on those who persist in pursuing environmentally destructive courses in defiance of ecological principles, integrators are more concerned to find and co-operate with any operators in the area of natural resources who are ready to follow responsible policies, but often need help and guidance to find out how. Integrators are strong pragmatists, who seek to judge, by the scale of results obtainable through substituting co-operation for embattled deadlock, which course will most benefit the environment over a period.

Which will best perpetuate the still precarious support that public opinion gives to conservation? Which will most effectively secure the integration of conservation objectives in a healthier phase of civilisation? Which will enable most scientific and professional people to work together most effectively at technical levels, where real progress must depend on their trained efforts rather than propaganda or political muscle?

I added that while I ranged myself among the integrators, parting company with the polarisers where they appear to me to be carried away by their own emotions or dogmatic beliefs, I recognise the validity of their natural suspicion that they risk being conned into accepting some disingenuous or flimsy compromise, leading to a renewed breach or a surrender of essential values.

It must be conceded, too, that polarisers play a necessary role in keeping the care of environment high on the agenda of public affairs. It is sad that friendly and constructive co-operation is never news, but strife and heated words always are; so unless the pot is kept boiling somewhere there is little to keep people alert and aware. It is bad luck for those, especially in industry and administration, who consider themselves unjustly pilloried; but their sufferings are not in vain – they help the more far-sighted managers to carry the less responsive with them in taking wise action while there is still time.

Reflecting now on these remarks of mine more than a dozen years ago I see no reason to amend them, and I believe the role-playing aspect of the debate has come to be better accepted and understood, while the polarisers have learnt how to produce their act more smoothly and to accompany it with a more effective and disarming display of expert knowledge, which has won some notable victories. At the same time, in view of what has been shown earlier about the disease of environmental blindness, and in view of our continuing inability to find a treatment for it, the blunt instrument of the polarisers may at times prove to be the only means of awakening the patient to the facts of his incapacity.

The spectacle of many groups of intelligent people doing their utmost to destroy the vital life support systems of their posterity on earth, and angrily opposing efforts by more enlightened groups to mitigate or prevent the mischief, is a truly remarkable phenomenon of our age, and one which we can be sure our successors, if they are permitted to survive on earth, will find it difficult to credit. What is the nature and cause of this perversity? How can it be corrected or cured, short of locking up those affected in secure homes for the environmentally blind?

Our natural environment is inexorably prescribed as the scenario for the search for reality which man as a questing animal pursues with his senses, and especially with his vision. Blockages in this field must have been uncommon or unknown among our hunting–gathering primitive fore-fathers, who could hardly have survived them, and indeed were ever busy sharpening their environmental perceptions. Unfortunately, during the past 5000 years or so, a bunch of priests, pedagogues, intellectuals and power-crazed or money-crazed cliques have not only turned their backs on these natural insights but have inculcated idea-systems and assumptions which inhibit their functioning, not, fortunately, in all of us, but in a great many. They fail to recognise that our gift of sight is not a matter of taking endless still photographs, but is an unceasing search of our lively visible environment for the rewards that it so richly offers and for the cautions that it signals to us. We have only to watch a dog out for a walk to understand what may come naturally, although in our case with sights rather than with scents, and only if we do not allow ourselves or our teachers and mentors artificially to inhibit the process.

This goes far to explain the unnecessary violence and alienation that we have allowed our architects and planners to create in our inner cities, by adopting what we may term the vandalesque (rather than the modern) style of architecture and civic design. Our questing eyes are programmed to seek rewarding habitats, blending fertile open spaces, rich in living creatures, interspersed with sheltering woodland or rocks, and with streams, pools or expanses of refreshing water. Instead, our civic designers, full of self-congratulation, present us with the precise opposite of our profound human need – an environment that is hard, sterile and lacking in greenery, or offered only in stiff mathematical unnatural strips, and which threateningly overhangs us with structures too tall, too geometrical, too uniform and too coldly surfaced to give any human satisfaction. They could not be more wrong, yet the consequent vandalism, criminality, alienation and even rioting often fails to convey to them that something is radically at fault with their whole approach.

Surely, enough is enough: is it not now clear that no one ought to be let loose as a planner or architect who has not had his or her environmental sight tested and found to be functioning properly, as an initial process in his or her professional training?

As our eyes search for rewarding habitats, and also for friendly fellow-beings, they are impelled and guided not merely by the hope of obtaining tangible satisfactions but also by the immediate enjoyment which they find in the process. It is widely accepted that landscape painters and their followers derive pleasure and fulfilment from simply looking at landscape, but it is less widely recognised that not only famous viewpoints but countless ordinary scenes, even townscapes, bring profound if inarticulate satisfactions to ordinary people going about their ordinary pursuits.

Still less is it recognised that such satisfactions are not dispensable luxuries but are psychological necessities, deprivation of which can cumulatively bring about frustrations and sufferings similar in kind, if not in degree, to those of a prisoner in solitary confinement. Some minimum daily ration of environmental quality above a certain threshold level is for many a precondition of healthy and happy living.

Those responsible for the redevelopment of many of our inner city quarters are guilty of inflicting psychological malnutrition on the inhabitants. Conversely, even despised suburban environments, with enough open space and greenery, can disseminate palpable if invisible satisfactions to suburbanites. Failure to appreciate such positive and healing properties of the environment underlies many modern ills and tensions. It would be helpful if the right specialists could trace and publicise the evident linkages between the programming of human vision and the rewards or turn-offs presented to it by different types of modern environment.

As we grope our way towards the New Environmental Age we need to become aware that the health of our environment is not just a matter of sound ecological management and of preventing damage and destruction; it also involves human mental health, the state of which it tends to mirror. In limited areas, such as indiscriminate tobacco smoking and noise-making. It is now socially accepted that becoming a prey to some weakness is no excuse for inflicting gratuitous suffering and damage on one's fellows. The same is coming to be felt about drunken driving of motor vehicles, addiction to heroin and similar drugs, and loutish behaviour by sports fans.

Should not the same apply also to those who seek to impose on the community as normality the consequences of their own mental ill-health in environmental matters, for which they ought instead to be seeking cures in their own interest? Is not their pollution, their vandalism at the expense of environmental quality, and their misuse of power and exploitation of the tolerance of the community similar in principle to the other evils mentioned, which the community in self-defence is finding it necessary to outlaw? Far from continuing to permit themselves to be branded as peculiar, environmentalists should now begin to turn the tables, and to expose the anti-social abnormalities of the sponsors of many of the misguided projects which they are having to fight. This should be done not by direct confrontation, but by promoting much wider and keener awareness of some of the conditions that have been briefly discussed above. What is the use of moving over to a much healthier and more nutritional diet on our tables if we remain exposed to the cripplingly unhealthy environmental quality that is foisted upon us once we emerge from our doors?

Environmental conservation has risen within three brief decades from an obscure and almost laughable fad of a small minority to a widely respected and accepted principle of national policy, whose exponents are consulted and enlisted in many areas of public affairs, almost as if they were becoming an Estate of the Realm. Its task is far from complete, and its approach and practice will need to be extended to many areas that it has so far barely touched, in order that future life on earth may be safely and happily assured to our children and to their surviving fellow-creatures, to whom they will owe profound apologies on our behalf.

Meanwhile, environmentalists should be aware that, in the pursuit of their special interest, they have stumbled upon, and begun crudely to avail themselves of, fundamental evolutionary processes which are much more widely relevant, but have been missed by others in their search up evolutionary blind alleys. Julian Huxley touched upon these when he wrote of Teilhard de Chardin's psycho-social phase of evolution, based on the cumulative growth of knowledge and calling for the utmost realisation individually of the possibilities of knowing, feeling and willing. Those would be the most powerful religious motivation in the next stage of our evolution and which he termed transhumanism.

He named the process involved psychometabolism, and compared it with physical metabolism, enabling more types to utilise more efficiently more of the world's resources:

> Just as the physiological metabolic systems of organisms utilize as a raw material the physico-chemical resources of the environment, so brains utilize the raw materials of experience and transform them into special systems of organized awareness, or 'idea-systems', which then play important roles affecting both individual behaviour and social evolution.

These emerging processes, now visible in environmental conservation, are bound, barring catastrophes, to prevail over obsolete traditional habits of thought still enshrined so widely in the arts and in education. It may be that, with the aid of computerised data banks and electronic communications, their lateral spread as processes may be more influential in finally breaking the grip of adversarial institutions than any direct attack based on the latters' mistaken policies and practices.

In any event it is important to keep to the fore not only the point that environmental conservation is promoting new attitudes and ways of living that are essential to survival but also that it is doing so by fresh processes that make those used in many other contemporary activities obsolete and inefficient. The more those out-dated processes are clung to, the more often and thoroughly their practitioners are going to be beaten when they tangle with conservationists. As they come to understand this some of the damaging pressures will be relieved without the tiresome necessity of fighting every case. To concentrate too much on the 'what' and the 'why' of conservation may lead us to underrate the importance of the 'how'.

5

Organisation and resources of the movement

The many and diverse achievements of the environmental conservation movement, especially over the past three decades, could evidently not have occurred in the absence of efficient leadership, management and organisation to fulfil well-defined goals. Yet there has been no great multinational Environmental Conservation Corporation Unlimited behind these achievements – only a cluster of smallish, disunited, grossly underfunded and understaffed bodies, which by normal standards could not possibly have been expected to deliver such a scale and quality of performance.

It is important, at least for conservationists, that the reasons should be explained and digested. We need to dissect the operative structure of the movement in order to learn how it has come to deliver its actual performance, and where its limitations and weaknesses lie, as well as its strengths. How have the key teams been recruited and deployed? How has policy been formed and public opinion shaped? How has partnership been developed with governments and internationally? How have environmental requirements been converted into law and then enforced? How is the movement influencing others, and securing its integration in the body politic? How has it been able to advance from one stage to another, facing previously unheard-of problems? These are the kinds of question that need to be asked and answered.

In certain countries, as has been shown earlier, a number of lively voluntary environmental bodies came into existence a century or more ago. Over several decades they felt their way towards a coherent grasp of the problems then facing them, and began to reach a mature and settled status. In most countries, however, it has only been much more lately that pressing needs have compelled a response, often involving the hurried importation of models developed elsewhere. Thus, different countries are at different stages of maturity as regards their environment, some showing a bewildering wealth of competing or co-operating organisations, while in others there is a contrasting poverty. In some of these, pressure to fulfil a role internationally has played a greater part than any domestic concern within the country.

An early impetus to organised field natural history arose from the

Conservation sprang from ecology and natural history, which in turn developed and became organised through the need to identify and gather medicinal herbs. Chelsea Physic Garden, shown here, is one of the oldest places devoted to this purpose, dating from 1673, and having served to train many of the pioneers during the prehistory of ecology.

dependence of early medicine on locating, identifying and collecting therapeutic herbs. In Britain, special forays for this purpose, or 'herbarizings', had begun to be organised at least by 1620, combining the gathering of specimens with training of budding apothecaries in their recognition and use, plus social pleasures thrown in. From these it was a natural step to the creation of botanic gardens, such as the Chelsea Physic Garden, which has survived since 1673; such gardens needed paid keepers or demonstrators, who became prototypes of the professional botanist, and custodians of a growing technical literature. Before long roving botanists were seeking new specimens right across the earth, collecting and cultivating exotic species, studying their distribution and numbers and learning to draw and paint them faithfully.

Apart from professional involvement, such initiatives stirred the interest of curious amateurs, and already by 1689 a group of friends in London had joined together informally in the Temple Coffee House Botanic Club, with a membership of forty, meeting on Friday evenings and also making field excursions. Was this the world's first natural history society? The leisure, sometimes wealth, and enthusiasm of such pioneers ensured that the taste would spread, and that there would always be plenty of knowledgeable amateurs to balance and civilise the band of narrower professionals, based especially on the new systematic museums that became necessary to assemble and analyse the expanding scientific material. Concern for fauna and flora thus escaped the exclusion of the amateur, which occurred in other sciences such as physics and chemistry, and also avoided becoming too academic.

From such roots environmental conservation was able to grow with the informality and looseness of organisation that characterise it still. Working in the field rather than the laboratory enabled and encouraged the amateurs to hold their own, in a reasonably harmonious blend with the professionals to whom they served as eyes and ears at large, as well as attracting public support and funds. The professionals, meanwhile, digested data into worthwhile contributions to science, and ensured that scientific standards were respected and observed.

It did not prove easy, however, to resolve the incidental problems of organisation. Although natural history attracted a variety of followers, some of them were botanists, some entomologists, some geologists and as time went on more and more became ornithologists. They shared common needs, but not common interests, and effort was required to merge them together, as in the case of the nineteenth-century London Natural History Society, whose 1300 members are now brigaded in sections for ornithology, botany, ecology and entomology, geology and archaeology, plus Recorders for mammals, reptiles and amphibians, fish, molluscs, dragonflies, butter-flies, moths and miscellaneous invertebrates, and spiders. There have always been some who preferred to belong to more compact and homogeneous clubs devoted to a single branch, and others who paddled their own canoes, unwilling to join any organised group.

Until matters had been sorted out in the realm of natural history there could be no sound base for organising conservation. Luckily the pursuit of knowledge reached a stage, just in time, when field investigation demanded national co-ordination and the creation of modern data banks. That was where I came in, as a founder in 1933 of the British Trust for Ornithology (BTO). It was doubly innovative, both on account of its programmed scope and methods for filling gaps in knowledge systematically, and as a national organisation to mobilise and put to work those whom H.F. Witherby had appealed to when he had launched the monthly journal *British Birds* a quarter of a century earlier.

Its functions have been well outlined in Dr D.A. Ratcliffe's Foreword to *Enjoying Ornithology*, the book celebrating the first fifty years of the BTO. He writes of:

> the development of British ornithology during the twentieth century as a science, a hobby, and a key element in nature conservation practice. The role of the British Trust for Ornithology has involved all three aspects. In particular it has been the means of capitalising on the fieldwork of energetic and dedicated amateur birdwatchers, and welding together much of their effort in a co-ordinated form that has greatly advanced the science of ornitho-logy. . . . catalysing and focussing the interests of the membership in a highly productive way that has been the envy of other countries. The collecting urge has been poured creatively into bird ringing and recording, with the result that the distribution, numbers, movements and biology of our avifauna are probably better known than those of any other group of organisms . . . .
>
> The outstanding feature of the British Trust for Ornithology has, indeed, been its primary concern for advancement of knowledge through corporate research projects. There has always been the need for a full-time professional staff of trained ornithologists to organise and collate the field contributions of the Trust member-ship in these collective investigations.

By such means, he adds, the Nature Conservancy (now the NCC) has been provided with 'an assured flow of ornithological information tailored to the needs of its conservation programme'.

The success of the BTO was important in laying sound foundations for the conservation movement in Britain. Positively, it demonstrated that science could be significantly advanced by mobilising the carefully supervised efforts of the multiplying amateurs. It also proved to the amateurs themselves that participation in corporate inquiries could be just as much fun as unguided and usually unproductive recording. It also helped decisively to break down the deep prejudice against organisation among naturalists. As David Elliston Allen has explained in his excellent *The Naturalist in Britain* (1976):

> There were many naturalists who were frankly hostile to what they saw as the advent of a bureaucratization of the subject . . . For some, form-filling of any kind is deeply distasteful; it bears the mark of the official and seems out of keeping with a subject that for so many represents a thankful escape from the routines of the office. There are others, too, who claim to detect in all this emphasis on drills and discipline, on team-work and training, the nasty smell of over-organization, sufficient to stifle the essential spontaneity.

I myself was not immune from such reactions, but in me they were cancelled out by perception that the price would be justified by the gains. As I wrote later, 'fuller organization has released more abundant energy and ideas in an unprecedented wave of vitality and creative growth . . . . Within this supple and responsive system . . . the influence of the individual is not diminished but intensified.'

In retrospect, the timeliness of the BTO's pace-setting example has been confirmed and greatly increased by two subsequent developments undreamed of at its launch in the 1930s: the advent of the computer, with its potential for storing and analysing data banks, and the arrival of urgent demands by conservation for evidence that only such methods as the Trust's could provide, and keep up to date, as the above quotation from Ratcliffe indicates.

While parallel movements such as those for development and the relief of poverty in the Third World, or for peace and disarmament, have had to create their own often sketchy foundations, environmental conservation differs in resting upon a comprehensive and profound set prepared for it in

Logo of the British Trust for Ornithology.

advance by the natural history movement. It has inherited scientific principles and knowledge, rich practical experience, and a widespread band of keen, expert and co-operative practitioners.

Building upon that foundation, however, has not been straightforward. Many, initially a clear majority of naturalists, belonged to the escapist school who strongly reacted against any attempt to divert them from their excursions away from it all, and to enrol them in kinds of work which seemed to them distasteful and doubtfully necessary, or at least best left to government action. Others, who were less unwilling, proved to have so little sense of urgency, method and management that their help was of negative value to conservation. What was it then that created out of this worthy but essentially impotent and unconcerned movement the force that environmental conservation now is?

Perhaps three key factors may be traced. First, the naturalists were led to observe intently what was happening in their beloved world of nature, and as time went on a minority of them became more and more frequently distressed and angry over what they saw.

Second, the cumulative effects of their observations and records of trends led them to draw conclusions and to pursue inquiries that were bound to point to the need for and means of corrective action, and to raise the question who was to undertake it? Many shrank back, but those who accepted the logic and the challenge became pioneer conservationists. I was originally among the former of these groups, and I took care to ensure that the British Trust for Ornithology steered clear of conservation. We did, however, lay essential foundations for it by taking advantage of the compact size and dense observer coverage of Great Britain to build up a data bank, soon outmatched for a period by the Botanical Society of the British Isles with its *National Plant Atlas*, and later developed into the national Biological Records Centre, covering many groups of animals as well as plants, and extending to inventories of thousands of sites of scientific interest.

A third key factor was the ever commoner and greater impact of development and technology, presenting urgent specific challenges in terms of habitat destruction, pollution or mortality of wildlife. Thus spurred into action, *ad hoc* groups, often local, brought great pressure on even unenthusiastic naturalists to join in, if only with expert advice. Such new groups created new fellowships and loyalties, and threw together the more responsive naturalists with public-spirited people who were ready and able to go into action, unlike some of the naturalists, who were too meek, too preoccupied or otherwise unsuited. This dualism between dedicated but aloof naturalists and the robust soldiery of conservation has often persisted, and indeed has developed further as conservationists have themselves budded out into distinct types, sometimes adhering to distinct kinds of organisation.

While environmental conservation has therefore arisen on the scientific, social and organisational base of natural history, it has neither taken over that base nor been fettered by it from striking out on new lines. Indeed, it has had to do so, being much more involved with complex and even political kinds of action, demanding quite distinct techniques, organisation and times and scales of response.

Perhaps the most fundamental requirement, and the one which best bridges the gap between ecology and its application in conservation is what may be called a 'Think Tank' to digest, analyse and synthesise the body of relevant knowledge, and to develop strategies based on it. In Britain, A.G. Tansley had been the leader in profound thought on the subject, through such channels during World War II as the Conference on Nature Preservation in Post-War Reconstruction, its successor the Nature Reserves Investigation Committee, the Committee on Nature Conservation and Nature Reserves of the British Ecological Society, and the Biological Committee of the Royal Society. Such a plethora of committees sounds bad, but all were able to follow the lead given thirty years earlier by Charles Rothschild with his thorough list of elite sites, and the work of his Society for the Promotion of Nature Reserves.

The government-appointed Wild Life Special Committee of 1945–7, of which I was a member and Tansley the effective leader, was thus able to look at the whole field in much more breadth and depth than might have been expected from its apparently restrictive terms of reference. It functioned, indeed, as a Think Tank to such effect that decades were to pass before its Report (Cmd 7122 of 1947) showed any sign of ceasing to serve as a positive and reliable guide to the way ahead. Indeed it was not until the World Conservation Strategy was prepared internationally and followed through at national levels that any comparably comprehensive and far-seeing intellectual effort was repeated. An important and continuing Think Tank was, however, founded in New York in 1948 by Fairfield Osborn, and its major contribution to the worldwide movement will be summarised in Chapter 7 (p. 174).

Although the Wild Life Special Committee was shortlived, fate decreed that decisions about action on it rested with the Lord President of the Council, and that the new head of his office – myself – happened to have been a member of the Committee. Its recommendations accordingly received a more sympathetic understanding than usual in Whitehall, being steered gently through mechanisms which would normally have quietly buried them. They were given effect by a Royal Charter of March 1949 creating the official Nature Conservancy, and accorded wide additional scope by an Act of Parliament, which I helped to draft, in December 1949.

From that date, nature conservation in Britain became an official responsibility, although those who imagined that this ended the necessity for voluntary bodies to busy themselves with it were soon disillusioned. There was, however, no precedent to guide us, anywhere in the world, and apart from our clear mandate to build up a network of National Nature Reserves the rest of our functions were left somewhat open.

I say *our* because, in common with six other members of the former Wild Life Special Committee and eight newcomers, I became a Charter Member of the Nature Conservancy, while remaining head of the Lord President's

On a field inspection for the Wild Life Conservation Special Committee in 1946: A.G. Tansley standing with A.S. Watt, watched by Cyril Diver, with E.B. Ford looking at something on the ground. From a painting by L.J. Watson.

Office, to which it reported. Six of my colleagues were Fellows of the Royal Society, four more were senior professors, three were Members of Parliament, from both the main parties, one was Chairman of the National Parks Commission and another a senior officer of the Forestry Commission. Our views and decisions, therefore, could not be readily gainsaid in any serious quarter, especially since no one knew at the time what such an agency ought and ought not to do.

In view of our membership and our status as a Research Council we placed strong emphasis upon research. It had, however, to be focussed on the kinds of decision we would have to make about the creation and running of nature reserves, and on our advisory duties concerning such wider problems as animal populations and control of invading vegetation. After a somewhat wobbly start, with no assurance that the experiment would work, the early retirement of its first chief executive created a crisis which was resolved only by my agreeing under pressure to take on the task.

The foundation of the Nature Conservancy as the first official science-based environmental conservation agency in the world was undertaken, so far as the administrative aspects were concerned, in an oddly light-hearted spirit. Hardly any of my senior colleagues when we received the Charter had any real experience of management or administration, and even I, despite my wartime shipping experience and my headship of small offices with picked high-grade staffs, had little to go on as regards many of the problems

A tower block, the result of bad planning in the 1950s, being demolished at Rochester, Kent.

we were to face in developing our nationwide activities. I soon found that neither the Research Council nor the Civil Service model would serve our purpose, and that we needed to devise a new structure, and above all a new style.

I fear I sometimes went so far as to say to my officers, 'If in doubt, try to think what the Treasury would do in such circumstances, and then just do the opposite. That way you will rarely be wrong!' I was never trained in management or organisation, but I found that what came naturally to me usually worked, especially in delegating responsibility down the line, coupled with careful briefing about policies and programs.

In the Civil Service it was axiomatic that the expert should be on tap not on top, but both the Conservancy's tasks and my own impressions from Whitehall convinced me that this needed to be altered drastically, if not reversed. I impressed on my administrators that their role was to absorb and implement the requirements which came from our largely scientific governing body, and were spelt out by the senior scientific staff, rather than to let their heads be troubled by policy formation or struggling on their own account for a more important role.

I also emphasised that we were to have no part in the illusion that people at desks around Whitehall necessarily know better than people who sit (or better still move around) at a distance. At least in conservation it was more rather than less likely that the man in the field would know best. I pointed out in the same vein that there is no valid evidence that posting people from England, especially the south-east, to positions where they have to deal with northerners, Scots or Welsh gives as good results as entrusting posts in these areas to people who have more appropriate backgrounds and accents. When appointing a Director for Wales I insisted on a Welsh speaker, with a more than ample vocabulary. My Finance and Establishment officers were both women, and I also promoted a woman as (I believe) the first of her sex to head an official research station in Britain.

I even attempted for a few weeks to run the whole Great Britain operation from Edinburgh, until I found that my absence from Whitehall was being taken advantage of by other departments which needed to be shown how they should toe the line. So far as the public was concerned the Conservancy tended to be personified by Regional Officers, wardens and others, who ranked low in the hierarchy but whose skill and tact with our neighbours in remote places and with the public were of vital importance. I spent many hours travelling about with them in one or other of our large fleet of Land Rovers, absorbing their experiences and gently conveying to them the kind of image we wanted to put across.

How rarely in management one encounters the word 'style' and how important it can be! As a new and often suspect body we needed to convey immediately our readiness to listen, our desire to fit in as well as possible with our neighbours, whoever and wherever they might be, and our hope that we would each learn from the other. In the special case of those National Nature Reserves subject to statutory management agreements with landowners, we were especially aware that they had much longer experience of land management than ourselves; except in strictly ecological and conservation matters, we thought of ourselves as their junior partners.

The conservancy itself delegated many decisions to a high-level Scientific Policy Committee, to territorial committees for England, Scotland and Wales and to a number of others. At one stage when there was a campaign against excessive reliance on committees in the public service, it turned out that I was the grossest example, being advised by no less than 49 unpaid members. I saw no reason to change my practice, which was to submit in advance brief papers outlining policy options and suggested lines, and thereafter to take immediate action on these lines, insofar as they had survived committee discussion, if necessary consulting the Chairman.

The Nature Conservancy in session at its Belgrave Square headquarters in 1959. Left to right: Colonel H. Morrey Salmon, Lord Hurcomb (Chairman, Committee for England), Arthur Blenkinsop MP, Professor W.H. Pearsall (Chairman, Scientific Policy Committee), Dr L. Dudley Stamp, P.H. Cooper (Administrative Secretary), E.M. Nicholson (Director-General), A.B. Duncan (Chairman), Dr E.B. Worthington (Deputy Director-General, Scientific), Professor A.R. Clapham, Lord Strang, Professor P.W. Richards (Chairman, Committee for Wales), Colonel J.C. Wynne Finch, Major John Morrison MP.

It was the practice of Conservancy Chairmen, especially Sir Arthur Duncan and Lord Howick, to spend much time personally visiting Nature Reserves, Research Stations and other outposts, and encouraging even junior staff to speak freely to them, often in my absence. Some of my bureaucratic colleagues considered this mad, but I had the utmost trust in my Chairman, and never once did I find cause to regret this freedom. It was all part of the cultivation of teamwork. I mention these points because I attach such importance to good management in conservation, and to its style as well as its textbook features.

The problem of acquiring National Nature Reserves was not seriously hampered, as it would have been later, by competition for the kind of land in question, or by high prices. Leaseholds or agreements with landowners could often be negotiated at nominal rates. Although finance was never easy, the Conservancy was in the favoured position at that time of coming under the Science vote, and its actual spending during its first decade expanded more than ten-fold. Since then it has multiplied, in real terms, more than seven times.

Despite its generally low profile, the young Nature Conservancy was presented with public relations gifts by the failure both of the chemical industry to anticipate how sensitive public opinion would be about spraying with toxic products, and of other interests on oil spills, nuclear power stations, fires on forests, heath and moorland, encroachments on common land and river pollution. Objections to the Conservancy's own activities were thus overshadowed by public perception of the usefulness of having an independently minded Crown body, able and ready to champion popular concerns in this field.

At a number of Public Inquiries and other confrontations, voluntary bodies came to see the makings of a mutually profitable alliance, in which they could benefit by the Conservancy's official status, contacts and information, while it could gain no less advantage from their ability overtly to campaign against misbehaving official bodies, and to whip up political and other support. By tacit agreement, new rules of the game were worked out which greatly increased the difficulties of those who wished to steamroller through projects injurious to conservation.

The confidence thus established, reinforced by grant aid to key voluntary bodies, prepared the way for the movement to embark on a series of important complementary initiatives. These strengthened public support for the Conservancy and in turn encouraged big increases in memberships for the societies. They had hitherto remained at levels absurdly low in relation to the numbers of people interested.

By an unconventional kind of official initiative, I promoted the creation of a confederation, named the Council for Nature, to encourage co-operative developments such as a Conservation Corps (employed to undertake practical tasks on nature reserves), an Intelligence Unit, gathering and disseminating a much increased range and volume of news for the media, and a National Nature Week, including a fairly ambitious exhibition, in 1963.

Far from superseding the voluntary movement, as had wrongly been assumed by some of its earlier leaders, the Nature Conservancy under my direction had opened up new fields of opportunity that enabled the enrolled membership to expand on a scale hitherto undreamt of, and in so doing to promote and sustain an increased role and support for the Conservancy itself.

On this basis the Conservancy, which had from the outset given substantial aid to the International Union, was able to provide a launching pad for the World Wildlife Fund, an essential instrument for spreading worldwide the necessary large-scale fund-raising and grant-making effort, and employing professional techniques to get the message over on a mass basis. A virtuous spiral had replaced the previous vicious circle. Inspiration had been bolstered by organisation.

In the United States the nearest counterpart at the time was the Federal Fish and Wildlife Service, rooted in the nineteenth-century United States Biological Service but reoriented towards a natural resource role in

A gorge near Ashkabad, USSR, showing deforested mountains, with surviving trees in the valley.

combination with its Fisheries sister body. It was accordingly dedicated to ensuring satisfactory crops of fish and of birds subject to hunting, just as was the parallel National Park Service to the establishment and running of the United States National Parks. (The American Nature Conservancy is not an official agency but a confusingly rechristened version of the Committee on Natural Areas of the Ecological Society of America.)

Theodore Roosevelt's initiatives as President towards establishing a National Resources Committee and a National Conservation Commission (1908) proved politically premature, but Franklin' Roosevelt's launch in 1936 of a regular North American Wildlife Conference, sponsored by a permanent Wildlife Management Institute, proved more viable. It has provided a model for initiating and monitoring many valuable protection measures, at both national and international levels. Its special significance in the field of organisation is its effective integration of operations at all stages from research and management on the ground to national adminis-tration, and then to the fulfilment of international treaty obligations. Its success in rebuilding the waterfowl populations of the continent has been won through massive financial support, ensured by the widespread popularity of duck-shooting and the readiness of the hunters to pay for it.

More general and disinterested measures for conservation had to await the epoch-making Environmental Policy Act of 1969, which 'committed the United States government and its agencies to a policy of international co-operation in environmental affairs' and directed them to

> recognize the world-wide and long-range character of environ-mental problems and, where consistent with the foreign policy of the United States, lend appropriate support to initiatives, resolu-tions and programs designed to maximize international co-operation in anticipating and preventing a decline in the quality of mankind's world environment. (*International Environmental Policy*, L.K. Caldwell, 1984)

Here was a unique kind of law, sweeping up the ineffectual aspirations of many conferences, programs of voluntary bodies and voices of public opinion with a flexible, if vague and uncertain, blanket endorsement extending beyond national legislation to govern participation in inter-national environmental decisions. To this there seems as yet to be no counterpart in any other country, least of all the United Kingdom. Another innovation was the creation of the independent high-level Council on Environmental Quality to advise the President, and to fill the long-standing gap in the Federal Administration concerning broader functions which in the United Kingdom were shared between the Department of the Environ-ment, the Nature Conservancy and the Countryside Commissions.

Perhaps the most internationally influential of this cluster of American environmental initiatives of the late 1960s was that of the Environmental Impact Assessment (EIA), a device for preceding major new development projects by a comprehensive statement reviewing all their foreseeable effects upon the environment. This was made mandatory upon the promoters, and gave rise to vast professional and legal activity, of varying quality and usefulness.

As it has also been much imitated in other countries, and led to discussions that have sometimes clouded the issue, it is worth quoting the original wording of Sec. 102 of the National Environmental Policy Act of 1969:

> all agencies of the Federal Government shall . . . include in every recommendation or report on proposals for legislation and other major Federal actions significantly affecting the quality of the human environment a detailed statement by the responsible official on –
>
> (i) the environmental impact of the proposed action,
> (ii) any adverse environmental effects which cannot be avoided should the proposal be implemented,
> (iii) alternatives to the proposed action,
> (iv) the relationship between local short-term uses of man's environment and the maintenance and enhancement of long-term productivity, and
> (v) any irreversible and irretrievable commitments of resources which would be involved in the proposed action should it be implemented. Prior to making any detailed statement, the responsible Federal official shall consult with and obtain the comments of any Federal agency which has jurisdiction by law or special expertise with respect to any environmental impact involved.

This handsome row of teeth in the Act distinguishes it sharply from other allegedly equivalent processes such as the British planning system, in that it compels all Federal government agencies *before* proposing legislation or major projects to perform detailed environmental homework, in consultation with all others concerned, and to make the results available in a structured and unambiguous form, failing which any such proposal will lack legal validity. While this EIA provision has justly been criticised for some of its verbose consequences the main point is the duty that it imposes to consider first, in all agencies concerned, what the environmental impact will be in the long as well as the short run. It is this inescapable obligation, laid upon many who previously would never have given a thought to the environment, which is so significant in the essential process of spreading environmental responsibility through the areas in which most environmental injury has its origin.

We must not, however, forget that for American constitutional reasons the Act does not apply to the individual states, or to any privately sponsored projects not involving Federal participation. (The belated adoption of an EIA requirement by members of the European Community in 1985 took a somewhat different form.) The requirements of the Act were further spelt out in Interim Guidelines promulgated by the Council on Environmental Quality on 30 April 1970.

Shortly afterwards, by Reorganization Plan No. 3 of 1970, President Nixon established the important Environmental Protection Agency and transferred to it a sweeping range of powers hitherto held by the Interior, Health Education and Welfare, Agriculture and other Departments and agencies, thus abolishing endless sources of delay, inconsistency and confusion in administering the relevant laws, and giving fresh drive to their reform and enforcement. Fortunately the entire decade of the 1970s was available for working out of these great advances, before the election of President Reagan, and the failure of the United States conservationists to stand up effectively to his retrograde policies ushered in a new environmental phase as shameful as its predecessor had been glorious.

Unfortunately space does not permit discussion here of the many contemporary advances in other countries, such as the formation of the Department of the Environment and the further legislation in the United Kingdom, the development of the Bundesanstalt für Vegetationskunde, Naturschutz und Landschaftspflege in the Federal Republic of Germany and the transformation of the Spanish Forestry service under the Ministry of Agriculture into the new nature conservation agency, the Instituto Nacional para la Conservacion de la Naturaleza (ICONA).

It is necessary rather to proceed to some description of the international development of conservation in terms of its structure, organisation and legal aspects, starting at the end of World War II and thus excluding the early history, already reviewed in *The Environmental Revolution*, and also in Keith Caldwell's *International Environmental Policy; Emergence and Dimensions*, which is required reading for any study of this field. The focus here will be strictly upon the progressive embodiment of major principles and strategies of the environmental movement in legislation and conventions and in international agencies, including those of non-governmental status only where they have exercised global influence and served as vehicles of fundamental change.

Julian Huxley, while still acting less than a year after World War II ended as Chairman of the British Wild Life Special Committee, early in 1946 met

Professor E. Handschin of Basel, the president of the Scientific Commission for the Swiss National Park in the Engadine. He concluded that, in view of its successful functioning over many years, it would offer the best example to show members of the Special Committee some of the problems of managing and using a natural area for research.

On hearing of this project, which was arranged for the week between 30 June and 7 July 1946, the president and chargé d'affaires of the Swiss League for the Protection of Nature seized the opportunity to expand the party to include participants from Belgium, France, Norway, the Netherlands and Czechoslovakia (apart from others from Denmark, Poland, Canada and the United States who were unable to come, as in the end was Julian Huxley himself).

While the six British representatives came on an official visit of inspection, unwarned of any other business, the Swiss hosts and some of their other guests were deeply concerned over the long interregnum in implementing the mandate of the Advisory Commission for International Protection of Nature, to be established in Basel by intergovernmental agreement in 1913 (see p. 30). This had been signed by delegates of seventeen governments, all European except the United States and Argentina. Although the prime mover, Paul Sarasin, tried to revive the project when the war ended, he was frustrated. After his death the initiative passed to Dr P.G. van Tienhoven, who initiated three national committees for the purpose in the Netherlands, Belgium and France.

As lack of agreement prevented reactivation of the Advisory Commission it was decided to create in Brussels an interim International Office for the Protection of Nature to collect worldwide documentation, to publish an international bibliography and to link together many Corresponding Members. The Office had to move to Amsterdam in March 1940, and by 1945 it was in abeyance. The ambitious leaders of the Swiss League, ensconced in a country that had escaped the ravages of World War II, could scarcely disguise their eagerness to undertake the prestigious role of running a revivified International Union.

At first this was evidently a shock to the elderly Dr van Tienhoven, who denied the competence of the meeting to discuss the affairs of the apparently moribund International Office, which he stressed had been privately funded. He favoured enlisting the help of UNESCO, which was in the course of creation, with Julian Huxley shortly to become its first director-general. (Just before the group broke up, however, he withdrew at least part of his objection.)

Having by chance been present at these first modern discussions on international nature protection, a subject of which up to then I knew nothing, it seems appropriate to tell here the impression it left with me. I felt that there were many pressing tasks at national level, not least to organise efficient and expert teams competent to establish well-managed national voluntary agencies.

I could envisage that a time might come when there would be enough of such national bodies, with sufficient knowledge and experience to exchange and, with enough common problems, to justify some sort of international meeting-ground or clearing-house. I was not, however, impressed with the capabilities in this respect of any of the evidently feeble and amateurish societies represented at these talks. I suspected that any early launching of a new International Union would either prove as abortive as its forerunners or could only be brought up to standard by an input of specialist and managerial effort and money from the United Kingdom, which was entirely out of the question, it being nearly three years before we were in a position to start up our own official national organisation.

The idea that a mere link-up of national societies in their existing state could advance matters, or that their admitted state of disarray was the sole obstacle to important progress seemed to me illusory. Assuming, which seemed still questionable, that there were serious problems needing to be tackled on the international plane, a much more substantial and better-conceived program would be essential, for which definite and credible commitments would need to be lined up in advance. My contribution to the discussion was therefore more cautionary and sceptical than supportive.

My opinion, as thus outlined, was openly biassed by short-term considerations relating to the inevitable priorities of post-war reconstruction in Europe on a vast scale, the new realisation of the complexity of the problem that we were gaining in our Wild Life Special Committee, and the obvious inadequacy of our prospective partners to measure up to the global tasks until some much stronger national bases had been built.

In retrospect, and in all fairness, I must now accept that despite the cogency of these reservations there were equally strong reasons for going ahead. One of these was the vigour and competence of the Swiss team, which are permanently on record in their detailed account of the meeting, and of the quickly ensuing International Conference for the Protection of Nature at Brunnen 1947.

These fully outline the antecedent international meetings and conventions and describe the choices which had to be made between becoming a new member Union of the International Council of Scientific Unions (or even a branch of the existing International Union of Biological Sciences) and becoming a new autonomous organisation under the umbrella of the United Nations, specifically of UNESCO, and including both governments and non-governmental members. Experience has shown that the 1947 Brunnen conclusions, blending these different concepts with the initial objective of an international federation of conservation bodies, found the right answer, and fulfilled the blunt demand of the Danish delegate, who told it:

> This Conference must show that it is composed of men and women of action and has both the desire and the capacity to act. It is necessary to work in a practical manner and to establish a living organisation for the international protection of nature.

That contrasted with my own message to the Conference from London that:

> we may hope that as soon as the most pressing and immediate problems have been disposed of, a satisfactory basis for international wild life protection will be found.

I can now plead only that my subsequent exertions for the Union may be held to have atoned for these pusillanimous sentiments at its birth. (I must add that in the event I was proved right in my fear that getting the Union on its feet would demand from the United Kingdom a disproportionate share of the effort.) A provisional International Union for the Protection of Nature was in fact constituted by the representatives of the twenty-four countries present on 3 July 1947. My friend Julian Huxley, who had championed the inclusion of Science as well as Education and Culture in the main objects of UNESCO, took this up with an enthusiasm that I did not wholly share. His term of office as Director-General of UNESCO lasted only two years, and the foundation of IUPN – as it originally styled itself – was one of his most enduring achievements there.

The Union was an uncommon if not unique animal, having as members governments, official agencies and many non-governmental bodies such as societies. Its first impulse was to meet, with unrealistic frequency, at a widely spread series of cities, and to pass with carefree abandon a copious set of urgent resolutions calling for action on varied controversial issues by bodies who were in no way obliged to give heed to them. After some years I had the curiosity to check how many of these resolutions had been followed by action on the lines demanded, and was astonished to find that, for reasons which I was at a loss to explain, a rather high proportion of them had resulted in, or coincidentally been soon accompanied by action of the type indicated.

As I had feared, the launch of the Union in 1948 was ill-prepared and premature. I had taken the precaution of persuading the British Foreign Office to put the draft constitution into sound legal form, but the finances remained in a mess, with hopes of worthwhile funding from the Swiss sponsors, UNESCO or the Americans being quickly disappointed, Fortunately, however, there proved to be substance in rumours that the Belgians had an excellent candidate to serve as secretary-general – Jean-Paul Harroy, Secretary General of the Institut pour la Recherche Scientifique en Afrique Centrale – and that the Belgians would give accommodation in their National Museum. Another bonus was that the very able and effective Marguerite Caram would be available to back him up.

We therefore shed no tears in bidding farewell to the Swiss League, whose consolation prize was that their politically astute and highly diplomatic president became president of the new Union for its first half-dozen years. Charles Bernard represented what I class as the missionary and rhetorical element. Although he contributed much to the initial international recruitment and enthusiasm, he had to be replaced at the Copenhagen Assembly of 1954 by a scientist of standing, Professor Roger Heim, head of the Natural History Museum of Paris, who enabled the Union to qualify for acceptance in the International Council of Scientific Unions.

This meant that its image and policies became sufficiently distanced from that of an eco-nut or environmental lobby outfit, and it was able to hold and expand its governmental membership, above all by recruiting strongly within the Third World – a far-sighted initiative which was later to stand it in good stead.

With creditable despatch, and aided by Huxley at UNESCO, the Union was able to put in a strong appearance, within a year of its foundation, at Lake Success, New York. Here it paralleled the United Nations Scientific Conference on the Conservation and Utilization of Resources with a special meeting on nature conservation aspects, the first International Technical Conference on the Protection of Nature. This meeting was notable for what has proved to be an outstandingly well-balanced review of the impact of chemical pesticides and insecticides, which were then a complete novelty.

During its first decade, and indeed later, the Union bewildered and pained its supporters by a baffling blend of achievement and incompetence, and by staggering from one financial crisis to another. Despite repeated invitations I consistently declined to serve on its Executive Board or to accept higher office, maintaining that my role as official adviser to the United Kingdom government would be compromised if I were not able to speak independently on IUCN and international affairs. It would be disingenuous to conceal that this alibi suited me personally, but I took trouble to give close support to successive presidents.

I had to concede that, especially during the latter 1950s, IUCN had performed creditably in picking the right issues and in sorting out what should be done about them, and that it had shown on the whole good judgment and sensitivity in its presentations and its relations with important interest groups. On the other hand it became increasingly apparent that the types forming the executive board had neither the capability nor the interest to create and operate a sound financial base or to develop a mass supporting movement. They did not think strategically, or plan realistic programs related to their priorities and resources, and they were content to engage in dialogues and confrontations at levels not high enough to bring results.

There was no point in blaming them for these faults, which were the natural counterpart of their virtues. Logically the right corrective was to establish a twin body to take care of the matters that the Union was unable or unwilling to handle. This became urgent at the outset of the 1960s, partly owing to the deepening of the Union's chronic insolvency, partly because the environmental challenges to be faced were fast multiplying and expanding in scale, and partly because the idea that there was a favourable opportunity to raise funds for wildlife was occurring to a number of people who would shortly launch a proliferation of wastefully competing and sometimes irresponsible schemes, unless a generally acceptable worldwide alternative was formed without delay.

Such was the situation that gave rise in 1961 to the World Wildlife Fund (WWF), plans for which were worked out by a group under my

The launch in 1961 of the World Wildlife Fund was heralded by a notable meeting with leading Africans from territories shortly to become independent. This group in the Ngorongoro Crater in Tanganyika includes Sir Julian Huxley (fifth from left).

chairmanship between April and September, when the Fund was duly registered in Zurich as an international charity, and was launched by meetings at Arusha in East Africa and in London.

There were obvious problems about the concept of two complementary international bodies, composed of sharply distinct types of people, each needing the other but each biassed against achieving full harmony and mutual understanding. The very idea implied a degree of organisational optimism for which I must take responsibility, while the credit for somehow at intervals making it work belongs to others.

Among the newcomers to the leadership group were a bevy of royals, headed by Prince Philip, who was to become the most dedicated and effective of all, and his partner Prince Bernhard of the Netherlands, who, during a long stint as international president, travelled round a remarkable number of countries and used his *entrée* to their government leaders to get conservation firmly on their agenda, often for the first time. Top bankers and business men, and some influential ladies, helped to consolidate the enhanced status of the movement in ways beyond the reach of the Union's Executive Board.

The growing inflow of funds spoke its own language, and enabled deals to be struck for a number of projects, matching national contributions. Land Rovers and other vehicles bearing the Panda symbol of WWF became a familiar sight in many parts of the world, and a steady stream of news releases made conservation of wildlife and its habitat an everyday topic of talk and interest. WWF, with its galaxy of energetic National Appeals, also helped to compensate for the Union's lack of grassroots representation.

All depended, however, on the progressive transformation of the Union from its initial talking-shop function to a decentralised group of hard-working expert teams or Commissions. These took care of: the expansion and upgrading of National Parks – the one on which I personally served; the promotion of applied ecology as a scientific base for all else; the Species Survival effort, involving the famous and effective series of *Red Books of Endangered Species*; the mainstay International Law Centre at Bonn under the Burhennes; and the Education Program, decentralised in regions of the world. Other special efforts included that leading to the Convention of International Trade in Endangered Species (CITES), which bit hard on the fashion world and on such trades as those in furs and crocodile handbags. There was also the great Tropical Forests campaign, which still hangs in the balance. At the Delhi Assembly in 1969, Mrs Indira Gandhi not only gave an inspiring address but also put her drive and influence squarely behind the launch of Operation Tiger. This successfully and quickly reversed the alarming decline of that notable species, and safeguarded the natural habitat of many lesser-known animals and plants. It has also had important local spin-offs in improving water supplies. Through such advances in organisation, involving in some cases hundreds of international collaborators, the countless words uttered and written in favour of conservation, and also the countless donations and subscriptions, were given a real cutting edge. This was reflected in an impressive rate of progress in many countries and in many aspects.

The 1960s proved a decisive decade, and due credit must be given to the many brilliant film-makers, radio and TV performers, writers, lecturers and others who turned conservation from a dull term confined to an earnest minority and made it everybody's business. (Some of them incidentally got valuable conservation projects started as well.) Nevertheless, it was essentially these advances in organisation, enabling the movement to identify and prescribe the necessary actions and to start them moving all over the world, which won confidence and dedication and harnessed so many effective activist supporters and participants to the environmental program.

Environmentalists did not succumb to the modern illusion that talk engendering 'charters' and 'decades' and demonstrations suffices to bring about change. So many worthy citizens and their leaders have not yet learned that if action is needed there is no substitute for themselves embarking upon it, and that action does not mean just emitting hot air into the already polluted atmosphere. It was the combination of the words and

A tiger in the Kanha National Park, India, the scene of some of the exploratory work leading to the successful Operation Tiger.

the music which enabled the environmental movement to take off and to gain an impetus that, to the astonishment of many outside its ranks, it has never lost. If that is to remain the case, it must not be taken for granted; in particular all those responsible for running the movement, in its happily loose and decentralised form need to understand what makes it tick. It is a main function of this book to further such understanding.

It was no accident that the 1970s opened with a wave of dismay and horror over the situation of our small planet earth, and with a responsive wave of administrative and legislative action by governments. That culminated in 1972 with the Stockholm United Nations Conference on the Human Environment, probably among the most successful international conferences ever held. Once more this was due to superb preparation and organisation, under its Secretary-General Maurice Strong. As Keith Caldwell explains 'it legitimised environmental policy as a universal concern among nations, and so created a place for environmental issues on many national agendas where they had been previously unrecognised.'

It responded to a changing view of mankind's relationship to the earth, from that of unlimited abundance created for man's exclusive exploitation to a domain of life, or biosphere, for which mankind is a temporary resident custodian. Getting this on the agenda, however, did not mean its ready acceptance by the rigid institutional upholders of traditional or new vested interests. On the contrary it simply involved environmentalists in facing the full horror of the greed, corruption, self-indulgence, materialism and complacency of the world's ruling groups, Left, Right and Centre.

In some areas, notably control of pollution, public opinion was already sufficiently prepared and articulate for sound and effective legislation to be fairly easily enacted at both national and international levels. Indeed, a strong minority of progressive industrial leaders saw it as in their interest to have their less scrupulous competitors put under legal restraint. When it came, however, to conservation of energy and other resources, and to curbs on land use, the going proved more difficult.

The bombshell sprung by the Oil Producing and Exporting Countries (OPEC) in 1973, and the ensuing oil shortage, administered to the economic *ancien régime* of the mid-century world a shock from which it could never recover. It reinforced the intellectual impact of the statements of the Club of Rome, and other influential spokesmen for the new message.

The lines of battle were now clearly drawn, yet the 1970s proved to be a decade largely of stalemate, broken only by limited skirmishes and a number of specific victories. Among these were Conventions to protect the seas and the seabed and their living resources from pollution and harmful uses, and for the control of Long-Range Trans-boundary Air Pollution. Above all, the

United Nations Law of the Sea Convention, signed at last in 1982, enshrined a complex but decisive move to recognise the global commons of the seas and seabeds as meriting international legal status, free from the greed and stupidity of persisting nationalism, and of interests operating under its cover.

Despite the delays and often infantile manoeuvres of spokesmen of east and west, or north and south, and the obstruction of defence interests, resource 'developers' and others, it is now pretty well established, thanks to the environmentalists, that the greater part of the earth's surface and all of its atmosphere belongs to the earth's people as a whole, leaving obsolescent sovereign states for the time being to squabble over the rest as they will.

Although, as recently as thirty years ago, the environment had not qualified for inclusion in the Treaty of Rome, circumstances have increasingly forced the European Community to take account of it, and by 1985 it even had to be allowed a place in the funding of the Common Agricultural Policy. The Commission's First Action Programme for the Environment, in 1973, recognised that 'improvement in the quality of life and protection of the natural environment are among the fundamental tasks of the Community' – a phrase which would have been harder to justify historically or legally than politically, in the light of the advantages of getting on the bandwagon. It is worth quoting here as a marker of time marching on.

The Community showed commendable if belated activity, among other things in participating in such Conventions as those on the Protection of the Mediterranean Sea against Pollution (1976), the Protection of the Rhine against Chemical Pollution (1976) and the Berne Convention on the Conservation of European Wildlife and Natural Habitats (1982). After a century of foot-dragging by the Mediterranean countries over conservation, they were now compelled to fall into line with their northern neighbours, which they did with good grace. The Council of Europe, which had sponsored European Conservation Year in 1970 with considerable success, at the time when activity over the environment was becoming a status symbol, has continued, with its wider membership but less operational character, to maintain interest in this field.

Policy review and research has not ceased to attract attention, in Europe through the independent European Environmental Bureau set up in Brussels in 1974, and globally through the International Institute for Environment and Development. An important legacy of the Stockholm Conference was the creation of the United Nations Environmental Programme (UNEP), which has tried hard but has not altogether fulfilled the intentions with which it was set up. Indeed, given the background of inconsistencies and deep reservations, that is hardly surprising.

The Conference itself was a *tour de force*, at which strong pressures of public opinion appeared to some extent to reconcile the conflicting approaches of the politicians and diplomats, the scientists and the many brands of non-governmental environmentalists who contributed to its unique brew.

When the follow-up came to be arranged, the suspicious and mostly ill-informed representatives of the Third World successfully insisted on locating UNEP at Nairobi, in the middle of Africa, far away from its environmental and political roots and contacts.

Its mission to reconcile environment and development was hampered during the years required by the Third World to overcome its own suspicions and to understand the vital role of environmental conservation – a lesson that many African states and others have since been learning the hard way. Its natural task of co-ordinating the environmental aspects of other United Nations agencies was handicapped by the latters' strong suspicions, and by its status as one of the smallest, poorest and most junior among them. While theoretically there were some sound arguments for putting it in Africa, that could hardly have been done at a worse time, when with few exceptions African governments were hellbent on a collision course with their environment, and were hardly disposed to give moral and material support, or even tolerance to its message.

(a) Collision course in Africa: Botswana 1970. A dead buffalo lies by a waterhole in devastated terrain, where no life-support system remains, yet the message still goes unheeded, both on the spot and internationally.

(a)

In the circumstances, governments of developed countries were unenthusiastic in making the running, as some might have done had the headquarters been in Europe. The wide gap between the surge of public opinion that had launched it and the stubborn adverse trends persisting even in the developed world would in any case have made UNEP's task unenviable. Even the impressive talents of Maurice Strong as its first Executive Director could not regain the Stockholm impetus, and the defeat on its doorstep over the catastrophic desertification of the Sahel countries was a bitter setback. Nevertheless UNEP has struggled manfully to establish such valuable services as GEMS (the Global Environmental Monitoring System) and INFOTERRA (the International Referral System), which form a base for a global service of information essential to environmental management.

On more general aspects UNEP has found it expedient to work closely with the much longer established and more experienced IUCN, itself not an NGO but a GONGO – a hybrid between a governmental and a non-governmental body, with discreet access to highly diverse sources of intelligence and support worldwide, and with many interests in common. The International Council of Scientific Unions, which earlier promoted the International Geophysical Year and the International Biological Program, is another natural ally.

In the former case the potential of a joint campaign has been well

(b) Ten years later and much further north, an Ethiopian and his son regard the skeletons of their starved livestock on once fertile ground; a few years yet and the skeletons will be human.

(b)

demonstrated by the World Conservation Strategy (1980). This was a natural sequel to a number of earlier exercises, starting with the IBP and its takeover by UNESCO in the subsequent Man and Biosphere Program. It had become obvious during the 1970s that there was no real hope of politicians, administrators, business men and other self-appointed public leaders taking sufficient interest in the urgent threats to survival on earth to consider and to draw conclusions about their own wrong attitudes and potentially catastrophic decisions affecting natural resources and the biosphere.

The connection between the conditions of survival and the policies, attitudes and practices that were hazarding them would need to be spelt out much more plainly and urgently, in terms of the physical carrying capacity of the earth, the destruction of soils and essential forest cover, the rising costs of meeting expanding material requirements and the shrinking resource base for energy and other needs such as fisheries.

There would have to be a plain warning against treating living resource conservation as a limited sector; against failing to integrate conservation in development; against needlessly destructive development through short-sightedness and ignorance; against lack of the capacity and skills to conserve; against lack of understanding of the benefits and responsibilities of conservation, with consequent lack of support; and against the failure to deliver conservation-based development where it is most needed, notably in the rural areas of developing countries.

The World Conservation Strategy, therefore, explained living resource conservation, its aims, its contribution to human survival and development and the main obstacles to its achievement. It determined the priority requirements for achieving each of the objectives, and proposed a frame-work and principles for supporting strategies at national level and below. It made recommendations for environmental policies spanning sectional areas and involving a broader system of national accounting to integrate conservation with development. It also proposed methods of evaluation and environmental assessment as a means to the rational allocation of land and water resources. It tackled legislation, organisation, management and training. It urged greater public participation in resource decision-making, together with environmental education. It recommended international action for more comprehensive conservation law, more assistance for living resource conservation, as well as action to conserve tropical forests and drylands, genetic resources, the open ocean, the atmosphere, and Antarctica. It urged regional strategies for shared living resources such as international river basins and seas. Finally it outlined the main requirements for sustainable development, including conservation priorities for the Third Development Decade. Where it most conspicuously failed was in omitting to tackle the grave implications of grossly excessive human population increases upon the health of the biosphere.

Launched simultaneously in many world capitals in March 1980, the Strategy had a friendly but somewhat low-key reception, and was handicapped by the imminence in the United States of an election that brought in the most unsympathetic and the least understanding administration in respect to conservation for at least half a century. This soon cast its shadow over the international environmental scene.

In these circumstances, the follow-through of the Strategy depended mainly on national programs to implement its relevant principles and proposals. In many countries there was some delay in appreciating and acting upon this. In the United Kingdom, in the absence of any government initiative, a Conservation and Development Program was prepared by a mixed group of agencies and voluntary bodies, supervised by a representative Standing Committee under my chairmanship. The work was done by an Organising Committee and seven specialist groups, contributing comprehensive and balanced reports on the main aspects of concern.

This, with parallel responses in other countries, gave practical guidance towards making the generalities of the World Conservation Strategy effective, and in setting targets for progress in developing conservation from a narrowly ecological and wildlife survival effort towards a broader integrated role in public policy.

It was three years later, and six years after the launch of the World Conservation Strategy itself, that the United Kingdom government published a glossy fifty-six-page popular illustrated booklet *Conservation and Development: The British Approach* announced as 'The United Kingdom Government's Response to the World Conservation Strategy' (1986). The belatedness of that response, and its bland public relations format, plainly revealed the government's attitude towards these grave matters, as did the heavy emphasis on particular measures already adopted, and the near avoidance of issues still controversial or neglected. Nevertheless, when critically decoded, the statement gives a useful and comprehensive situation report and outline of policy. It shows recognition of the growing power of the environmental movement, and readiness to respond to it and work with it. It also accords a welcome degree of priority to scientific research and thorough monitoring as a basis for public policy, and to positive attitudes towards international co-operation on broader environmental problems. In effect it is a halfway house between *ad hoc* piecemeal reactive measures and the ultimately necessary acceptance of the paramountcy of the essential needs of the biosphere and of sustainable yield principles over previously dominant economic and social dogma. Implicitly it confirms that the government will go along with the movement to the full extent that the movement can prove its case to public opinion, but no faster.

At the meeting in Ottawa in 1986, for which this statement was prepared, the World Conservation Strategy received its eventual international endorsement at government level, but without sufficient political emphasis or publicity to add very much to the degree of acceptance already attained. A disturbing factor was the hesitancy shown at the Ottawa Conference on Conservation and Development: Implementing the World Conservation Strategy, in regard to supplementing the Strategy with a recommendation to add the stabilisation of human population as an element within national conservation and development strategies. It is understood, however, that this will go forward.

Although the international conservation movement is essentially non-political in any party sense, the recent broadening of its field has involved more overlap with parts of the substance of politics. In the hands of the politically naive this has sometimes led to direct entry into the political arena as a Green or, worse still, as an 'Ecology' party. Under some types of proportional representation it has proved possible to win just enough votes to become a serious nuisance to conventional parliamentary parties, and even to secure inclusion in a coalition. The term nuisance, however, can apply both ways, especially since these Green parties tend to lack even the necessary minimum of political cohesion and working discipline to function effectively and with credit in the tedious parliamentary game. Their one major benefit to the movement is that their presence makes their conventional rivals so uncomfortable as to be willing to offer environmentalists a high political price to keep out of the parliamentary arena and leave them alone. A keen rivalry for the environmental vote, and a compulsion to work hard to earn it, does no one any harm.

That problem arises only at a late phase in the evolution of the movement, as an internationally and nationally organised force. We are now in a position to see in perspective what the earlier phases have been, and how each has contributed to the whole. The first phase, up to about 1948, was a prehistory of exploring, pioneering, and experimenting here and there.

The second phase, which passed through rapidly between 1948 and 1956, was one of actively organising up to national and international levels, and of intensive missionary propaganda, protest and discussion, creating a core of mature activist leaders and thinkers.

The third phase, even briefer, between about 1956 and 1960, saw the centre of gravity shift towards a professional ecological base, ready to develop a realistic conservation program and the beginnings of a trained staff, able to work alongside many keen volunteers.

In the fourth phase, throughout the 1960s, a consensus on programs to meet the alarmingly developing challenges was brilliantly disseminated through the media, attracting a mass influx of active supporters of all ages, surprisingly quick at learning the message and at improvising ways of spreading it and acting upon it.

Simultaneously, the twinning of IUCN with the new supportive WWF enabled an effective presence and track record to be established quickly in many remote parts of the world, lending credibility to the hope of actually

On the platform at the 25th Anniversary Meeting of the World Wildlife Fund at Assisi, Italy, in September 1986 – reunion of the founding members with Charles de Haes, Director-General. Left to right from him: the Duke of Edinburgh, Max Nicholson, Sir Peter Scott, Guy Mountfort, Luc Hoffman, Prince Bernhard of the Netherlands, John Loudon, and Hans Huessy.

Below are shown the past (left) and present (right) WWF logos.

saving threatened wildlife and habitat on a worthwhile scale. Nearer home a series of pollution threats were fought with gratifying success, and politicians were led to take notice and to begin adopting the term 'environment' in their programs, institutions and legislation. The movement was thus establishing itself as a real force, while at the same time, through the IBP and its important offshoot the Scientific Committee on Problems of the Environment, a much expanded and developed scientific basis was made available, including a capability for worldwide environmental monitoring.

On this vastly reinforced base, the fifth phase began with the Stockholm United Nations Conference on the Human Environment. This took full advantage of worldwide alarm at the threat of Doomsday, in order to bring together politicians, scientists, conservationists and young activists. They embarked on an exercise which began to translate public opinion into an agenda for legislation and action by governments and international agencies, including the creation of UNEP. The cleaning up of surface pollution was still a dominant theme, although threats in the atmosphere to climate, and a struggle for the safeguarding of the global commons, were emerging strongly as issues carrying the movement further beyond national boundaries. It was now better organised, more sophisticated and respected, more confident, and better aware of the strengths and weaknesses of its opponents, and of how to tackle them.

The stage was accordingly set for the sixth phase, during about 1978–83, when the World Conservation Strategy was prepared by a worldwide team effort, formulating for the movement a profound and realistic basis for its further evolution and activity as a force in world affairs. The simultaneous emergence of Green political groups and parties confirmed that, if it so chose, the movement was now strong enough to intervene in the political arena, but on the whole this course was not favoured.

Rather it was felt that the *ancien régime* of the political and economic Establishment of the mid-century was now fighting for survival against its own inherent contradictions, such as indefinite material growth, perpetually expanding but unusable and unaffordable nuclear armaments, unwise and excessive overseas lending for often corruptly sponsored and inappropriate prestige projects, currency and budgetary instabilities on a painful scale, and a failure to live up to promises of full employment and social welfare. The onset of plain ecological bankruptcy in the Sahel, Ethiopia and elsewhere opened many eyes and purses to the misdirection of world resources by greed, vanity, and neglect of the clear needs of sustainability and thus led to the next stage.

In this, the seventh phase, the movement would begin seeking to seize the strategic initiative, taking advantage of the disarray and disillusionment among its main adversaries and of the opportunities for integration with newly emerging adaptable groupings looking for new approaches and new life-styles compatible with the earth's limited life support systems. At the same time even greater environmental battles would be fought to save the remnants of tropical forests, to repulse the spread of environmentally destructive agriculture and fisheries, and to compel a reorientation of Third World development practices in relation to ecological principles.

As this book goes to press, the International Council of Scientific Unions (ICSU) is holding a meeting in Bern on plans to launch an environmental successor to the International Geophysical Year and the International Biological Programme. Entitled the International Geosphere–Biosphere Programme (IGBP), this is framed to enable scientists worldwide to produce within a decade an authoritative and integrated assessment of probable future interactions between the global natural environment and current human activities. The aim is to enable predictions to be made in critical areas, valid for around a century ahead, and thus to make a decisive step towards sound management of the planet, always provided that the necessary funding can be raised.

At the same time, a distinguished group of American academic ecologists is launching a Club of Earth. The Club aims to check the threats to global biological diversity, particularly through destruction of tropical rainforests, by making effective representations to political and economic decision-makers; this will lead to firm use of international leverage against ecological disruption (*Nature*, vol. 323, pp. 189 and 193 (1986)). If successful, these initiatives should contribute significantly to answering our final question: how will this seventh phase turn out, and to what kind of eighth phase will it lead?

6

Interactions

So far, as is the custom of environmentalists, this account of the conservation movement has been on lines self-centred from its own standpoint. There is justification for that, in as much as it has developed historically by organic, progressive and complex evolution from traceable roots, like a mature tree. But such a standpoint is no longer sufficient, as the movement increasingly has to co-exist and interact with other groupings in different but converging subject areas. The simile changes to that of a tree reaching maturity within a forest of competitors, and needing to disseminate progeny that can look forward to vigorously surviving and spreading. As Andrew Marvell put it, in his *Horatian Ode upon Cromwell's Return from Ireland* (1650):

> Nature, that hateth emptiness
> Allows of penetration less
> And therefore must make room
> Where greater spirits come.

How does and should the world make room for the integration of the environmental movement's contribution in a more civilised and sustainable pattern of living? Who and where are the movement's potential allies and its persisting adversaries? In what conditions can they be led to form constructive alliances, or to adjust their attitudes and programs as far as necessary?

It seems most practical to review, sector by sector, the main activity groupings that most clearly interrelate with environmental conservation, starting with those which are in some way intermeshed with it, before proceeding to those which are extraneous, either adversarial or setting constraints.

Historically and philosophically the appropriate starting point is the world of science (see Chapter 4, p. 68), which itself originated in the pursuit of 'natural philosophy', and was early preoccupied with the heavens, with living resources, especially through botany, and with geology. One of the first projects of the Royal Society of London, under John Evelyn, was a prescription for the conservation of trees, entitled *Sylva* (1664). The cultural climate was favourable, except in countries dominated by the Papacy.

Principles soon became internationally accepted for the advancement of knowledge by experimental testing of theories, by precise measurement and recording, including both extensive surveys and explorations and the monitoring of changes over time, and by the free communication of data and findings with fellow-scientists, regardless of national boundaries.

Studies of the environment and the problems of its conservation became rooted in science, although during the century before Charles Darwin's *Origin of Species* (1859) the scientific centre of gravity shifted away from the biosphere. Natural history was left largely to amateurs, and was starved of resources except for the amassing and analysis of museum collections. The shock administered to received religion by Darwinism resulted in universities, which had remained largely under church influence, viewing with grave suspicion the study and discussion of biology, and exiling natural history to the status of a hobby interest.

Science, with its henchman technology, had itself to fight long battles for acceptance and support, and has only during this century won admission to the Establishment, despite its initial royal patronage three centuries ago. Unfortunately the price exacted by its applications in industry, and above all in warfare, has been a regrettable dependence for funding and support upon those social and economic circles most dedicated to materialist exploitation and to the pursuit of naked power.

Its contributions, even to wealth creation, have often been diverted, through high technology, into channels inimical to the welfare of the biosphere and into triggering off ecological disasters. In such areas as nuclear research it has been fettered with rules of secrecy, and acceptance of outside interference, contrary at least to a scientific spirit and to its free development.

In comparison with other, increasingly sophisticated, laboratory research, purporting to yield definitive and permanently valid results, ecology long tended to be viewed as little better than marginally scientific. The work of Tansley, Pearsall, Elton and others in Britain, and their peers in other countries, won grudging recognition, but was almost pushed aside in the excitement about molecular biology. This threatened in the late 1950s to relegate the biology of living animals and plants in nature to the status of a mere sub-science. The threat, however, was successfully resisted, and was reversed in the 1960s by the fortunate chance that the International

Council of Scientific Unions felt obliged to give biology a turn after the International Geophysical Year, and the only suitable field for an international biological program proved to be ecology.

Although the IBP was not a brilliant success it soon led on to the Man and Biosphere Program, and then to the United Nations Stockholm Conference, which established ecology as a substantial partner within the scientific community. This was helped by the creation of the Charles Darwin

Charles Darwin, as an amateur naturalist, did much to shape biology towards ecological and environmental lines of development and to ensure that, like astronomy, it would find a place for the curious and exploring non-professional. He also left it a legacy of challenging fundamental beliefs and ideas that carries on in the environmental movement.

Foundation on the Galapagos Islands, the Royal Society station on Aldabra in the Indian Ocean, and the large-scale biome studies and biological productivity researches carried out for example at Port Barrow in Alaska, at Seronera in the Serengeti National Park, Tanzania, at Barro Colorado on the Panama Canal, and elsewhere. In these ways, a respectable degree of cross-fertilisation was established between mainstream science and its ecological and kindred environmental offshoots.

Indeed, considered within the framework of science, these are among the most vigorous growing points, commanding a rate of increase in financial backing and a freedom of initiative which scientists in a number of more conventional fields may well envy. Sharing the same basic principles, and the same uninhibited internationalism and open communications, environmental conservation has derived much of its strength from its scientific origins and from its resolution in sticking to them, as is evidenced by the

Final meeting of the Special Committee for the International Biological Programme of the International Council of Scientific Unions at the Royal Society of London in 1974. At rear: Professor F. Bourlière (France), President; with W.F. Blair (USA), a Vice-President; M.J. Dunbar (Canada) and J.S. Weiner (UK), Section Conveners; H. Tamiya (Japan), a Vice-President; and R.W.J. Keay (UK), Chairman, Finance. Front row (left to right): Max Nicholson (UK), Convener, Conservation section; G.K. Davis (USA); C.H. Waddington (UK) and J.G. Baer (Switzerland), former Vice-Presdient and President, respectively; G. Montalenti (Italy), former Vice-President; Livia Tonolli (Italy), Section Convener; and Sir Otto Frankel (Australia), a Vice-President.

IUCN's status as a member of the International Council of Scientific Unions.

As 'certainty' in science assumes a less certain meaning, ecology finds itself moving imperceptibly away from the margin and more towards the changing, less mechanistic mainstream. It may therefore be hoped that environmental science and conservation may look forward to a further development of the *rapprochement* with science generally that has become evident in most recent years, sluggish and chilly as it still remains. Ecology enshrines an independence, an integrity and a vitality which our somewhat jaded world of modern science badly needs.

Historically, much of the original work leading up to the modern environmental movement was done as a spare-time occupation by members of a number of professions, including clergymen such as John Ray and Gilbert White of Selborne, plenty of medical men, foresters, district administrators, surveyors, engineers, and others whose duties took them out into the field. Such influence as they exercised in this direction seems unfortunately not to have been matched by any corresponding success in turning the minds of their own professional colleagues towards an appreciation of the environment.

On the contrary, too often we find that environmentally damaging projects have been recommended and put into shape by, for example, civil engineers and surveyors. In extreme cases, where clients are given advice foreseeably involving them in environmental liabilities, against the modern background of officially recognised environmental obligations, it might well be argued before long that the professional men responsible have been guilty of dereliction of duty, for which they deserve to be sued.

In 1970 The Standing Committee for the Third 'Countryside in 1970' Conference (see pp. 133–4) had recommended that 'an inter-professional committee should be established with adequate means to encourage the inclusion of conservation in professional and academic qualifying courses' and to promote better understanding of conservation by the professions. The resulting action was very disappointing, and the task remains to be tackled seriously. Meanwhile few if any of the relevant professions, with the exception of landscaping, can be exonerated from having contributed to the recent and continuing degradation of the environment.

Although they meet to confer internationally, the professions are normally organised within a national framework, with fairly tight rules. Has not the time come when all those having functions that may be critical for the environment should be urged to include among these rules an unequivocal obligation that their advice and decisions should at all times be guided by the need to conserve its quality and to respect its value to mankind? Public opinion, which has come to rather harsh judgments on the recent performance of certain professions, would no doubt feel at least some reassurance if such an ethical obligation could be known to be undertaken by those who look to being retained by clients.

Much, indeed far too much, has been written about environmental education, which should be a major ally and reinforcement of the environmental movement but somehow has so far proved a grave disappointment. In the United States, which has by far the most experience, it was early found that educating or brain-washing the young to accept conservation as something they ought to believe in and support was not the same as genuinely educating them about the nature of the environment or the biosphere, and its significance and workings. During the 1960s the Biological Sciences Curriculum Study, based in Boulder, Colorado, made a strong effort to correct the deficiency, with fair but only limited success. The achievements of the environmental movement have demonstrated that proselytising can to a large extent be done among adults, while demonstrating how nature works is a more educational and necessary use of the time of school children, provided that it can be done, at least in large measure, out of doors.

It appears that sensible broad conclusions about environmental education can be reached without undue difficulty at international or national conferences, but are often impossible to carry out in practice in the schools. A good example of this is afforded by the Tbilisi Declaration of October 1977, which agreed on eight guiding principles for international action:

> Environmental education should consider the environment in its totality – natural and man-made, ecological, political, economic, technological, social, legislative, cultural and aesthetic.
>
> Environmental education should be a continuous life-long process, in-school and out-of-school.
>
> Environmental education should be interdisciplinary in its approach.
>
> Environmental education should emphasize active participation in preventing and solving environmental problems.
>
> Environmental education should examine major environmental issues from a world point of view, while paying due regard to regional differences.
>
> Environmental education should focus on current and future environmental situations.
>
> Environmental education should examine all development and growth from an environmental perspective.
>
> Environmental education should promote the value and necessity of local, national, and international co-operation in the solution of environmental problems.

These are admirable sentiments, but they leave one wondering how justice is to be done to them within the tight framework of a school curriculum, and by the teachers to whom the task must fall. One must also wonder just how much meaning can be attached to such lofty abstractions by children who have not first been led into the field and skilfully shown how to look at and comprehend the animals and plants whose living communities form the tangible basis of that elusive generality 'the environment.'

The potential exists within environmental education to trigger the kind of revolution or renaissance in all educational thought and practice that is so badly missed in so many adult worlds. Trying to fit environmental education into the rigidities of the present educational establishment is, however, a thankless task, and I personally suspect it is time wasted.

Much of what the educationists have failed to contribute to environmental conservation has been made good by the excellent performance of the media, led by television, films and radio. These have, to their own surprise, found endless attractive material that can hold worthwhile and sometimes even very large audiences, week after week. While, in principle, the media deserve to be treated as one of the main partner interests of the environmental movement, their role needs no further discussion here as the process of transferring material from the field to the screen, the microphone, the periodical or newspaper, the disc, the exhibition or the museum occurs spontaneously, without calling for any remote or high-level negotiations or bargaining.

A much less tractable area, and one of immense importance, is that which is somewhat oddly termed development, and is primarily concerned with those regions of Central and South America, Africa, south Asia and the Pacific and Indian Oceans that are, scarcely less oddly, now known as the Third World. Among the many great tragedies of human history few have been more painful than the accidental coincidence of the universal opportunity for freeing most of the human family from their long bondage to ignorance and poverty with a brief period of impatient, insensitive, greedy and aggressive mass intervention on the part of an ostensibly civilised group of advanced countries, who ought to have known better. In ecological terms the damage done by the more high-minded and charitable of the interveners has been hardly less than that of the greediest.

Among the few who both perceived this situation and felt able and willing to try to tackle it intelligently and constructively was Barbara Ward, who forged the small International Institute for Environment and Development into a remarkably influential instrument for reconciling these two worlds. Her first brilliant approach was by taking the succession of United Nations Conferences of the 1970's on the Human Environment, Habitat, Water,

Food and so forth, and converting them into major world occasions for awakening public opinion and ensuring a follow-up, rather than leaving their proceedings to gather dust.

Unfortunately, despite a series of futile Development Decades and similar non-events, the great sums poured into this worthy cause were largely wasted through being entrusted to the blind leading the blind. To give just one personal example, I made a great effort in the later 1960s to persuade the United Nations Development Program (UNDP) in New York to allocate

Barbara Ward, economist, champion of Third World development, and conservationist, whose globally embracing perspective and sure touch so greatly influenced the international spread of the environmental movement.

an absurdly modest sum for a co-ordinated program in the Saharan countries, based in Tunisia where the necessary scientific expertise and facilities were ready, to demonstrate how to stop the spread of desertification. Although I was politely listened to, no support was forthcoming, and, by the end of the decade which would have been required for the study, the people of the desert fringes began to die in catastrophic numbers, together with their crops and livestock. If those in charge had listened, the Sahel famine might still have been averted, but the UNDP had to prove once more that where there is no vision the people perish.

Although this is the only major example within my own experience it could be matched many times elsewhere. Among the culpable blunders that were allowed to recur were:

Failure to seek and use scientific advice in designing and executing development projects, especially as regards ecological and social science aspects (p. 62).

Failure to adopt appropriate alternative technology, and an obsession with the big and sophisticated approach rather than 'small is beautiful'.

Failure to learn the basics of providing food, firewood and shelter in terms of local culture and local economies, and to decline support for more ostentatious projects where these essentials were neglected.

Failure to recognise and take better precautions against the misuse of international aid to bolster power-seekers and corrupt elements in Third World countries.

Failure to identify the shortcomings and counterproductive contributions of western-trained economists, engineers, lawyers and others, and to deny them opportunities for harming local communities with the leverage afforded them by aid programs and funding.

Indulgence in bureaucratic and long-winded procedures inappropriate to the direct and urgent tasks.

Failure to educate, train and back up the more practical and adaptable potential leaders and workhorses at local level, as against emissaries from the centre and outside 'experts'.

Failure to give recognition and encouragement to other elements in local culture with potential for effective self-help.

This sorry list could be extended, but what would be the point? The arrogance, ignorance, lack of due humility and sensitivity, and the persistent unwillingness to listen on the part of those who were entrusted with the handling of aid to the Third World will stand in history as one of the major blots on the record of this century. It needed the colossal tragedy of the Ethiopian famine, conveyed to the world largely by environmental film crews, and responded to by a magnificent band of young pop musicians, to begin to show the full horror of the situation created by the folly and ineptitude of the development movement, and the practical way to deal with it. Even now, the lessons of this vast fiasco are only slowly and reluctantly being absorbed by some of those on whose consciences the famines should lie. If only they could have listened!

Thanks to the International Institute for Environment and Development (IIED), and to other independent bodies such as the Intermediate Technology Development Group, much valuable work has been done in devising genuine and practical long-term solutions costing much less than the grandiose, overcentralised and inappropriate policies and prescriptions that have now to be superseded. The need for drastic reorientation in the harsh light of Ethiopia still remains to be squarely and honestly faced. Had this been a situation in war, a number of battle-losing generals would have been summarily replaced. We treat people with great sympathy, except those who need it most.

The situation has been aptly expressed by Brian W. Walker, the president of IIED, in his Introduction to its *1985 Annual Report*:

> 1985 was a critical year for environmentalists and practitioners of development alike. The focus was Africa. Many agencies, and not a few experts, were forced to rethink their positions. Two interlocking and terrible trends dominated that great continent. Environmental bankruptcy, on a continental scale hitherto unrecorded in the history of the human family, underscored the futility of much of what has passed for 'development' over the last four decades . . . . And we were forced to contemplate the agony of the malnourished mother and her innocent, dying child. Both are the victims of the failure of development.

As was quickly realised by Bob Geldof in using his vast fund of Live Aid, it makes no sense to forget about rehabilitating the life support systems, natural and human, and to pour money simply into day-by-day salvage operations. The sloppiness of the term development has been fully analysed by Professor Keith Caldwell, who was reduced to finding that 'as a practical matter "development" is defined by what it is . . . . Development is as development does'. This undefined nature of the interest which is the recipient of so much money, and the agent for so much human welfare is scarcely creditable, even if we are bound to accept it as credible. Muddled thinking leads to muddled action, and eventually to muddled holocausts.

What is the remedy? It has already been foreshadowed in insincere and unfulfilled declarations by the United Nations Development Program, on one occasion in conjunction with the World Bank and UNEP in 1980, promising the incorporation of environmental considerations in development policies. No more such prevarications can be accepted. It is now essential that the appropriate environmental agencies at each level be given

Bob Geldof, guided by no more than a big heart and plenty of horse sense, put to shame the United Nations agencies and experts who were paid to anticipate and prevent just the kind of blunders and horrors which were to shock the world in the mid eighties.

an equal voice in decision-making and that 'development' shall be officially and mandatorily redefined in terms which make plain sense, not least ecologically.

Such a combined movement for actively promoting the health and welfare of people and of living resources, wherever on the planet these are at risk, is evidently essential. No more funds should be voted for the proponents of old-style 'development' to continue to go it alone. Given the will, this merger could be brought into operation without delay, with existing institutions and programs being progressively overhauled. The process would be comparable to that familiar in many large industrial mergers, and like them it would need an injection of tough, fresh, top management.

Is it too much to hope that the United Nations leaders, who have so badly disappointed mankind's expectations, and have wasted so many lives and so much money in this field, will make the necessary decisions, aided and pushed, we may hope, by the world environmental movement? Human needs, the battered biosphere, and both logic and common sense cry out for such action.

While the United Nations and many donors as well as recipient governments bear responsibility for the 'development' fiasco, comparable damage has been inflicted on the planet by the irresponsibility and incompetence of world bankers. They have encouraged dishonest, corrupt and ill-advised governments and agencies in the Third World to overborrow for the ostensible funding of dubious large-scale projects in ways that have not only gravely undermined the natural resources base and life-support systems of many vulnerable countries but have hazarded the world monetary system entrusted to their custodianship. They have thus squandered immense sums, which should have been much more soundly invested in other enterprises. Although it is now nearly a half-century since Fairfield Osborn began demonstrating to American bankers the prudence and benefits of obtaining ecological advice on investments in land and resources, bankers generally still throw away *our* money by failing in that respect.

Even the World Bank – the Bank for International Settlements – which after much persuasion did establish an internal ecological advisory service, and has, under such Presidents as Robert MacNamara, tried quite hard to ensure that its investments are not damaging to the environment, has too often allowed itself to become misled. The subject was thoroughly explored in conjunction with the international banks concerned in the IIED study *Banking on the Biosphere: Environmental Procedures and Practices of Nine Multilateral Development Agencies* in 1979. It is surely time for more vigorous public pressure to establish the environmental accountability of banking, and thus to provide an overdue reinforcement to the solvency of the banking system. Going environmentally into the red often means going financially into the red also.

Since the environmental movement rose to importance it has provided substantial employment directly; it has also encouraged the creation and expansion of environmental industries such as equipment for measuring and controlling pollution, energy conservation devices, recycling wastes, saving paper, reducing noise and consequential engine inefficiencies, and much else. Yet the world of business, whose environmentally blind population is great enough to wring the heart, is still only grudgingly and gradually beginning to understand, first that ignoring environmental factors is no longer civilised or tolerable as a business practice, and further that taking full account of them helps profits, in the vast majority of cases.

In Britain, efforts have been made to spoon-feed business people with relevant environmental material by means of the regular briefing publication *Environmental Data Services* (*ENDS*) and more recently through the bridging organisation the Centre for Environment and Development (CEED), formed as a result of the World Conservation Strategy, which seeks to bring business people and environmentalists together, with particular attention to mutual problems and opportunities. While a number of major firms, especially in oil, chemicals and other science-based industries, are attentive, the majority of manufacturing and service industries show little interest.

In the United States, while the chemical industry, for example, has a far worse record than the British environmentally, a larger proportion of firms take care to show social responsibility. This has been especially marked in relation to the quality of urban environment, notably in such cities as Baltimore, Pittsburgh, Indianapolis, Denver and Boston, where business interests have undertaken a major share in projects to enhance environmental quality. Many rundown British inner cities would appreciate a similar enlightened involvement on the part of business. Indeed the environmental movement itself has played only a minor and peripheral role so far in contributing to the livability of British cities.

In the countryside, on the contrary, the British record has been one of much activity, and even of confrontation with champions of modern highly mechanised chemical agriculture and large impersonal agrobusiness. A prototype of environmental organisation was the Council for the Preservation of Rural England (CPRE), formed as early as 1926 under the inspiration of the planner Patrick Abercrombie and the lively architect Clough Williams-Ellis, who shortly afterwards wrote that delightfully combative little book *England and the Octopus* (1928; new edition, 1975).

This was not a unitary society, but an umbrella organisation covering many kindred interests; it was influential and fairly effective until World War II deprived it of momentum. Afterwards it suffered badly from the deaths or ageing of its prime movers, and from undue delay in recruiting young enough successors – a besetting sin of the earlier environmental bodies. Its recent revival is late but welcome.

The Ramblers Association put all it had into promoting the National Parks Act and, by playing its cards badly, suffered in 1949 a defeat that left it relatively impotent for a longish period. Through these historical accidents it fell largely to the nature conservationists to make the running during the 1950s. It was only in 1958 with the formation of their counterpart to CPRE, the Council for Nature, that the way was open for a triple alliance between nature conservation, the protection of rural amenities generally and the leisure users of the countryside. This was attempted through the three 'Countryside in 1970' Conferences of 1963, 1965 and 1970, with partial success.

Under the presidency, and at the instigation of, the Duke of Edinburgh this trio of meetings formed the first major effort to achieve a broad lateral

The Duke of Edinburgh opening the first Countryside in 1970 Conference in London, with (left to right) Dr R. Beeching (British Rail), Lord Strang (National Parks Commission), Lord Hurcomb (Council for Nature, (Lord Howick (Nature Conservancy), Sir Christopher Hinton (Central Electricity), Aubrey Buxton (Council for Nature) and Max Nicholson and R.E. Boote (Conference Secretary and Deputy Secretary, respectively).

consensus at high level between the many and varied owners, occupiers, and users of country land. The first conference had 220 participants, from ninety mainly national organisations. Its follow-up in 1965 was prepared by twelve Study Groups, each composed of a team of experts with an assessor, a convener secretary and a minuting secretary to report in depth on:

> the Training and Qualifications of Planners;
> the Training and Qualifications of the Professions concerned with Land and Water;
> Technology in Conservation;
> Countryside Planning Practice;
> Review of Legislation;
> Outdoor Recreation, Active and Passive;
> Traffic and its Impact on the Countryside;
> Preservation of Natural, Historic and other Treasures;
> Information and the Countryside;
> Living and Working in the Countryside;
> Reclamation and Clearance of Derelict Land;
> Planning and development in Scotland.

Each of these Study Groups included members, usually senior, from around ten or more specialised organisations, aided by nearly twenty assessors from government departments and agencies, working hard for months beforehand. In addition there was a major input from the Conference on Education, attended by representatives of some ninety educational bodies, who had met separately at the University of Keele, in order that they should contribute fully without swamping the main Conference. During the preparatory period several other important subjects were covered by, for example, the joint Institute of Landscape Architects/ Nature Conservancy conference on ecology and landscape at Attingham in September 1964.

Simultaneously, the Conservation Foundation held at Airlie House in Virginia a Conference on The Future Environments of North America. This had been organised by a small steering committee of which the Chairman and one other member (myself) had been concerned in the London 1963 Countryside Conference. It was followed in May 1965 by the White House Conference on Natural Beauty, covering a range of related problems through fifteen specialist panels, of one of which I was a member.

This bald list must suffice to indicate the scale and thoroughness of the concerted effort on both sides of the Atlantic to prepare the way, as it did, for the series of major advances towards more systematic care for the environment that ensued in both countries during the later 1960s. These include the creation of the two Countryside Commissions in Great Britain, and its new Department of the Environment, and the national Environmental Policy Act in the United States (see Chapter 5, p. 100).

Perhaps the most relevant point here is the progress achieved towards widening informed awareness of environmental problems, and making a start towards tackling them comprehensively through multi-lateral teamwork, extending far beyond the earlier limited world of environmental conservation. Nevertheless, I still had to emphasise, in my concluding conference appraisal in 1970, that too many decisions continued to be made on too narrow a base of expertise, especially by small groups of economists, lawyers and accountants. 'The input for the decision-making process', I said, 'is far too narrow, and that is one of the reasons why wrong decisions are made'. I fear I would still be in order in repeating that.

In my Introduction to the Nature Conservancy's *Annual Report to Parliament*, published in November 1964 I had stated:

> It has always been the Conservancy's view that conservation is much too great a task to be done by the Conservancy alone. They can merely study it, experiment with it, demonstrate the need and how to meet it and act as a pace-setter, guide and stimulus towards a nation-wide understanding and fulfilment of this great task.

I went on to welcome the start of broader co-operation, adding:

> When man seeks to preserve amenity, what he is basically trying to do is to perpetuate the natural variety of scenery which constitutes the landscape. The conservationist wants the same thing under a different name. He desires the greatest possible variety of habitats for the plants and animals which make up the natural resources of the countryside, but he understands something of the complex underlying process which the guardian of amenity may overlook. The conservationist, however, is still learning how to master his art and science, while the public are still learning that such an art and science exist.

Now, in this chapter, an attempt is being made to review even more broadly the field for lateral concerted effort. It is encouraging to be reminded what success (considering the difficulties of the times) attended a similar effort during the early 1960s. Experience shows that environmental conservation needs to advance in breadth as well as in depth, even though the former depends upon the latter.

A rather modest but effective example in Britain has been the creation since 1969 of a series of Farming and Wildlife Groups, combining enlightened agriculturalists with conservationists, based on the head-quarters at Sandy of the Royal Society for the Protection of Birds. In this effort, the farmers are in the forefront, with the conservationists in support. The work is decentralised, with branches in nearly every county, most of them supported by full-time advisers carefully picked for their blend of knowledge of both farming and conservation, as well as for their personality. A number of them are young women.

They have the support of the National Agricultural Advisory Service and of the Minister of Agriculture and the National Farmers' Union, as well as the Country Landowners. While it took more than a dozen years of preparation to get this fully in operation the experience confirms that, given enough patience and effort, and at no great cost, related separate interests can be brought to engage in combined operations with environmentalists, and to produce worthwhile results, although still on too small a scale.

Coincidentally with this quiet positive work on the ground, farmers and conservationists had become locked in a sometimes emotional confrontation over damage to scientific sites and to hedgerows, ponds and watercourses, through the demands of large-scale mechanised operations and the massive application of fertilisers, pesticides and herbicides. This controversy became entangled with another arising independently from the stimulus given by the European Community's Common Agricultural Policy to increase production of cereals and other products at high cost and in amounts far in excess of the needs of European consumers. Levying taxes and charging prices higher than should have been needed in order to store, at high interest rates, farm products that no one wanted, and which had been grown at the cost of severe damage to the countryside and to natural habitats, seemed for some years to make sense to many farmers and politicians.

It made no sense at all to the British public, but much needless damage was done, not least to the good name of the farmer, before wiser counsels prevailed. One disturbing feature was the extent to which the Ministry of Agriculture, employed to represent the nation, allowed itself to become a tool of blind sectional interest, and to prolong resistance to the adoption of more sensible policies on behalf of the public as a whole. Another noteworthy point was that, as in the case of oil on beaches and so much else, important consumer interests failed to pull their weight in correcting these evils, until much of the burden had been carried by environmentalists.

At international level again, and especially within the European Community, inexcusably long delays occurred before funding ceased to become available exclusively for the unbalanced development of the agricultural sector of the rural economy, and was grudgingly and most inadequately opened to other sectors, including conservation. While it can at last be said that the sound and publicly beneficial arguments championed by environmentalists are prevailing, no satisfaction can be felt that the process has taken so much too long that it has meanwhile squandered vast resources wrongfully withheld from the environment, and that the much larger interest groups which benefit from the reform should have defaulted on performing their proper share of the campaign.

It is surely time for environmentalists to insist publicly that, where they have to fight causes from which others stand to benefit, those others should not hang back and fail in their own plain duty. It is time for fingers to be pointed at the defaulters, and to make them blush in public. Those also who come forward belatedly, and under pressure which they should not have needed, would do well to keep a low profile, and not to expect to be given fulsome credit for eventually seeing reason.

Forestry, like farming, has adopted practices which have brought it into conflict with environmental conservation. In Great Britain the exposure in World War I of the grave national hazards resulting from generations of neglect to grow timber led to the panic creation of a State Forestry Commission, given virtual *carte blanche* by the Treasury to establish large

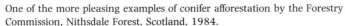

One of the more pleasing examples of conifer afforestation by the Forestry Commission, Nithsdale Forest, Scotland, 1984.

monocultural plantations of exotic softwoods on cheap land. It occurred neither to the Treasury nor to the Commission that changing technology in the coalmines might end the demand for timber pitprops, one of the largest elements in the expected market, by the time the trees had been able to grow. Nor were the true costs of the Commission's timber plantations, or the risks of arboreal diseases incidental to such monoculture realistically assessed. The damage to landscape in areas of outstanding tourist value was also ignored until environmental clamour forced greater restraint in such areas as the Lake District.

Under heavy and sustained pressure, the Forestry Commission has incorporated landscaping, recreational provision and wildlife conservation into its practices, many decades after the United States Forest Service had led the way in multipurpose use. It has also become less centralised, unhappily too late to avoid being compelled under political pressure to unload to private purchasers many woodlands of wildlife and amenity value that conservation bodies are forced to purchase at high cost in order to save them from ecologically unsound exploitation or from unacceptable damage to amenities.

Some day it would be interesting to make a thorough financial audit of the cost to public funds and to the national environmental resource as a result of Forestry Commission policies and practice during the half-century 1920–70, before the environmental message began gradually to be heard and acted upon, as happily it now has. Such an audit should also evaluate the costs and benefits, to the nation, of tax concessions to wealthy individuals that enable forestry companies to benefit at the expense of frequent encroachment on environmentally sensitive areas.

Over-centralisation was also the pattern in many other countries, especially those formerly in the British Empire, such as India, where it has perhaps had even more catastrophic results owing to the clear felling of what should have been conserved as protection forests on the Himalayas and other ranges, and the consequential release of vast floods and loss of irreplaceable topsoil.

In a few countries, notably Switzerland, which had the visual aid of annual avalanches, people learnt early that trees must be taken care of on pain of intolerable suffering. The care and wise use of Swiss forests was entrusted to the local communes, for whom they have proved a great economic as well as ecological and cultural asset. The Swiss are by no means averse to making money, but in the case of their forests they have long since learnt not to do it by sawing off the branch on which they are sitting.

That is just what the modern world is continuing to do with the reckless destruction of its tropical forests, inspired by an unholy alliance of greedy

Coast-protecting mangrove forests are key natural resources for some of the world's poorest countries; this is all that remains of one in Haiti that was needed for charcoal.

Logging in Sabah, Malaysia, 1983 – an example of the destruction of tropical forest.

developers, irresponsible bank lenders, ecologically illiterate governments and exploding human populations. Only fools forget the respect due by people to trees.

Until recently it was widely believed that, with the exception of spillages of oil, the seas and oceans were broad enough to have unloaded into them with impunity every kind of noxious effluent and refuse which the stupidity of man could devise. Seafarers for many generations have got away with this while articles of refuse were less enduring, less damaging and less conspicuous. The International Maritime Organization, which has not much else to do, but which has a habit of responding only very belatedly to external pressures, has a shameful record in this area, the more embarrassing as it is the only United Nations Agency with headquarters in London. It has, however, joined in as a fellow traveller in the Regional Seas Program of its younger sister agency UNEP. It is arguable that the marine environment would have been no worse off if the International Maritime Organization had never existed.

One of the earliest areas to experience the need for conservation was the yield and management of marine fisheries. Those in the North Sea were already declining in the late nineteenth century, sufficiently to induce establishment of an International Council for the Exploration of the Sea,

The misuse of the Royal Navy in a vain attempt to frustrate Icelandic efforts for rational fisheries conservation in their surrounding waters contrasts oddly with its current much more difficult assignment to enforce similar conservation over a controversial but internationally important zone round the Falkland Islands.

which since 1902 has had its headquarters in Copenhagen, and has won respect for its researches. In 1926, at the request of the League of Nations, it produced a Report recommending international regulation with close seasons and rotation of fishing zones to ensure sustainable yield. This proved abortive, as have nearly all subsequent attempts towards enforceable conservation measures for marine fisheries, despite the excellent scientific base which marine biologists have developed for the purpose. For a further half-century irresponsible and greedy overfishing has been countenanced by short-sighted governments, to the point beyond which the fishery itself could not economically survive. One of the most discreditable episodes in this sorry history was the final 'Cod War', in which the United Kingdom's Royal Navy was employed in a futile attempt to prevent Iceland from enforcing necessary conservation measures in its surrounding seas.

The vast expansion recently of international tourism has inflicted immense harm on vulnerable and hitherto unspoiled environments. Possible mitigating measures have been internationally reviewed many times since the International Union for the Protection of Nature's Technical Meeting at Salzburg in 1953, but owing to the amorphous character of the travel, hotel and other services involved, and their reckless disregard of the importance of safeguarding their own raw material in scenery, landscape, coastline and other amenities, it has proved impossible to get to grips with

A Spanish coastal strip of sand dunes appropriated by developers for excessive and unsuitable exploitation as a tourist centre.

any meaningful negotiations. The one happy exception has been in East Africa, where, by providing attractive facilities for safari trips in the National Parks, a disciplined and mutually beneficial traffic has been developed to a stage where it represents one of the most important contributions to local balances of payments, for example in Kenya. (The unhappy civil conflicts in Uganda over recent years have destroyed an equally valuable connection there.) A growing number of specialist tours relating to wildlife and the environment exert a limited degree of influence in favour of conservation, but the ignorance and irresponsibility of the mainstream tourist industry persists.

While development for tourism tends to choose sites of high environmental quality, and to plan to erect on them conspicuous structures such as hotels, restaurants and swimming pools attracting busy traffic, the requirements of leisure facilities for the home population in some cases conflict less with environmental quality. Examples of this are golf courses and the use of inland waters for sailing. There are, however, many instances in which recreational uses conflict with conservation of wildlife or the environment, and much patient study and negotiation has been devoted to finding mutually acceptable solutions, not always with success.

Noisy or highly disturbing sports such as water skiing, speedboat trials, motor-cycling scrambles and hill-climbs, and low flying are special problems, as are anglers who discard lead weights, nylon lines and other objects lethal to wildlife. In the latter case repeated efforts in Britain to reach an amicable and workable agreement have obtained such a poor response that legislative prohibition under penalty appears the only alternative.

On the whole, competing users of the countryside appreciate the need for give-and-take co-operation, which may involve zoning in terms of space or times of use, and the acceptance of codes of conduct. This is often facilitated by the fact that areas of overlapping interest can fairly readily be identified and mapped, and the types, seasons and times of desired use can be specified. On both sides also, organisations often exist that have the status and interest to seek a *modus vivendi* rather than drift into a situation of irritation or confrontation, so that in most cases serious conflicts can be averted. This is a model which might well prove to be of service in other areas of competition for land use, apart from those that are normally settled by official planning decisions.

Graver and bigger problems often arise over the siting and operation of major public utility projects, such as airports, oil processing depots and ports, pipelines and power stations, especially nuclear.

In some ways the advent of aviation has been a help to environmental conservation. It has for the first time made possible a close inspection of the whole earth and its living resources, as well as its landforms and geology. Charles Lindbergh, who started his career as an air pilot and concluded it as a leading conservationist, told me that this change was brought about by the disturbing sights he saw flying about the planet.

Astronauts have confirmed the message, spellbound by the beauty of the living earth seen from space in contrast to so many lifeless planets around it. Aerial photography, from satellites as well as aircraft, is a powerful tool of information, and even for helping to heal environmental blindness. Without aviation the systematic monitoring and conservation of endangered species as we now practise it would not be possible.

These are big pluses, but there are also minuses. Posterity will look with horror on the commercial explosion of package tourism, which has suddenly let loose on so many vulnerable and unspoilt environments such a nasty human effluent of ignorant and ill-behaved visitors, whose trivial and ephemeral wants take precedence over the essential requirements of many generations to come.

More specific and limited pollution has come from the carelessly designed aircraft engines which, in wasting so much of their fuel, burden both the

(a) A warning, ostensibly temporary but in practice permanent, on a Kentish coastline once notable for the excellence of its free supply of healthy shellfish, ruined by what economists call an 'externality' of industrial production processes.
(b) Sewage discharge into the seas.

(a)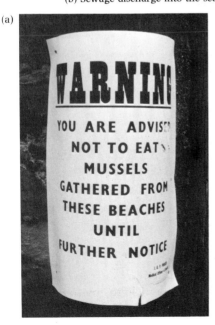

(b)

atmosphere and the stratosphere with chemical pollutants threatening climatic systems as well as breathing creatures below. It has been fortunate that some of these engines were so unreasonably noisy as to trigger off environmental protest strong enough to compel their restriction and redesign, with incidental improvements in efficiency and economy without which even more airlines would be in financial trouble to-day. For this, however, the 'environmental lobby' receives no thanks, and expects none.

Even now, improved design has scarcely begun to tackle the excessively long and solid runway requirements which make aviation so demanding in landtake and so ineffectual in conveying its host of passengers into the cities, which are their usual destination, rather than into what should be the surrounding green belt of countryside. Aviation is young, however, and not having become so fossilised as many other interests, is to some extent adaptable to the demands of the even younger environmental movement, for which it has learnt the hard way to show a proper respect. Looking back over the past two decades, we can see some grounds for hope that, in its own self-interest, it will become more of a partner and less of an adversary in the future.

In terms of environmental damage aviation is already matched, and in sheer potential far surpassed, by that other great gift of modern science, nuclear energy, in its various applications, civil and military. Sadly, however, it has come to to stay with us before we have had time to tame and civilise the barbarian military-industrial sovereign state; before the engineers and scientists had learnt how to harness it safely and to dispose of its alarmingly and enduringly radioactive residues, and incidentally before they become capable of fulfiling the promises they have been giving us for the past thirty years of reliable lower-cost energy, demonstrable on honest and comprehensive accounting methods. We are faced, therefore, with mankind's biggest-ever exercise in damage limitation, until civilisation and technology can regain control and put the genie back in its appropriate bottle. The situation has been made worse by the fact that no one responsible, since Christopher Hinton, has even tried to communicate about it, until 1986.

Thanks largely to their own hubris – the Greeks had a word for it, but engineers might find it more understandable to imagine a blend of complacency, arrogance and presumption – the builders of the nuclear power industry and their political, administrative and commercial sponsors failed to perceive how the time-bomb of nuclear war would tick ever more loudly in the ears of the public, and would concentrate their minds and fears on the two obvious weaknesses of peaceful nuclear power. These are, of course, its failure to guard adequately against forseeable human errors in design and operation at hazardous stages, and its unaccountable failure to wake up to, and deal credibly with, its growing output of radioactive waste. Perhaps nothing in the modern world so brightly illustrates the failure of its top technologists to give elementary thought to environmental problems as the fact that for decades after the generating of nuclear waste became an obvious and major practical problem, the engineers continued to accord it bottom priority by assuming that they could just dump it somewhere on land or beneath the sea. How can such minds have existed in this supposedly advanced twentieth century, our successors may well ask with incredulity and contempt?

Pending an answer, one of the much-heralded pathfinding exercises of glorious high technology is virtually brought to a halt, at immense cost to us all whose savings have been at least prematurely over-invested in this industry, which has now to go back to the drawing board for an indefinite period.

Its plight, however, is almost enviable compared with that of the vast overkill industry which continues to pile up nuclear weapons, now belatedly becoming recognised by even the dimmest minds as realistically unusable in

By an irony of fate, this unforgettable American nuclear test explosion at Bikini atoll immediately followed in July 1946 the initial discussions for the International Union for the Conservation of Nature and Natural Resources. From that date the race has been on, and so far it is by no means won.

any imaginable circumstances. Here the environmental movement has rightly left the running to be made by its sister Nuclear Disarmers, who have perforce had to resort to different tactics and organised demonstrations, civil and even marginally violent disobedience to the law, emotional mass appeals, and political pressures, sacrificing respectability to the attainment of more urgent and challenging impact. Some overlap occurs at the support base between the Nuclear Disarmament and Peace Movement and environ-mental conservation; I was myself briefly involved in both in the 1950s, until my talks with leading Establishment figures persuaded me that they could not be taught, without resort to measures too brutal to be harmonised with our environmentally prescribed strategy and tactics.

The career of Nuclear Disarmament from the days of Bertrand Russell and Aldermaston marches to the present has been of uneven activity and effectiveness, but it is not for environmentalists to criticise the fluctuating degrees of heroism, not seldom of the highest order, which our fellows in it of both sexes have displayed.

Recently a coming together has proved possible through the wise and bold leadership of the environmental action group Greenpeace, which switched methods hitherto used effectively against whaling and sealing to a challenging demonstration against French nuclear bomb tests at Muroroa

Greenham Common Peace Camp symbolises the concern and dedication shared with conservationists by anti-nuclear campaigners readier to adopt non-violent disobedience to policies which they find unacceptable. Run entirely by women, and successfully cultivating media attention, this campaign has undoubtedly influenced political views and shifted the topic higher up the agenda.

atoll in the nominally peaceful Pacific Ocean. To the eternal shame of the French nation, President Mitterand's personal office despatched a mission, scarcely credible between friendly nations, to affix demolition charges to the *Rainbow Warrior* in Auckland harbour, New Zealand.

Only after fierce argument was the secret plan changed from one of blowing it up at sea with all fifteen of its high-minded crew, to an explosion before it sailed, which in the event cost only one life. Thanks to the memorably prompt and efficient response of the New Zealand Prime Minister David Lange, who happened personally to be in charge of Foreign Affairs and of Security Intelligence Services, the whole sordid business was unravelled and the successive official lies from Paris were confuted to the extent that one of those responsible, the Minister of Defence, had reluctantly to be sacrificed, leaving the President and Prime Minister to carry on with their guilty now non-secret.

It is essential that this criminal act against conservation should never be allowed to be forgotten, and that the anniversary of 10 July 1985 shall long be remembered soberly as *Rainbow Warrior* Day, not least in France. Indeed the French secret service has set a record for the speed, thoroughness and accuracy with which any secret mission has ever been unmasked.

Let all those who may be tempted to resort to foul practice to counter the

The Greenpeace vessel *Rainbow Warrior* sunk at Marston Wharf, Auckland, New Zealand, by French limpet mines, with loss of a life.

legal and proper measures which they force upon the environmental movement think twice before acting similarly, and weigh the price for this outrage. The good name of France will yet have to pay, despite the short-term solution, since reached, of using blackmail against New Zealand exports to force handing over of the convicted agents in return for some cash compensation and a worthless official apology.

Oil, the other spectacular energy development of recent decades, has a vast potential for environmental damage, which was early made conspicuous by the irresponsibility with which it was allowed to escape into the sea. This led to one of the earliest major confrontations with environmentalists, and to a responsive development of awareness and sensitivity on the part of leading oil men that has made this one of the model examples of the possibilities of genuine and effective action by an industry to honour to the full its environmental responsibilities.

Unfortunately, when the Alaskan oilfield came to be developed, some of the American oilmen concerned turned a deaf ear to the wise environmental advice of their British colleagues, and as a result incurred vast losses before operations could finally go ahead with the necessary clearances. I recall the vivid impression made upon me, while visiting the Prudhoe Bay plant of BP at that time, by the fact that within a couple of metres of the edge of the great installation the surface of the virgin tundra lay undisturbed and just as it had been.

Natural gas, a similar type of industry, was slower to get the message in Britain but, having got it, was quick to develop a first-rate team for environmental appraisal and for embracing conservation in its new projects and operations. Both oil and gas provide encouraging evidence of the extent to which industrial and environmental interests can be harmonised where industrial managers have the wit to see the many advantages of so doing.

Health and safety in industry, together with sanitation and hygiene, were among the first environmental factors to attract public concern leading to government action. Provision of sewerage and refuse collection, and the supply of pure water, go back much beyond a century, even though the population explosion and the mass flocking of illiterate poor families to Third World cities are now reproducing risks and sufferings which had been expected to be a thing of the past.

The long, and on the whole creditable, history of environmental health and safety services does nevertheless show that people soon come to take environmental care for granted, and to fail to recognise when and where its principles need to be given extended application on account of hitherto unforseen menaces and problems. It is not enough to have brought under control this, that and the other specific situation; there must always be vigilance to detect in good time where the principles need to be applied to new circumstances, and this calls for comprehensive monitoring and survey of the environment as a whole.

In the case of health, there is now shown to be a need to manage intelligently not only the physical environment but that of our homes, and the nutrient and chemical content of our diet. Unfortunately, more scientists are employed in industries profiting by putting questionable additives into food than are free to use expert knowledge to safeguard and improve the nation's health. It is a sad reflection that in Britain it took World War II to mobilise the best scientific guidance to give the nation a healthy diet, and that since that effort ceased it has taken exploited consumers nearly four decades to learn for themselves how to find such a diet and to insist upon it being made available in the supermarkets. Some of those leading this campaign have learnt from experience as environmentalists that there are ways of resisting the policies and practices that are wrongly foisted on them by vested interests.

Having discussed as fully as space permits most of the main organised sectors of activity with which the environmental movement has to co-exist, it is time now to turn to people themselves – the beneficiaries or victims of those activities. First, who are the people whose future on earth is threatened by mismanagement and maltreatment of its natural environment? The most obvious point, which conservationists have been making with increasing vigour to their blind and deaf rulers for several decades, is that there is such a thing as carrying capacity, and that animals that multiply beyond it will be disciplined by famine and other unpleasant correctives. The people – not the governments – of a substantial number of nations, including the United Kingdom, have grasped and acted upon this message, and have adjusted the size of their families to zero population growth. All twelve of these nations so far are in Europe and – no thanks to the Pope – they include Italy with an increase in 1984 of only 0.1%, following Sweden and Austria with 0.0%. Half-a-dozen more European countries, as varied as France, the Netherlands, Czechoslovakia and Bulgaria are down below 0.5%. If they too cease growing, the zero-growth group will reach nearly one twelfth of mankind – a respectable if tragically belated start.

Compared with this bright European corner the rest of the global picture ranges from disturbing to horrific. China, the most populous, with more than a billion already, at least deserves credit for seeing the red light at last, and switching so far as possible to one-child families on a course calculated to bring about stability at just under 1.5 billions, or just under one-third of to-day's world total of 5 billion. (There are currently in the world some 133 million annual births, giving an increase of 80 million plus.) China has only half the arable land of the United States but already four times the population, and a prospect, on recent trends, of declining amounts of food per person within a few decades. The prescription adopted is drastic but is being applied as gently and persuasively as the situation permits, and promises to be largely effective.

Other Asian countries such as India, Indonesia and Thailand are responding less vigorously, and there are still some whose governments encourage a rise in fertility, not always with success. During the two closing decades of this century further world population increases will roughly equal the *total* population at 1900, which had already tripled in between.

Even these startling numbers fail to convey the gravity of the situation. Kenya, for example, which is already in trouble feeding its 19 million people and providing them with such necessities as fuel, faces a four-fold further growth by as soon as 2025. Densities which we have been accustomed to regard as high in Belgium, the Netherlands and Japan at 300 to 350 persons per square kilometre are already more than doubled in the case of Bangladesh, and will be doubled again by 2025, with an increase in existing misery there which is beyond computation.

Key facts about this race towards uninhabitability are (1) that it is still getting much less high-level or popular attention than many other issues of infinitely less menace, and (2) that we know how to check it by practical and

Example at Rio de Janeiro of the worldwide refugee movement of surplus rural population seeking a livelihood in improvised substandard accommodation within indiscriminately expanding cities.

acceptable means which are neither adequately encouraged and supported nor even freely available in many parts of the world. The environmental movement, with its many other preoccupations and overloads, has shrunk from giving it priority, but is at last doing so, partly under the stimulus of Common Ground International, a joint group under my chairmanship bringing together leaders of the International Planned Parenthood Federation and of the environmental conservation movement, to frame and disseminate a number of joint policy and situation statements, and to promote concerted efforts by followers of both movements in the field in many countries.

Progress, however, remains far too slow, and, although the rate of increase in most countries is beginning to decline, young populations, increasingly concentrated in unmanageably large cities unable to take proper care of them, point to aggravation of pressures and tensions for at least the next half-century. We only have to listen to each day's news to understand that the world is a much less secure, healthy and happy place than it was even thirty years ago, and yet we are gratuitously laying up for our children an intensification of that trend. Apart from the bill to be paid in universal misery and constraints, there is the even more ominous and enduring cut in essential life support systems, which are already becoming inadequate. Nature, also, has the power to hit back biologically at a plague species. And now the uncontrolled spread of AIDS, with its effects not only on the current generation but on the unborn in the womb, could be a first warning. Sex can bring life, but its abuse can also bring annihilation.

People do not live by bread alone, but public subsidies to the arts and to culture are often nullified by the nightmarish background which modern artists feel bound to reflect, and even by the difficulties and dangers of visiting performances or places where historical and aesthetic experiences have long been rewardingly sought. Widespread cancellations of vacation trips because of fears of terrorist attack are the latest symptom of this worsening. The conditions which generate international terrorism are being aggravated much faster than the often ineffectual countermeasures can be put into operation.

I had intended at this point to discuss the potential for renewing the almost interrupted communication between environmentalists and the arts, but I have regretfully concluded that this would not be timely or appropriate now. There are too few signs that a response would be forthcoming. I also despair of religious leaders and the churches contributing significantly towards the urgently needed renewal of our battered civilisation. Indeed they show little sign of appreciating even the existence of most of the pressing problems with which this book deals, and the influence in particular of Pope John Paul II probably more than cancels out such limited benefits as all the others put together may be able to contribute. Following the Inter-Faith Service held successfully at Assisi on 29 September 1986 during the WWF anniversary celebrations efforts will be made to prove me wrong on this; I devoutly hope they will succeed.

Although so incomplete, this chapter has made a first attempt to throw some light on the human ecology and context of the environmental conservation movement to-day, in terms of the parallel movements and activities which impinge on it, either beneficially or negatively. As has been shown, these comprise: sources of ideas and inspirations in science and philosophy; proponents and disseminators of knowledge and ideas through the media and education; research workers filling gaps and assisting lateral thinking between environmental and other movements; professionals, and managers of land and marine resources; providers of facilities for tourism and utilities, together with bankers and leaders of commerce and industry, including especially oil and nuclear power, and such services as health and family planning, and the generation of employment.

Some of these are shown to contribute positively, some neutrally as fellow-travellers, some negatively as making rather than easing the problems, some in more than one of these ways. In some of these areas, progress is visible through previously adversarial groups becoming less so, or even positively helpful. In others, persistence in environmentally destructive or damaging activities is having cumulatively worse and even irreversible effects. Whatever the situation, environmentalists need to monitor it – to identify allies, active adversaries and sheer inert masses in the way, and to study how most effectively to interact with them and to understand what is making them tick, if indeed they do tick. Tiresome as it is, special attention needs to be given to blockages within or surrounding the main problem groups, and how best to treat and relieve them. Our aim must be to bring about a situation where the principles and practices which we pursue will have been so fully and completely absorbed in all humanity and its institutions that promoters of environmental conservation as a separate entity will be found superfluous, and will gently and thankfully be able to fade away, greeting with reverence and appreciation the new environmental age, which can as yet be discerned only with the eye of faith. The struggle is vast and daunting, but, as this outline has shown, the barriers can be and are being gradually identified and surmounted. The dogs bark, but the caravan moves on.

7

Pioneers of conservation

Conservation takes care of the natural environment, but people take care of conservation. No discussion of its aims, scope and achievments can be complete unless it tells something of the diverse personalities whose talents, characters, careers and idiosyncracies, at different periods, within different nations and against different backgrounds, have by their thoughts, persuasion and actions helped to make the movement what it is. Any such essay cannot of course be more than a subjective sample, derived from limited knowledge. Having, however, had the privilege of knowing and working with a fair proportion of the recent protagonists, I owe it to them and to the reader to do my best to record some of their contributions in the light of the kind of people they were. Most of those included here are no longer living, except for a few who have more or less completed their contributions, although happily they are still with us. The account begins, however, with some who played a major part in shaping the emergence of the movement even before this century.

St Cuthbert, who founded in effect one of the earliest bird sanctuaries on record, 1300 years ago on the Farne Islands, should head the list, partly because he insisted that leaving wildlife unmolested was a religious obligation, and partly because his authority was such that his injunction still holds sway, and is in fact now backed by law. In that he has been more fortunate than St Francis, whose brotherhood with the birds remains to be re-established in Italy, despite all the efforts of conservationists. His love of nature, however, is still affectionately remembered, except perhaps in the Vatican. His contemporary, Emperor Frederic II, also merits mention as having done much by his interest, studies and publication to place the natural world on the agenda of princes, and to establish falconry. Indeed, various forms of hunting played a major role in ruling and landowning circles in keeping alive an interest in what we would now call conservation.

As has been seen earlier (Chapter 5, p. 89) concern with the medicinal properties of herbs led to the first professional and scientific interest in the subject. It was quickly followed by anxiety to conserve timber resources, and to plant and introduce trees. It is interesting to reflect that the earliest scientific work on this, John Evelyn's *Sylva*, arose from his deep sense of guilt at his family fortune having been derived from wholesale destruction of timber to manufacture gunpowder with the charcoal. This personal concern was reinforced by the Navy's anxiety at the scale of inroads into the stocks of mature oaks available for building its wooden ships. His initiative led both to positive conservation through planting and to regulatory laws restricting the depredations of iron-masters with their tree-felling. John Evelyn therefore personified no less than four of the main strands that have run through conservation ever since – personal feelings, remedial prescriptions based on science, proposals for curbing damage, and legislation to enforce changes of practice. In his case, as in others, the personal factor was probably decisive.

Trees have long stirred up ambivalent feelings as between the sense of achievement in clearing them for settlement or farming and the sense of guilt at destroying so rapidly so noble and mature a living thing. The moral conflict has been aggravated in recent times by appreciation of the role of trees in the landscape and opposition to growing them as mass commercial crops, often composed of alien species laid out in highly unnatural patterns. Europe has produced no such champion of great trees as the Californian John Muir, nor has it seen any such outrage as the cutting through a living tree of a passage for a horse-drawn vehicle. It is somewhat surprising that in this epoch of reckless destruction of forests, especially in the tropics, no outstanding personality has become specially identified with the conservation of trees.

In North America, Ralph Waldo Emerson and Henry David Thoreau gave influential leadership during the nineteenth century to a mystical view of nature intimately linked with trees and forests, while Frederick Law Olmstead made manifest in landscape and park design a similar group of values. In Europe, as the Romantic movement faded, such overtones were mainly lacking.

However, Europe responded more enthusiastically to a somewhat older American leader, of French origin, who perhaps contributed most from that time to the creative and practical evolution of the modern conservation movement – John James Audubon. Audubon originated three of the main approaches that continue to inspire and guide the progress of conservation. First, through his vivid fresh perceptions, skills and exploration in the field, and his talents as an illustrator, he replaced the previous wooden and uninspiring pictures of wildlife with life-like and moving scenes. He began the process, completed by colour television, of enabling everyone to share in the wildlife heritage, and in the enjoyment of watching it with understanding and emotional satisfaction.

His second gift to us was to put birds in particular into their distinctive natural habitats, breaking away from the artificial, museum-style detachment of previous misrepresentations of animals, and showing plainly where each species belonged.

After failing to secure a publisher in the United States for his great illustrated work *The Birds of America*, he was luckier in Edinburgh and London in obtaining worthy technical and financial backing, although he never lived, as we have, to see the day when a single copy of it would fetch the astonishing sum of one million pounds. In his time, few could personally enjoy, let alone possess this great work, but the fact of its existence transformed the ways of looking at nature. No longer were museum skins, laboured written descriptions or pictures based upon them, the basis for visualising the habits and habitats of the living world. A new pattern for its interpretation had been demonstrated; it was to be elaborated through still and cinema photography, colour printing, radio, television, video and other techniques. The breakthrough to a fresh and true perception of nature had

John James Audubon, painted by his sons during the 1840s.

been made with the issue in London, between 1827 and 1838, of the plates for *The Birds of America*.

Out of the richness of his originality, Audubon went on to bequeath us another splendid endowment. He observed, thought about, and warned about the risks of decline and even extinction of treasured species, and the need for positive conservation measures, long before the word conservation had won currency even in America. Had he been listened to there would still have been time to save the passenger pigeon and others, but it took their disappearance to awaken the nation to his message. The adoption of his name for the national network of conservation societies hardly atoned for the sluggishness with which his advice had eventually been taken, but at least it reminds us that his contribution was by no means confined to observing and painting birds, brilliantly as he did both of those.

Audubon was a great pathfinder, but, if credit for the successful *establishment* of the modern conservation movement belongs to any man, above all others it must be accorded to the American President Theodore Roosevelt. Although as a boy near-sighted, and unable to see much until belatedly provided with spectacles, he became a dedicated naturalist. He would have embraced a scientific career had he not been frustrated by his inability to get training other than as a laboratory worker in biology. His family being well off, he had no need to earn money. Entering politics as a young man in New York, he also acquired in 1883 two cattle ranches, in what was still the Wild West, amid sporadic outbreaks of fighting with bands of Red Indian braves, and much lawlessness among the cowboys and buffalo hunters.

Dividing his time between these two contrasting life-styles he got a grasp both of nature and of human nature, which stood him in good stead later. He was drafted for the almost sinecure Vice-Presidency of the United States, through interests wishing to avoid having him for a further term as governor of New York. Within a few months, the assassination of President McKinley resulted in his becoming President, and during his eight years of office he put conservation on the map, being, even to this day, the only major head of government on earth to really understand its significance and its necessity.

At this period, land and natural resources of vast potential value belonging to the federal government were virtually up for grabs from predatory private interests. This problem could only be coped with by promulgating policies that would vindicate the principle that the public interest in the wise use of natural resources should come first, and by establishing competent professional agencies for the purpose, such as Commissions on Public Lands, on Inland Waterways and on National

Conservation. In the conflicts that arose there were many casualties, including the jailing of two United States Senators and two leading bankers.

His Wild West experience, both of people and of natural resources, proved invaluable, however. Aided by a first-rate team of public servants he broke through public apathy and ignorance about 'the relation of the conservation of natural resources to the problems of national welfare and national efficiency'. Finding that all forests belonging to the United States were run by one Department while all government foresters belonged to another, he set up the United States Forest Service, with responsibility for some 60 million acres of forest lands, under Gifford Pinchot.

Roosevelt wrote of him:

> He was the foremost leader in the great struggle to co-ordinate all our social and governmental forces in the effort to secure the adoption of a rational and far-seeing policy for securing the conservation of all our national resources . . . . The conservation movement was a direct outgrowth of the forest movement. It was nothing more than the application to our other natural resources of the principles which had been worked out in connection with the

Theodore Roosevelt in his less familiar indoor aspect, as a great executive.

forests. Without the basis of public sentiment which had been built up for the protection of the forests, and without the example of public foresight in the protection of this, one of the great natural resources, the conservation movement would have been impossible.

The other national resources mentioned included large Reclamation Act projects, comprising dams higher than any ever built before; a great program under the Inland Waterways Commission, the creation of 36 State Conservation Commissions, reinforcing the National Conservation Commission. The creation of five new National Parks, four big game preserves (including that of $1\frac{1}{2}$ million acres at the Grand Canyon), National Monuments such as the Muir Woods giant sequoias, and fifty-one bird reserves, from Hawaii to Florida, were only part of this great personal accomplishment. It demonstrated a vast new vision, given shape on the ground by uncommon political courage and tenacity, skilful public leadership and superb administrative drive and competence. After the expiry of his term the rats got in, under his successor Taft, and unfinished business such as his international initiative (see Chapter 2, p. 30) was dropped. Most of the agency advances were maintained, and even pursued, but except for the belated establishment of the National Park Service in 1917 and the 1916 Treaty for the Protection of Migratory Birds (itself a Roosevelt legacy) little more was achieved until the 1930s. There was virtually no further White House initiative until his cousin, Franklin Delano Roosevelt, launched the Civilian Conservation Corps as part of his 'New Deal'. In the words of Senator la Follette at the end of Theodore Roosevelt's presidency in 1909:

> This immense idea Roosevelt with high statesmanship dinned into the ears of the nation until the nation heeded. He held it so high that it attracted the attention of the neighboring nations . . . . His greatest work was inspiring and actually beginning a world movement for staying terrestrial waste and saving for the human race the things upon which . . . a great and peaceful and progressive and happy race life can be founded.

The world conservation movement has never again had the luck to be furthered by any such combination of supreme political power, knowledge and wise judgment, and by the opportunity of carrying through with public consensus so many innovative measures covering, in more senses than one, so much ground. There is no better example of the dependence on a single great personality of so much that even conservationists take for granted.

After Theodore Roosevelt, conservation was pursued at a lower level by heads of federal agencies, and by many leaders of the voluntary movement, although somewhat fitfully and with limited effect. In contrast to European experience, conservation in the United States had started at the top and had no way to go but downwards.

In Britain responsibility for conservation had traditionally rested with private landowners, who created and maintained a wide range of agreeable landscapes and, with the exception of persecuted predators, also of native wildlife. As the nineteenth century went on, however, it became clear that this would not be enough, but with the notable exception of environmental health, and locally of access to commons and open spaces, concern was mainly confined to private individuals and groups. Among these, four may be identified as having left a substantial personal stamp on the emerging movement – W.H. Hudson, A.G. Tansley, Charles Rothschild and more recently Julian Huxley.

It may seem odd to class the often solitary Hudson as having a power base, but he became closely linked with the (later Royal) Society for the Protection of Birds, and implanted on it his (fortunately too pessimistic) assessments of the impending loss of rare species. In *Birds and Man* (1901) he wrote:

> Within the last few years we have seen the disappearance (as breeding species) of the ruff and reeve, marsh harrier and honey buzzard soon to be followed by the sea-eagle, osprey, kite, hen

A conservation campaign to end the ignorant prejudice against birds of prey that has destroyed so many of them is now bearing fruit, but in the case of the white-tailed sea eagle in Britain it came too late to obviate the need for artificial re-introduction from Norway to recolonise former territories, now successfully underway.

Decline of the sea eagle in Britain

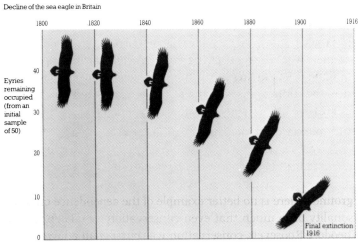

1800   1820   1840   1860   1880   1900   1916

40

Eyries
remaining
occupied
(from an
initial   30
sample
of 50)

20

10

0

Final extinction
1916

harrier, Montagu's harrier, stone curlew, Kentish plover, dotterel, red-necked phalarope, roseate tern, bearded tit, grey-lag goose and great skua. These in their turn will be followed by the chough, hobby, great black-backed gull, furze wren, crested tit and others. These are the species which, as things are going, will absolutely and for ever disappear, as residents and breeders, from off the British Islands . . . Finally, we have among our annual visitants a considerable number of species which . . . would probably remain to breed if they were not immediately killed on arrival – bittern, little bittern, night heron, spoonbill, stork, avocet, black tern, hoopoe, golden oriole . . . . This is the case . . . . Nevertheless I believe that it may be possible to find a remedy.

It *was* possible, thanks above all to his efforts, and we have the satisfaction of knowing that in the 1980s every species on this list of the doomed is breeding successfully in Britain, except for the sea-eagle (reintroduced in the 1980s and just beginning to breed), Kentish plover, and five of those mentioned as possible colonisers.

Yet Hudson's judgment at the outset of this century was far from being wild speculation; it was extremely well informed and with minor corrections may be taken as what probably would have happened but for the vigour, skill, and tenacity with which bird protection has meanwhile been pursued. It gives us some measure of what is owed to those who took on the struggle against heavy odds, and refused to be defeated.

Perhaps Hudson's greatest contribution was the use he made of his keen perceptions and his talents as a writer to win over a wide circle of readers to a lively appreciation of the English countryside and its wildlife. He strongly appealed to the influential and the educated, and no small part of the favourable and informed public opinion on which environmental conservation has been built stems from his persuasive and enlightening efforts.

He condemned speculation as to the causes of phenomena with insufficient knowledge of the precise facts and commended the idea that in order to find the true causes of bird migration 'astronomers, physiologists and men of all stems in biology and physics should be called in to consider the question from all points of view'. In this he was anticipating modern co-ordinated investigations. In many ways his influence has contributed to the substance, the atmosphere and the resolution of environmental conservation to-day. I cannot forbear to add that no other writer so greatly influenced my own early responses to nature.

Sir Arthur (A.G.) Tansley made an equally significant contribution to the movement, at a later period and in very different ways. Like Hudson, he was not easy to get to know, and although my acquaintance with him began in the 1920s, and I worked quite closely with him during the later 1940s and the 1950s, much about him remained a mystery. Tansley had a profound philosophic bent, which set him apart from his fellows, and at times made for loneliness and melancholy. A long period of 'Disillusion and Disaffection' as Sir Harry Godwin called it in his excellent appreciation (*Sir Arthur Tansley: the Man and the Subject, Journal of Ecology* **69**, 1–26 (1977)) prevailed in his middle life, from 1914 to 1927, just before Oxford came to his rescue with a professorship. From then on he found continuous scope for his talents; this was well epitomised by Godwin as:

> the capacity to recognise a need, a hiatus in the course of scientific development or its proper communication; here his sense of timing was almost infallible. . . . . He had the capacity and drive to act to fill this need, most commonly by bringing together and inspiring men of like opinion, organizing them effectively and bringing their objectives into scientific or public notice . . . . He had the vision to perceive the primary aims of an enterprise, the judgment to assess its timeliness and its political and financial practicability, together with command of clear direct language that convinced others. Surely herein lay all the attributes of *leadership*, a quality that enabled him to be the creator of so many enterprises whose permanent usefulness has been both national and international.

Yet even in 1939 he told Godwin that he saw his life's effort, to convince scientists and the public at large of the validity and importance of the ecological viewpoint, as a failure. He had spent 'lonely years "in the doghouse" and had to suffer the loneliness of the long-distance runner.'

Long before I knew him he had founded two key journals – the *New Phytologist* in 1901 and the *Journal of Ecology*, which he edited for over 20 years for the British Ecological Society, of which he was the founder President in 1913. Two years earlier he had published his classic work on *Types of British Vegetation*, and in the same year he had promoted the first international phyto-geographical excursion, bringing together in the field a number of leading ecologists and botanists from different European countries and through these personal relations damping down tendencies to fracture ecology into adversarial schools. For a time his interest had switched to psychology, which he studied under Freud in Vienna, but after returning to the fold he took up the Sherardian Professsorship of Botany at Oxford, while I was there. He took some part in a team from mixed disciplines undertaking field surveys, which were among the first of that kind. Later he turned his attention increasingly to conservation, and became its father figure, as he already was for ecology in Britain. As chairman of the British

Ecological Society's Committee, he made, in 1943, the case for an official service for nature conservation in Britain, going on to lead the official Wild Life Conservation Special Committee, the precursor of the Nature Conservancy, of which he was the first chairman until 1953. He also pioneered university and school field studies, never forgetting the link between ecology and conservation and the world of human activities. He loved the chalk grasslands, and after his death aged 84 in 1956 the Nature Conservancy commemorated him with a Sarsen Stone monument at Kingley Vale National Nature Reserve in Sussex, a favourite haunt of his. The inscription, which I wrote for it, reads:

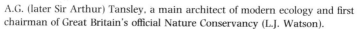

A.G. (later Sir Arthur) Tansley, a main architect of modern ecology and first chairman of Great Britain's official Nature Conservancy (L.J. Watson).

In the midst of this Nature Reserve which he brought into being this stone calls to memory Sir Arthur George Tansley F.R.S, who during a long lifetime strove with success to widen the knowledge, to deepen the love and to safeguard the heritage of nature in the British Islands.

While most botanists were preoccupied with plants or groups of plants and their characteristics, Tansley was a pathfinder in surveying all vegetation, in analysing the principles and methods governing its spread and its ecological survival, and then in showing how these could be applied practically in the tasks of conservation. He was also a great human being. Few men so gentle and modest have by insight and endurance brought about so great a transformation.

Although not classed as a conservationist Sir Patrick Geddes (1854–1932) certainly ranks as a pioneer environmentalist whose contribution should not be overlooked. Studying biology under T.H. Huxley at University College London he went on to Aberdeen University as a demonstrator in zoology before becoming successively a demonstrator in botany at Edinburgh and Professor of Botany at Dundee. His interest shifted, however, to the fields of sociology, regional survey and the evolution of cities, in which he was an influential pioneer, applying his biological knowledge to laying the foundations of physical planning, and anticipating the convergence that is only now assuming a dominant role. He was, in fact, an environmentalist before his time.

His profound and broad approach to the application of ecology in human affairs, and above all in cities has been pursued and further developed into our own time by his disciple Lewis Mumford, who has written of the distinction between the world of organisms and the world of machines as giving rise to a new vision:

> profoundly different from the one offered by those who left out of their world picture the essential qualitative attribute of life: its expectancy, its inner impetus, its creativity, its ability under exceptional circumstances to transcend either physical or organic limitations. The name given to this new vision of life was bestowed belatedly, only when it began to be systematically pursued; it is ecology.

As the environmental movement broadens out the relevance of Mumford's still underrated contributions will surely become better appreciated.

The legacy of T.H. Huxley, and indirectly of his co-fighter Charles Darwin, emerged again even more decisively for the movement in the work of his grandson Julian Huxley, a founder of international conservation, whose contribution is not easy to disentangle from his many other activities and inspirations. A gifted polymath, eagerly turning from one subject to another, he was not only a profound contributor to evolutionary science and a leading humanist but a founder of ethology and behavioural studies, a keen ornithologist, a talented populariser of science and practitioner on radio and in journalism, and author of many books and papers.

He was also a poet and artist, an avid traveller, and a man of deep and broad culture, always open to new ideas and new facets of life. He was endowed with a fertile imagination, rich creativity, a questioning, probing and exploring mind, quickness of perception and expression of thoughts, a persuasive manner, a schoolboyish sense of humour and, except in his periods of depression, an inexhaustible energy. He kept up a great diversity of friendships and correspondences, exhibiting much critical discernment, yet he never found the necessary self-criticism to curb the dissipation of his energies and his readiness to be diverted from one unfinished task to another. He was unable to learn to be realistic in organising his time and priorities and not to accept at face value 'trendies' and their pet projects. Nor did he always appreciate when he was needlessly estranging people who might have proved to have been valuable allies.

At intervals from boyhood on he would focus on conservation, rarely for long but sometimes with dazzling success. His early experiences in, and continuing attachment to, East Africa were perhaps most basic in this respect. On a lecture trip to Switzerland in 1946, during his fleeting role as Chairman of the London Wild Life Conservation Special Committee he, almost in passing, triggered off the initiation of the International Union, and then as first Director-General of UNESCO he as it were caught it on the rebound by sponsoring its official launch at Fontainebleau and simultaneously gave it a key role, as an infant less than one year old, in organising and running the first great International Technical Conference on the Protection of Nature, at the United Nations Headquarters at Lake Success in 1949 (see Chapter 5, p. 106).

Twelve years later he reappeared and played a decisive role in pulling out of the air the concept of the World Wildlife Fund, which he then helped to launch successfully at the Arusha Conference and in London in September 1961. He never held office, either in the International Union or in the WWF, but he was active in many other ways, for instance on the 1957 Coto Doñana Expedition, which led to the establishment with WWF aid of the Parque Nacional de Doñana in Spain, and the 1963 Jordan Expedition, whose initiatives for national parks were soon afterwards sadly nullified by the Israeli wars in the region.

Like Fairfield Osborn (see pp. 173–4) he saw restraint of the growth of human population as of overriding importance to conservation, and was active in promoting family planning and related programs. With his multifarious interests and contacts he did as much as any man, perhaps even more, to put conservation on the map as a major concern of world citizens, and as having a central place in human evolution and culture. If he had been more narrowly a conservationist he might well have achieved less for the movement. Unlike nearly all his peers he never had a real power-base, but the lively network of which he was personally at the centre went far to compensate for that lack.

Among his early students who made a special personal contribution to conservation was Charles Elton, effectively the founder of animal ecology as a counterpart and in some ways a corrective and amplification of the almost

Sir Julian Huxley, one of the most creative of conservationists, who inspired the launching of the International Union for the Conservation of Nature and the World Wildlife Fund, and through his countless friends in various subjects and countries did much to put conservation of natural resources on the world map.

exclusively vegetation-based ecology of the subject's earlier phases. Quiet, modest and allergic to committees, Charles played a role that was none the less formative and influential for being acted in such a low key.

In contrast, Julian's protégé James Fisher was extrovert and almost flamboyant; taking up conservation rather late in life he certainly made up for lost time. His outstanding gifts as a radio performer were eventually outshone by Peter Scott's on television; together they convinced sceptical media magnates that nature and its conservation could draw and hold audiences comparable to almost any other programs, except of course soap opera. Peter, however, from the launch of the WWF in which he took a leading part, took on for more than two decades perhaps the greatest single burden in building up the global conservation movement, not only travelling and preaching the message untiringly but presiding over countless meetings of all kinds through which the pace and scale of action were well warmed up.

It is necessary, however, to backtrack here to other important contributions, earlier in the century, which have also proved important for the growth of environmental conservation. On the European continent much of the pioneering fell to leaders in three of the smaller countries: the Netherlands, Switzerland and Belgium. In the Netherlands a classic reactive situation arose in 1904 when a project by the city of Amsterdam to use the

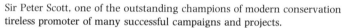

Sir Peter Scott, one of the outstanding champions of modern conservation tireless promoter of many successful campaigns and projects.

scientifically valuable Naardermeer for dumping refuse was defeated by the formation of the Vereniging tot Behoud van Naturmonumenten in Nederland, which purchased it as the first of a great series of Dutch nature reserves. The crisis brought forth the man, and until past the turn of the century the impressive figure of Dr Pieter van Tienhoven dominated the Dutch scene, although his devoted efforts towards establishing an International Office for the Protection of Nature were largely frustrated by political and economic events (see Chapter 5, p. 103).

That frustration had earlier overtaken the Swiss attempt, led by Dr Paul Sarasin of Basel, whose bold plan to 'extend protection of nature to the whole world from the north pole to the south pole' seemed on the verge of reaching fruition when World War I cut it short. Thirty years later other Swiss naturalists, Dr Charles Bernard and Johann Büttikofer, returned to it with more success, as is described in Chapter 5 (pp. 103–6).

Sarasin, however had succeeded in establishing in the Engadine a Swiss National Park that was, almost uniquely, under scientific supervision and used for research. It proved to some extent a prototype for the similarly oriented National Nature Reserves in Great Britain. Although this account is so largely preoccupied with terrestrial habitats mention must be made here of F.A. Forel, the nineteenth-century pioneer of limnology, based at Morges on Lake Geneva, which was long afterwards to become for a time the seat both of the IUCN and of the WWF.

The Union's transfer there from Brussels was through the initiative of its president, Professor Jean Baer of Neuchâtel, another Swiss (born in London) who contributed much to the development of conservation. As president-elect of the International Zoological Conference at its Darwin Centenary meeting in London in 1958 he was instrumental in the establishment of the Charles Darwin Research Station on Galapagos, the world's first international biological station. He followed this later by taking a leading part in the launching of the IBP, the critical meeting for which was held at Morges in May 1962 with him as host – he became president two years afterwards. Jean Baer was a tall, breezy fellow, radiating confidence and leadership – I recall that at the end of the Darwin Centenary meeting his predecessor as president, Sir Gavin de Beer, who at a guess was little over five feet tall, looked up at him and told the Conference, 'and now it is time for me to conclude my duties – little bear hands over to big bear'!

The other pathfinder from a small country was the Belgian Professor Victor van Straelen, who had done, on a much larger scale, for the Parc National Albert in the then Belgian Congo what Sarasin had tried to do in Switzerland, by establishing l'Institut des Parcs Nationaux du Congo Belge, which, between its foundation in 1933 and the independence of the territory in 1960, was to publish some 300 scientific volumes. Van Straelen was one of those who early personified the concept of conservation as being rooted in science, and also as being global in its concerns – concepts which are now taken for granted.

He had a no less important successor, Jean-Paul Harroy, who successfully ran the International Union through its formative years, and later developed its United Nations World Parks program in partnership with Hal Coolidge (see pp. 36–7). He left IUCN to become vice-governor of the Belgian Congo and then a professor at Brussels University, once more demonstrating the many-sidedness of the makers of the movement.

In Britain, leaders of the Fauna Society were active in the promotion of National Parks overseas, but at home there was more interest in nature reserves. The Society for the Promotion of Nature Reserves was founded in 1912, almost simultaneously with the British Ecological Society, by Charles Rothschild, who compiled an excellent national list of sites meriting conservation. Unfortunately the Society lost momentum in World War I, and through his early death, although it held together as an influential rallying point, attracting such energetic figures as George Claridge Druce, Herbert Smith and Cyril Diver.

Meanwhile a parallel movement, quite unrelated to ecology and indeed to science, had arisen from outdoor and amenity interests in favour of what were called National Parks, but bore little relation to those so designated in the rest of the world. The protagonist was John Dower, an architect and town planner whom I knew and liked for some fifteen years before his early death in 1947. It is probable that the series of National Parks which his efforts called into existence represented the closest attainable in England and Wales to the international concept, in view of geographical, political and land use constraints. It was only after his death, as the worldwide concept and network of National Parks expanded and took firm shape, that it became apparent how unfortunate and confusing a choice had been made in calling these National Parks, instead of something more appropriate to their distinctive character. It was embarrassing to conservationists to find that in this single but prominent case Britain had become the odd man out, through the well-meaning but ill thought-out decisions of an isolated group, well outside the mainstream of scientifically based conservation.

A parallel group, the bird protectionists of Britain, had been heavily engaged with their problems from early in the century, although in scientifically and practically based efforts the running was for some years made by special groups concerned with wildfowl, oil pollution and other specific topics tending to be handled internationally. Jean Delacour, born in France but, like Audubon, based in America, proved an ideal head for the

International Council for Bird Preservation, magnificently partnered by Phyllis Barclay-Smith of London. As the earliest established body in the field the Council felt justified in retaining 'Preservation' in its title long after everyone else had gone over to 'Conservation'.

Jean was a man of the world, suave, unruffled, but a master of his subject

Charles Rothschild, founder of the Society for the Promotion of Nature Reserves, now the Royal Society for nature Conservation.

and an impressive presence at international meetings. Phyllis managed to combine being almost absurdly English with a capacity for immediately and enduringly making surprising international friendships – she would appear, for example, as the accredited representative of the Hungarians, who were devoted to her. Almost a workaholic, she put on a successful act that it was all being done for fun, although woe betide anyone who took that as an excuse for sloppy or unprofessional contributions.

A marked change took place in Britain when diverse characters who had taken some kind of interest in conservation became swept into the ambit of the official Nature Conservancy, and had to take responsibility for decision-making and to learn to work with other members and with staff of different backgrounds and different specialities. Some of these, such as Professor W.H. Pearsall, were robust scientists and seasoned teachers, always ready to tackle and explain not only technical points but the ecological and other principles governing broad approaches. Others, such as Lord Hurcomb, were knowledgeable as amateurs about, say, birds, but made their main contribution through ripe experience of handling public affairs at high levels.

Others had special knowledge of one aspect of conservation, as with Professor J.A. Steers for the coastline or C.M. Yonge for marine biology. Sir Arthur Duncan, Chairman of the Conservancy for eight of its early years

Phyllis Barclay-Smith, moving spirit of the first international conservation organisation, the International Council for Bird Preservation.

was a farmer, head of the Galloway Cattle Breeders, and also Convenor of his County Council, but an expert also on birds and several groups of insects, with a fund of wisdom and good humour that could bring the best out of a meeting, in his own or another country. Good with people, and a good listener, he had a clear grasp of essential principles, and consistently upheld them with firmness but with conciliation to other views.

In sharp contrast, Frank Fraser Darling brought to conservation great gifts for observation and profound reflection on ecology, conservation and their relation to human life and ethics. He lacked, however, a number of more mundane capacities that would have fitted him better to serve as a member either of a staff or of a senior committee, and his efforts to adapt to such environments tended to finish in mutual frustration. Fortunately his value as a guru and as a detached assessor of complex problems in the field was recognised before too late by the Conservation Foundation in America, who assigned to him between 1959 and 1972 the right kind of roving commission in which he did some of his best work, crowned near the end by his Reith Lectures on Wilderness and Plenty for the BBC, at exactly the right time, in 1969. I knew him for thirty years, and had sometimes to share his sufferings over actual or imagined setbacks, but in the end he more or less came into his own, and found a receptive audience for a contribution that was partly scientific, partly ethical or philosophical, and at times even mystical. He belongs at the far end of a spectrum that extends all the way from the most practical or political of conservationists to the poets and dreamers. Both extremes are needed even if the task of getting them to mix can be demanding.

Returning to the American scene of the 1930s, it required the Dustbowl disaster, when the blown topsoil of the farm states literally darkened the sky over Washington, to give conservation fresh impetus. At last action began on the logical follow-up of the Roosevelt land reforms through the injection of applied ecology into a more comprehensive and positive style of land management, and of land use capability assessment.

Among several pathfinders in this field, perhaps the most creative and influential in the long run was Dr Edward H. Graham, Chief of the Biology Division of the Soil Conservation Service, an innovative Federal agency created in 1935 and supported by many State services. At last the land resource was scientifically studied, surveyed and supervised by principles and techniques far in advance of those adopted in Europe, and in most other parts of the world.

Ed Graham personified what were to become key qualities in the later movement. As an ecologist he had an outstanding breadth and depth of perception; as a land manager he added a practical common-sense dimension to his scientific judgment and his expertise on plants and animals significant for the environment. He was ever responsive and appreciative concerning the contributions and problems of people living on the land, however unsophisticated and slow-spoken.

Modest to a fault, he made perhaps his most lasting contribution through

Frank Fraser Darling personified some of the rarer elements vital to modern conservation, particularly the dedicated mission to learn all about the habits of large mammals in the wild and the urge to discover and communicate a set of ethics able to match and to replace in part more material reasons for establishing worldwide conservation of nature.

such notable books as *Natural Principles of Land Use* (1944), which gave new meaning to the natural resource approach by showing both the damage that could be done by unsound methods and the possibilities of remedial treatment. Through IUCN and the IBP he was also one of the most hard-working American contributors to the development of the world movement on ecologically sound lines.

Some four years after *Natural Principles of Land Use* there appeared almost simultaneously in America three seminal and immensely influential books – Fairfield Osborn's *Our Plundered Planet*, William Vogt's *Road to Survival* and Aldo Leopold's *A Sand County Almanac*. Each of these in its own way spelt out vividly and persuasively the essentials of the required new attitude, which we can now see, nearly forty years later, beginning to take hold.

In *Our Plundered Planet*, for example, Osborn wrote of 'this other world-wide war, still continuing' and bringing more widespread distress to the human race than has resulted from armed conflict. This was man's conflict with nature. 'If we continue to disregard nature and its principles the days of our civilization are numbered'. He dismissed the view 'that there are great possibilities of gaining additional subsistence from the earth through the *development* of the tropical areas', which he stated 'would be a stopgap and not a cure' in face of 'the constantly growing pressures of increasing populations in every continent of the world' – this at a time when global population was still less than half what it has now become.

In criticising the wishfulness of the then currently fashionable 'Four Freedoms', he stressed that no rhetoric or expedients could

> offset the present terrific attack upon the natural life-giving elements of the earth. There is only one solution: Man must recognize the necessity of co-operating with nature. He must temper his demands and use and conserve the natural living resources of this earth in a manner that alone can provide for the continuation of his civilization. The final answer is to be found only through comprehension of the enduring processes of nature. The time for defiance is at an end.

Shortly afterwards, in his keynote address to the International Technical Conference on the Protection of Nature, at Lake Success on 22 August 1949, he blamed the revolutionary burst in the mathematical and physical sciences for having 'tricked mankind into believing that we are the "masters of the universe", and to overlook, if not forget, our essentiality and oneness with the natural world.' 'The only great danger', he argued,' lies in the possibility that man may endeavour to disassociate himself, or to consider himself exempt from natural laws'.

Coming from a vintage New Yorker, full of the tangy, robust flavour of that great city's early twentieth-century phase of looking the future in its face, but delivered at perhaps the zenith of American power and material achievement, these were arresting words. I quote them at some length because I see them as vindicating Fair Osborn's claim to be honoured as a central figure in formulating and expressing the core message of the modern conservation movment at its earliest formative stage.

At this pivotal moment of the half-century he was redeploying his formidable talents and influence partly away from his powerbase as head of the New York Zoological Society and into his new creation, the unique Conservation Foundation, which was to focus outstanding resources of scholarship and learning and a mature grasp of public service on devising guidelines for public policy and action upon the new problems of global conservation.

Osborn was tenaciously constructive, cautious and critical but impatient, eager to gather round him the best minds which his persuasive powers could assemble and set to work under so hard a taskmaster. With his commanding presence and his quizzical teasing manner went a certain theatrical streak; faced by hard differences or uncertainties he would look intently at the company and challenge them: 'Let us reason together!'

In contrast to his forerunners he was not especially interested in wildlife and habitat, but rather in the interaction between people or population and resources. He believed intensely in harnessing knowledge to action, but his regard for research wore thin unless it was clearly leading somewhere quite soon – he had no time for intellectual pursuits in a vacuum. Nevertheless, through the talented team that he assembled and led, he vindicated the science-based and study-based approach to conservation as the only sound route to policy formation and to enduring and incontestable progress. In his company the hunt was always on, but its rules were demanding and had to be observed.

Fairfield Osborn was drawn into international conservation by the force of his global diagnosis, but his outlook was Anglo-American rather than cosmopolitan, unlike that of his equally energetic contemporary from New England, Hal Coolidge. Hal seemed actually to like foreigners and to be at home with them, especially in the Pacific and South-East Asia, but also widely elsewhere. He too was scientifically based, and he too had a power-base, in his case in Washington, DC, with the National Research Council and the Pacific Science Association of whose vast and impressive Congresses he was the tireless impresario. He was a rare combination of an American Establishment figure, a keen internationalist, a capable scientific administrator, and one of the earliest of dedicated conservationists.

That combination, backed by his skill as a fixer and to some extent as a fund-raiser, was of outstanding value to the infant international movement, of which he was at times the most effective champion in the United States. His special concern with National Parks, and his organisation of the IUCN Commission on National Parks and of the First and Second World Conferences on National Parks at Seattle in 1962 and at Yellowstone in 1972, together with the prestigious United Nations List of National Parks in its accurately revised editions, were of incalculable value. They helped to give conservation a high and admired profile in the world, and also to give it roots in many countries, otherwise well out of the mainstream.

Without Hal's unfailing energies and enthusiasm throughout its growth pains the world conservation movement would have lacked some of its most important present assets. His taste for back-room activities, and his unselfish and unassuming character, put his contribution at risk of being underestimated. To do that would be a great error.

Another American, less of an internationalist but also most influential in the build-up of the conservation movement from an early stage, was Ira N. Gabrielson, a former chief of the Bureau of Biological Survey and director of the United States Fish and Wildlife Service, and later president of the Wildlife Management Institute. 'Gabe's' devoted following, experience and authority were always helpfully available in retaining American interest.

Newcomers to conservation may easily overlook the extent to which, during the 1950s especially, other parts of the world had to rely on the then immensely greater experience of so many of the practical aspects which was available in America. For example, in January 1955 I invited Professor Gustav A. Swanson, a leading American authority with experience also in Scandinavia, to make a tour of wildfowl wintering areas and centres of research in Great Britain and to give advice on the pending establishment of a national system of Wildfowl Refuges. Not only his expertise, but his familiarity with the help afforded by such refuges to maintaining stocks of quarry species, contributed to the successful establishment of the network with full support from previously suspicious shooting interests. His readiness to listen, and his evident wisdom on the subject made a deep impression, and helped to defuse a difficult situation.

In 1959 I toured several North American universities to seek their help, which was freely given, in settling the best pattern for the Post-Graduate Diploma Course in Conservation which was set up at University College London in the following year. It was much influenced by plans made available by Professor Starker Leopold of the University of California. The London course has run successfully ever since, and has made an important contribution to the provision of trained men and women for environmental responsibilities, not only from Britain.

Having been much impressed, on a field trip with the First World Conference on National Parks, by the Nature Trails in the Olympic National Park on the coast of the Pacific I applied for technical aid to introduce this then unknown invention to Britain. I managed to persuade the National Park Service to send us for this purpose Louis Kirk, the Park Naturalist of Olympic, and his equally experienced wife. In a tour from April to June 1963 they were able to see many British reserves and their wardens, and to give much valuable advice on practical interpretive programs and techniques, which formed the start of much that is now taken for granted.

It has been my hope in this chapter to complement the accounts given earlier of the evolutionary background of conservation, of its progressive response to destructive challenges, of its developing organisation, and of its interactions among other movements, with a review of the part which leading individuals, their characters, capabilities, and preferences have had in shaping the movement into the form that it now takes. Looking back, I am unsure whether I have succeeded. Evidently there are makers of the movement who are hardly represented at all, including those working in the field as wardens, interpreters, surveyors, researchers or managers, or reporting on threats to wildlife and sites, or campaigning, film-making or fund-raising. Even within the range of participants included, many equally meritorious have had to be omitted, while among those named treatment has often had to be unduly summary and inadequate.

Nevertheless, with all its faults, this chapter has seemed worth including to remind us all of the vast team effort and investment by dedicated men and women which environmental conservation represents, and of its relative success in enabling so many diverse people to come together and to stay together amicably for the fulfilment of the great task. The subject would need a long book to do it justice, but even thus cursorily to touch upon it must elicit feelings of humility, of admiration, and of encouragement. Our cause is great, and it has enlisted great people.

8

A critical appraisal of the movement to-day

In the light of this attempt at a rough comprehensive appraisal, what are we to conclude about the nature of the environmental movement, its progress and significance? Is the movement a reality or a figment of our imagination? If it is real, what is its true substance? To where is it supposed to be heading, and is it showing signs of getting there? If it succeeds, what kinds of change will be required in attitudes, life-styles, and in what is done, and refrained from being done, on earth?

How long will the essential changes take, and how much more damage will have been inflicted meanwhile? How much of that damage will prove to be irreparable, and what scope will there be for some kind of salvage program to help in eventually restoring ecological equilibrium and health? Is mankind really capable of rising to the scale and urgency of the challenge? What are the strategic priorities, and where are they located? How much further must the movement be strengthened if it is to succeed, and on what lines?

Questions, questions. Take heart, however. Man is a questioning animal, and one of the conspicuous attributes of the environmental conservation movement is its readiness to question, and not least to question itself. Indeed it may be claimed that this questioning propensity is one of the main reasons for the movement's success, not only because those who fail to ask the right questions must also fail to find the right answers, but also because, like hunting, questioning is fun. It elicits qualities of awareness, of teamwork and of communication that are enjoyable as well as constructive. There are plenty of stick-in-the-mud never-questioners who, once they get over the first shock of exposure to environmental questioning, find the experience invigorating, and become ready for more of it.

Those who have dismissed environmental conservation as a passing phase have been proved to be wrong in terms of their own analysis and timescale, but they are right to the extent that it is inherently transient, in the longer term, and has continuously to take on new forms in order to stay in business. More fundamentally, they are wrong in their assumption that it answers no permanent and far-reaching need, and may therefore be expected to go away without that need having been met. They also overlook the fact that, although called into existence to remedy current follies threatening human survival, conservation is part of the true substance of mankind, implanted by countless generations of evolution before a few hundred generations of arrogant and misguided teachers and leaders led us away on a suicidal path. Man is reawakening to his true role as an ecological animal, unique in being consciously and perceptively an ecologist, when he so chooses.

It is a main function of this book to show that environmental conservation, having established its immediate narrow role, is destined to proceed to broader and deeper assignments. The dominance of intellectuals, politicians, business men, publicists, and others in leading positions who persist in ignoring the paramountcy of ecological principles is already passing. Not one of them can any longer stand up before his peers and credibly refute the proposition. The arithmetic of natural resources will soon make them admit that two into one won't go. Meanwhile, however, they evade the issue, talking and acting as if they seriously expect it to go away, and striving to hold together their dwindling flock of dupes. Perhaps they hope that environmentalists will soon become bored pointing out the obvious to the deaf and blind.

The remaining answers to the initial fundamental questions concerning our future must await the next chapter. Our tasks in our own time must continue to be down-to-earth. They can and must be monitored, and their progress checked and evaluated to ensure that we stay on course, and that progress is as fast as can reasonably be expected. We must not lapse into the mental confusion and sloppy ways of those who have got us into this mess. Their practice is to drift without measuring in which direction they are drifting, or how fast.

The tasks which the movement has in hand, and which must be ever more vigorously pursued, fall into four classes. First, it must identify and bring to a halt the persistent practical interventions and harmful activities that are continuing to worsen the natural and even the man-made environment.

Second, it must labour positively to change the wrong attitudes behind these harmful interventions, and to replace them by conservation-friendly approaches, at least to the point where these become accepted as right and as appropriate to be followed generally, even if some backsliding persists.

Third, all possible encouragement should be given, especially among the young, to the adoption of new life-styles, attitudes and where necessary codes of conduct consistent with, or favourable to, conservation. Social payments should be weighted accordingly, while provisions such as community service in lieu of other penalties should be used to foster positive uses of leisure and to employ the environmental potential for discouraging anti-social conduct. Much more should be done to exploit the therapeutic uses of the environment, and to invest public money in these.

The fourth class of task to be continued is of course that of creating new environmental assets, including national parks and nature reserves, nature trails, city farms, school outdoor study areas, open-air museums, field study centres, urban study centres and many more. Also, we must not forget the need to send far more well-led expeditions of keen young people to neglected sites and regions, especially in the Third World, on lines pioneered by the Brathay Trust and Earthwatch. Countless supporters and activists of various kinds in environmental conservation were first inspired by seeing things going on at such places, and by the dawning of awareness of the fulfilment and satisfaction which something of the kind could give them.

The number of such opportunities has multiplied immensely during the past two decades, and many more people now know how to set them up and run them to a high standard, while funds are more and more freely available for them. Yet many more are still needed, both to expand the coverage of conservation and to inspire and recruit more conservationists, many of whom will be needed to take active parts in the three earlier classes of work. At a rough guess we need at least four times as many active conservationists to ensure success in the coming decade, let alone to finish the job. We have done pretty well in both quantity and quality of recruitment and expansion since 1960, but the curve must be held at least as steeply up to the coming century.

Reverting to the first class it is particularly urgent to identify, attack and root out the really harmful attitudes and ideas that motivate and trigger off so much environmental damage. The movement has been too ready to wait until harmful projects or programs are actually developed or even launched before counter-attacking. That is doing it the hard way. We need not only Environmental Impact Assessments of mischiefs already planned and funded, but Environmental Impact Preventives, to be administered in advance to developers, financiers, technologists and professional advisers who can be diagnosed as prone to think up environmentally inacceptable projects. We need much more timely prevention, and less preoccupation with cure, which often comes too late.

Every time a plainly inacceptable scheme is put forward we should insist, not only on its rejection but also on an inquest into the circumstances in which, and the background of the persons by whom, it was proposed. Originators of such schemes should be noted, and invited to give assurances that they will be more careful in future.

Those who will not learn either to perceive what is environmentally wrong for themselves, or take timely advice from others who can, must in future expect to be regarded as black sheep, and that might even apply to whole sections of professions, who wilfully misbehave environmentally. As public-spirited environmentalists have so often been contemptuously smeared as 'the environmental lobby' the other side may have to learn that what is sauce for the goose is sauce for the gander, as public opinion swings more and more against them. They must expect to reform quickly or to be labelled as eco-louts.

While it is easy to list the attitudes which will have no place in a New Environmental Age – such as careless waste, selfish exploitation of scarce resources, pollution, and the throwaway society – it is perhaps less easy to define life-styles and attitudes that should be encouraged. Many young people, however, are shaping the right course, finding pleasure in experiences and immaterial services rather than in acquisition of little-used or redundant articles, and in ostentatious consumption. While hopes of replacing lost conventional manufacturing jobs by similar jobs in services may be exaggerated, many service industries are less environmentally wasteful and give opportunities for part-time and seasonal employment that can be fitted in with the life-styles of many people, especially women. There is great scope too for manufacturing industry to inject more research, better design and more attention to consumer needs, while cutting down on jobs better done by machines. Conservation calls for such a switch.

There are also welcome signs that more caring attitudes towards the environment are being echoed in greater readiness to care for other people, especially the sick, the elderly and the unfortunate. It can now be seen that the ideal of the welfare state was faulty in that it confused the concept of a benevolent community taking on the burden with a merely bureaucratic and financial surrogate being created for what are essentially human and neighbourly obligations. Under trade union pressure even pre-existing voluntary and philanthropic groups tended to be elbowed out by often uncaring and less helpful so-called public servants.

Voluntary care is at the root of the environmental movement, and there is no reason why, as it spreads, the less fortunate members of the human species should not also benefit by the new spirit now extended to other animals. Indeed the fact that 'uncaring' is becoming a current term of opprobium in politics shows which way the wind is blowing.

A weakness prevalent among voluntary bodies, and not unknown within the environmental movement, is that of amateurism and a tendency to personal or group feuding. In comparison with the neighbouring animal welfare movement, these vices are not too much in evidence, but there have been cases where loyalty to some dominant individual has prevailed over loyalty to the cause and the declared principles, and where personalities who have not been able to fit in within a given body have founded a rival breakaway group of a diversionary character largely to suit their personal predilections. It is indeed a frequent criticism that there are too many distinct organisations, with more or less the same aims and scope, duplicating or dissipating effort and confusing the public as well. Often such criticisms overlook subtle differences and needs which justify the diversity, but not always.

Some may find it easier to paddle their own canoes than to help to crew a more disciplined and better navigated vessel, and it is important that the justification for separate bodies should be kept in mind and openly discussed, especially as increasing public support makes it less difficult to find some backing for a plausible but unjustified new venture. On the other hand, tidy-mindedness has sometimes been taken too far, in efforts to amalgamate well-established and well-run bodies, with distinct functions, styles and supporting members, numbers of whom would feel unhappy to find themselves brigaded together in some new impersonal and possibly more bureaucratic organisation.

An adequate or even slightly excessive diversity also permits and encourages the taking of responsibility earlier and by more people. It thus promotes vitality and provides a richer base of recruits for leadership, which sometimes tends to be monopolised by too few for too long in larger bodies. Diversity also sharpens competition, and is some protection against small highly motivated cliques, sometimes with incompatible or even disingenuous objectives, who may plot to take over some influential and possibly well-funded organisation, which can then serve as a platform for their ulterior aims. That has happened.

Infiltration is not a tactic which can be overlooked nowadays. Where it is suspected it can create problems also where it affects membership of national umbrella bodies or international organisations, which may be embarrassed by the appearance of representatives on them whose integrity cannot be relied upon. Fortunately the environment movement has so far got by with probably less than its fair share of such problems, but vigilance is always needed. In the context of rapid change and development it is perhaps most essential to verify that policies and customs which have come to be taken for granted are still valid in new conditions which may call for a rethink. But the *bona fides* of new reformist recruits need to be held up to the light.

Some parts of the field often tend to be more fully worked while others are neglected. Certain creatures, such as birds and butterflies, exert a degree of attraction that fewer feel for bats, snakes and earthworms. Until very recently the important potential of nature in inner cities has been generally neglected, and even marine reserves have suffered from lack of promotional interest. Many naturalists travel to watch wildlife in countries which are desperately short of competent people to record their species and ecological communities, and to make such material available to those responsible nationally or regionally for conservation, yet the necessary steps to link them up are not taken.

Often, attractive educational or informative booklets and posters are produced, copies of which would greatly assist conservationists elsewhere who lack such material. Many more examples could be given of a failure to discern and fill gaps the persistence of which weakens the performance of the environmental movement. It is easy to become complacent as we survey the vast number of good and successful initiatives, without giving a thought to what is not being done and urgently needs to be.

Training is also an area which needs attention, although informal happy-go-lucky methods have on the whole given surprisingly good results. This has been due partly to the good fortune of the movement in being led through its early stages by an outstandingly talented group of men, many of them with special educational or communicative gifts, who have quietly guided and instructed their disciples and supporters, at meetings and in the field. More formal provision is now becoming needed, from the highest levels (where the Julian Huxley Memorial Fellowship at Balliol College, Oxford, has been designed as a prototype) to the level of wardens and assistant wardens of nature reserves.

Relations with political parties form another area of concern and sometimes confusion. The environmental movement's success in bringing about action in so many ways is evidence that in modern conditions it is not essential to have influential political links for such purposes, provided the politicians are left in no doubt that enough of their voters are deeply concerned. Many of those who have not had direct experience of the workings of political mechanisms cling to a pathetic faith in their efficacy, and fail to understand how many competing interests and motives have a say in the event.

Even more naïve is the idea that returning a handful of Greens to parliament will transform the situation, except possibly in the direction of creating chaos in the entire political process, which is not adapted to functioning in terms of single-interest groups in a legislature. Fortunately, before such deviations have gone too far, it has become evident that the sheer voting numbers behind conservation require the earnest attention of politicians of all parties, to whom they convey a message which is impossible to ignore.

Underlying this situation is the more subtle and imponderable modern trend towards greater sophistication and scepticism, and at the same time a greater demand for consultation and participation, especially among the expanding sector of the public that has had higher education. Many politicians hanker vainly for a return to the days when simplistic appeals to muddled political creeds would usually evoke a predictable response. In their frustration they sometimes exclaim that the nation is becoming ungovernable, as indeed it rightly is, by such crude manipulative methods. For this marked and continuing change of climate the environmental movement can claim no mean share of the credit. It has shown people how to question and challenge shoddy and often improper decisions taken in back rooms and handed out by politicians as the only right course. This practice of talking back is spreading fast.

What has been said so far in this chapter relates clearly to the more advanced countries, and has special reference to the United Kingdom. Americans like to think, not without reason, that conservation is their own invention and that what happens in the rest of the world stems from it. Historically that is pretty well justified up to the early 1950s, but not since. Europe especially has become very active in conservation during the second half of this century, and has initiated new lines of thought and new paths of knowledge and practice of which Americans know little.

Indeed, the United States persists in remaining so provincially American that it finds great difficulty in maintaining genuine and two-way international communication in this field. American participation in such global bodies as the IUCN, the WWF and the IBP has often been strained and rarely central. It was a Canadian who steered to success the United Nations Stockholm Conference, and mainly Europeans who hammered into shape the World Conservation Strategy.

I find saying this painful and embarrassing, especially as I personally have made no secret of having originally learnt the greater part of what I know about conservation in and from the United States. Yet the retrograde policies of the Reagan Administration over the environment and over world population have proved the last straw, coupled with their astonishingly docile acceptance by the once formidable American conservation movement.

That movement has led the world in a number of key developments, including the build-up of National Parks, forest multipurpose use, management of wildfowl populations, environmental and ecological education, and the evolution of environmental law. It has, however, been less effective in control of land use, control of chemical and other pollution, creation of a strong comprehensive scientific base for nature conservation, and creation of a concerted environmental conservation movement involving strategic co-operation by many official and voluntary bodies.

While American conservationists are most friendly and helpful to visitors from other countries seeking enlightenment, and are most generous in providing and funding training opportunities for overseas candidates, they seem to find it harder to participate on equal terms in examining the comparative effectiveness and wider implications of their own and other approaches to conservation problems. Paradoxically, the best and most profound debates on the role and future of conservation have been staged in the United States, in such symposia as are cited in the Sources (see p. 217).

While it would be an exaggeration to picture the world conservation movement as actually split between American and non-American camps, there is undeniably some difficulty in obtaining really concerted thought and action, especially relating to Third World problems. As soon as some favourable opportunity can be found it would appear desirable to bring together, in frank discussion of a seminar character, a number of leaders who could pinpoint and try to resolve some of the conflicting assumptions and prescriptions which currently hamper global progress.

Reconciliation, however, will not be easy, owing to the deep-rooted nature of American conservation philosophy, in contrast to the more empirical and adaptable approach in Europe and elsewhere. I have experienced this in an unsuccessful attempt, made on American initiative, to harmonise the British model in co-operative field ornithology (pioneered by the British Trust for Ornithology) with the continuing American split between professionals and amateurs. Leading Americans sincerely wish to understand and move towards the British model, but, despite much goodwill and effort, progress continues to be inhibited by deep resistances. At least in this instance it is a gain that the difference has been openly faced and frankly discussed. Such efforts should not be abandoned.

As has already been shown, two of the greatest sources of global environmental damage are the failure of the New York-based United Nations Development Program and associated aid agencies, and of the largely American-based international lending bank system, to take notice of environmental advice that is freely available to them, and has been outlined in such works as the already cited *Ecological Principles for Economic Development* (1973) by R.F. Dasmann *et al.*, of which the Conservation Foundation of Washington DC was a co-sponsor.

There is a clear need for American conservation agencies with the necessary clout to make much stronger representations on the spot to those financial and aid organisations that persist in out-of-date practices tending to undermine sustainable resource use and life support systems. If American conservationists would work more closely with their counterparts in other countries (on the model of the International Institute for Environment and Development) such evils could be at least partly remedied.

Progress in the Third World remains depressingly slow, as is indicated by the near failure of international efforts to combat desertification, even in the African Sahel Zone, which has suffered so much from it. Still more is this so in the continuance of massive destruction of tropical rainforests, despite efforts to promote international measures for restraint which may with good fortune become partially operative within the next few years, after so much irreversible damage has been done. Even in the case of gathering fuel wood, which demands much longer journeys on foot for less result by the women on whom the task falls, remedial measures have been tackled on a pitiably inadequate scale and the desperate plight of these women has not been publicised as it should be. The developed countries and their environmental and aid movements cannot escape a substantial share of the responsibility.

A grave fault in the world environmental movement is its failure to start getting to grips with the need to build up in the Third World any counterpart to the network of team members out in the field, on which its successes elsewhere have been based. At a leadership level there have been some

Ras abu Hammas, Jordan. Planting on sand dunes to check desertification.

valuable American initiatives in recruiting and training Park managers and wardens, for example, both in the United States and in East Africa.

Some training of Third World personnel has also been undertaken by the British and others. One of the most promising of these, groomed to run Uganda's National Parks, stood up manfully against the government's attempt to curry favour tribally by initiating a power dam in the then Murchison Falls National Park; the outrage was averted but not before he had become the victim of a mysterious fatal road accident when he was forced over the edge of an embankment. Other African heroes who sacrificed their lives upholding the integrity of National Parks were certain wardens of the former Albert National Park during the Congo civil war, prior to the emergence of Zaïre. It would not be difficult for volunteers from Europe and North America, under suitable supervision, to train and motivate substantial numbers of, for example, Africans in some counterpart of the former United States Civilian Conservation Corps and its Peace Corps, or the British Trust for Conservation Volunteers and Voluntary Service Overseas. Passing resolutions and making gloomy reports in far-away capitals is no substitute

(a) Ethiopian women digging a well below a dry river bed in the hope of finding water.
(b) A river operation by the Swiss-based international trust Vivamos Mejor, which through local centres, especially in Latin America, helps and leads poor mothers and others to improve their lives by recourse to the best modern knowledge about nutrition, pure water supply, environmental improvements and getting better value for their little money. This grass-roots exercise is complementary to conservation strategy.

(b)

for organising conservation efforts on the ground in the Third World, which cannot make progress without more technical aid in this area.

Indeed, conservationists even in 'advanced' countries are often unaware of the scale and expertise of the joint efforts of public servants and private volunteers that ensure the relatively high effectiveness of enforcement of environmental law and other measures within their own nations. For example, in Great Britain the Royal Society for the Protection of Birds maintains a long established and professionally competent staff, which enforces unremittingly and toughly the laws of bird protection, backed up (where cruelty is a factor) by the national staff of the Royal Society for Prevention of Cruelty to Animals. Especially where protected species are collected in connection with international trading, there is close support from the official inspectorate (the Endangered Species Branch of the Department of the Environment) enforcing CITES – the Convention on International Trade in Endangered Species. That Branch operates a vigorous and vigilant control on the import (and thus indirectly on the killing and taking) of animals and plants, from any part of the world, which are sought by collectors or commercial interests. Collectors themselves are under vigilant and constant attention. Owing to the expertise required, the officers are backed up by a complex network of conservationist advisers, both professional and amateurs. These are actively engaged in day-to-day preventive work which has global benefits to wildlife – they, and many like them, are not content to push papers or to involve themselves in lobbying, valuable though those also are in the right circumstances.

CITES is indeed an outstanding example of the pathfinding international role of the environmental movement. It goes far to prevent greedy or thoughtless interests in the developed world from using their wealth and capabilities to raid the rare or vulnerable wildlife of the planet. Not long ago it was common to see the skins of rare species of wild cats adorning the backs of fashionable ladies, who now have to find some other outlet for their vanity, since the trade has been stopped internationally.

So many worthy objectives or good causes prove abortive by being entrusted simply to high-sounding charters, resolutions, policy statements or other pieces of paper disconnected from everyday affairs. The environmental movement stands out in its thoroughness in seeing things through. In the CITES example, this arose from a carefully prepared Convention on International Trade in Endangered Species of Wild Fauna and Flora in 1973 (itself following the American Endangered Species Conservation Act of 1969), backed by ratification of some seventy-six nations. Its executive responsibility has been vested in the United Nations Environment Programme and delegated, through the IUCN Survival Service (with WWF financial backing) to the appropriate national organisations, both governmental and non-governmental. The environmental movement does not sit back wringing its hands at the absence of a world government to fulfil environmental requirements – in case of need it improvises the necessary bits of world government, which are given effect from United Nations level down to the operations of nearly all international airports and what is sold in the high street.

It is true that, even after a decade, not all the objects of CITES can be fully enforced, and that there is still plenty to be done before commercial demand in the least co-operative countries is finally stopped from contributing to the plight of endangered species, but the record of achievement is already impressive. It is already assisting to mitigate destruction much more successfully than is yet the case with the accompanying efforts to safeguard threatened habitats, or belatedly to check the commercial traffic in heroin and other Third World products prohibited by law.

Such examples demonstrate that the environmental movement has been right not to succumb to defeatism, or to be discouraged from employing every ounce of its resourcefulness to find out quickly what is going wrong across the whole earth, and then to leave no stone unturned to get it remedied. Only thus can environmentalists hold up their heads and pursue their work with pride.

Despite all their achievements, and their prominence, environmentalists are not yet keenly self-aware, nor are others well-informed about them. It may be worth while, therefore, in the light of what has been said earlier, to attempt to outline the movement in profile, as it is to-day.

Environmental conservation is loosely structured, flexible and still rapidly developing and expanding, not hierarchical or subject to directives from any recognised higher authority. Internationally and nationally it has a dual organisation, both governmental and non-governmental, with unusually close reciprocal relations, from national, regional, functional and local levels to that of United Nations and other world agencies. Informal communication and partnership is reinforced by agreed codes of conduct, programs and policies, and by an extensive framework of national laws and regulations, and international treaties, conventions and programs. These are operated by agencies or federations, in the enforcement of many of which an important role is played by non-governmental partner bodies, to an extent not easily matched elsewhere.

The movement is at once global and down-to-earth, one of its favourite maxims being 'Think globally but act locally'. Although without formal or mandatory terms of reference, its actions are guided in some detail by a series of generally accepted statements of policy, notably the World Conservation

Strategy and the conclusions of UNEP, IUCN, WWF and other representative and respected bodies at international and national levels, which are intermeshed. Their discussions are forward-looking and far-reaching, producing guidelines that are usually, if flexibly, respected. Although not formally integrated, the movement is accordingly not in practice fragmented or self-contradictory.

The movement is keenly perceptive in regard to emerging challenges, trends, and changes in conditions around it, and is quick to question the continuing adequacy of its previous responses, and to see the need for new ideas and new initiatives. Initiatives come mainly from the non-governmental partners, but principles and programs are often formulated at a forum provided by governmental or international organisations. These perform a refereeing or co-ordinating, and sometimes restraining role, while relying for much of the required action on non-governmental bodies, with which they normally have relations of trust and confidence, and to which they furnish diplomatic and to some extent financial backing.

The movement is remarkable for its network of largely voluntary professional and lay observers and advisers all over the world, and for its capacity and speed of absorbing and interpreting a mass of relevant data of many kinds. Except in areas where the necessary research or survey is extremely complex, or is overtaken by events, as for example with 'acid rain', its expertise and knowledge are rarely found wanting. It is perhaps weakest in anticipating and initiating additional surveys and studies, especially where they are expensive and call for co-operation or resources that are not easily mobilised in advance. Nevertheless, few other world movements are less often caught napping.

This is partly because the movement has so far managed to stay young and avoid becoming rigidified between frozen blocks of ideas or schools of thought, and partly because of its varied and lively composition. It has a large nucleus of middle-class, often professional or scientific, educated and politically non-aligned members, middle-aged or youngish, with a fringe of supportive senior citizens and fully its fair share of enthusiastic young people. The arts, technology and much of industry and commerce are however, rarely well represented in it, as are most of the lower socio-economic layers.

It attracts a high proportion of activists, who are suspicious of being manipulated from either within or outside the movement, and of linking up with trendy, ideological or dubiously motivated allies. The articulate and sometimes keenly controversial activists are, however, outnumbered by more participatory and conciliatory types, no less concerned with results but more ready to see the need to fit in with other interests and outlooks. Nearly all, however, are tolerant of others pursuing in their own ways the aim of caring for the environment and its wildlife, and are impatient to see results, whatever their temperamental differences, which infrequently cause rifts of any severity.

It is a broad and unschismatic church, ready to accept those who prefer to further the cause in their own ways, sociably or unsociably, but impatient of seeing its time wasted by abstractions, generalisations or plain red herrings.

Its primary motivation is for saving and enjoying wildlife and habitats, or the quality of environment in landscape and scenery. It is, however, open-minded and not averse to embracing a wider range of objectives or partnership with natural allies, provided the case is well made and there is a prospect of even indirect benefit to the cause. Indeed, many of its members are also concerned with other kindred movements, although plenty are narrowly dedicated or one-track. It also, of course, embodies many whose interest is more passive, and who help mainly by subscribing, by reading about and discussing happenings, and by talking to others in their community and maintaining general interest.

This backs up the proficiency of the movement in securing publicity, predominantly favourable, in disseminating relevant information, and in taking advantage of newsworthy opportunities, or even creating them. Opinion polls show that the movement is unusually successful in impressing its message and its importance on public opinion, which is often in this area better aware and better informed than politicians or leaders in the arts, business or religion.

Indeed, there has been a noticeable tendency for the movement's habitual scepticism, and insistence upon responses enabling the facts to be plainly understood, to rub off on other sectors of public opinion.

Looking back over this profile it may be felt to give too flattering a view of environmentalists. Have they really no more faults? It is sometimes asserted that too many of them are mean, and are attracted to a pursuit to which they need not pay so much as if they were golfers, sailing people or engaged in field sports. This is clearly not without foundation. The keen, almost religious, dedication of the early-morning wildfowler, for example, does not often find a match in conservation circles. Putting the hand in the pocket is an art which has had to be taught rather persistently by the WWF and others providing the sinews. Conservationists may have been a bit slow to learn, but they are coming· to support appeals for funds with increasing readiness and not without generosity, even though they could still do better.

Another fault is probably that, considering so many of them are widely travelled and are internationally minded, too few take any trouble, in visiting countries with great environmental problems, to seek out the handful of hardpressed local environmentalists. They could then offer help or encouragement, or speak up for them among their influential country-men who need to be persuaded of their merits for support.

Criticisms that environmentalists are often unreasonable, or voice their complaints too stridently and aggressively, are no doubt sometimes justified, although probably less often now than in the past. Chronic environmental blindness and deafness on the part of many others sometimes left no practical alternative between submission to environmental mayhem and making so much fuss that action could no longer be shrugged off. Few environmentalists, however, actually enjoy quarreling and raising their voices, more than is strictly necessary in response to the attitude adopted by the other side. It is only necessary to glance at nuclear disarmament, or trade union disputes, to confirm that by and large environmentalists are not easily provoked into tense confrontation, let alone violence.

It is sometimes complained that resources are diverted into care of the environment that would be better devoted to human betterment and to the redress of human suffering. Such complaints, however, do not rightly lie against environmentalists, but against the inadequate performance of others who have chosen to concern themselves with those causes, but have failed to match the environmentalists in dealing with them. Rightly regarded, care for the environment should rank high as a contribution to human welfare and enjoyment, and deserves to be appreciated as such.

Another complaint has been that the retention of sites in the countryside for conservation of wildlife, natural beauty or landscape represents a loss of food production. Now that all can witness the mountains of unsaleable food whose production and later storage requires large subsidies from tax monies which could clearly be better spent, those who have made such criticisms will presumably refrain from repeating them, even if it is too much to hope that they will publicly apologise for the mischief which their arrogance and ignorance have caused.

It is much easier to characterise and appraise a movement that was most active a century or more ago than one which is at its peak to-day, especially if one is an actor within it. That much must be apparent to readers of this chapter. With whatever shortcomings, however, it is better to attempt such a profile than to stumble on unaware that there is a need for it, and that sooner or later it will be undertaken. Pending that day, this poor beginning may have its uses, if only in stimulating others to improve upon it.

9

A forward view

The task of environmental conservation is peculiar, if not unique. It has to achieve a vast and complex but definable result within a time limit that is relatively brief, although inconveniently longer than is customary for most normal human programs. That result, which will determine success or failure (or even disaster), involves nothing less than permanently arresting the deterioration in the functioning of the biosphere as a viable life support system for the earth. The time limit must permit the biosphere to recover its equilibrium, and to renew its vigour sufficiently to enable human, animal and plant life to continue to flourish into the indefinite future.

Precisely what that task will involve cannot yet be fully specified, partly because of the incompleteness of our present understanding of all the factors essential to the healthy continuing functioning of the biosphere, and partly because we are uncertain how much more damage, and of what kinds and dimensions, will yet be inflicted upon it as a result either of further harm flowing from past injuries or of new harm inevitable before sanity prevails. We know now, however, broadly what will be entailed.

During the late 1960s, when I was writing *The Environmental Revolution*, a number of fluent and imaginative authors let themselves be stampeded into an orgy of pessimism, with forecasts of imminent Doomsday. Although no less concerned than they, I refrained from joining them, and my judgment on the outlook at 1970 is on the record in my conclusion to that work, and in its preceding chapter 'The way ahead'. Unlike some of my colleagues, I need feel no embarrassment in summarising here what I wrote then, and in briefly reviewing how far it has been borne out during the past sixteen years. That will serve as a useful introduction to a more extended forward view into the twenty-first century. It might be entitled 'Doomsday Revisited'.

By way of introduction it should be explained that any attempt to forecast the future in this field must bear in mind five aspects. First, we have to consider the nature and present state of the biosphere, and its capacity to cope with and recover from injury. Second comes the scale and pace at which severe injury is being and will be inflicted upon it, in ways and to a degree calculated to impair or destroy its capacity for recovery and its resource yield. Third, we need to assess the existing and prospective strength of the environmental movement to perceive, check and where possible reverse such injury. Fourth, we also need to gauge the potential of the environmental movement for persuading or compelling the human groups mainly inflicting such injury to learn to desist from it, and to switch to due care of the environment. And fifth, we have to consider the longer-term prospects of a reorientation in our civilisation as a whole, in the direction of enduring harmony with its natural environment.

Around 1970 we had only just acquired a bare minimum of knowledge on the first of these aspects, but we had awakened to the horrific possibilities of the second, and were easily led to believe that these could bring fundamental catastrophe within quite a short period. That was the Doomsday syndrome, and fortunately it has proved grossly exaggerated, as I suspected, but could not be sure of, at the time. Accordingly I focussed rather on an assessment of the prospective strength of the environmental movement, which many at the time regarded as doomed to defeat, or even likely to prove a passing fashion. On the contrary, I reached the conclusion that it had come to stay and would increasingly prevail – an optimistic view that fortunately subsequent events have tended to confirm. I was scarcely less optimistic on the fourth aspect, and we now know that progress here, although by no means negligible, is proving much more gradual and disappointing than I had envisaged. That in turn has postponed success on the final aspect – the New Environmental Age.

'The way ahead' started by explaining that the first third of the twentieth century saw the infancy of the conservation movement, while the middle third had faced it with efforts and development taxing its limited energies, leaving the final third to risk defeat unless it could tackle a formidable range of problems, some cosmic and abstract, others specific and concrete.

More persuasion, demonstration and pilot projects would be needed before the required transformation could be attempted realistically. At the same time the main intellectual and moral forces that had contributed to modern man's appalling disregard of his responsibilities to his environment had now been thrown back on the defensive. (That, in retrospect, was clearly an overstatement.) Mankind must now finally and unequivocally renounce all claims to be above ecological laws. The moral and intellectual bases of outdated beliefs and practices must be challenged on their own ground. (That has partially been achieved by such initiatives as the Club of Rome, but the process is far from complete.)

Historically, religion has been the core of wrong cultural attitudes, and it remains so with negligible exceptions, ignoring the wiser tradition of a minority of leaders such as St Francis. The need for theological rethinking on man's place in nature is urgent. (It is still urgent, and still virtually ignored by the churches, but conservationists are now tackling it head-on at Assisi.) Education, however is now a greater stumbling-block, and although a start has been made towards comprehensive and fundamental revision of the role, methods and content of education it will, on the most optimistic expectation, take the rest of this century to bring the attitudes of the churches and the educationists into some reasonable degree of harmony with modern knowledge about man and his appropriate role in relation to nature. (Pessimistic as it seemed then, that forecast now looks somewhat optimistic.) Fortunately the mass media can powerfully assist meanwhile. (They have done this splendidly, and with far-reaching influence.)

By the middle 1970s this should have created a firm base for sustained and realistic policies for care of the environment, but there will be very difficult new problems, of combating self-indulgent and destructive tendencies. (Events have roughly borne this out, but the 'firm base', although

Procession to the World Wildlife Fund's Inter-faith Service at Assisi, 29 September 1986, led by the Duke of Edinburgh with Dr Karan Singh for the Hindus and Rabbi Arthur Herzberg for the Hebrews.

unshaken, has proved of limited use for launching large-scale advances.)

The conservation movement needs to be matched by some kind of human conservation movement to tackle the self-defeating and self-destructive tendencies of mankind, including delinquency, racialism, urban troubles, bureaucracy and dogmatic politics. Such a distinct and immense task was no part of the job of the conservation movement, but would enough human conservationists of high calibre be found for it? (The answer so far is a loud NO, although the need indicated is now even plainer. *Faute de mieux* conservationists are being compelled to move towards filling this disgraceful gap.)

There must be a fusion of ideas and a removal of obstacles to intercommunication, focussed by a new ecologically oriented culture, a starting point for which must be better integration of ecology in science generally, which it might be hoped would be largely achieved during the 1970s (It was not.) Ecology itself must be consolidated and absorbed into the practice of the land-linked and other relevant professions, giving reality to trusteeship for the land. 'There could, however, be a disastrously long time-lag . . . between the winning of new knowledge with revolutionary implications and its thorough application in world-wide practice.' (That is just what has happened.) Despite the Duke of Edinburgh's Conferences on the Countryside, and the parallel White House Conference on Natural Beauty, reconciliation of conservation and development evokes a tardy response.

Although there has been fair progress in treating environmental impacts of extractive industries, and towards planning major new works '*from the outset* with full knowledge of and regard for their total environmental repercussions' (Environmental Impact Assessment), progress since 1970 has been poor with the training of the land-linked professions and with agriculture, forestry and fisheries, while tourism and recreation have hardly yet begun to consider their environmental responsibilities. Interdisciplinary mixed teams were widely required, as were changes in governmental and international organisation and practice, for example in relation to prevention of pollution. (In this area progress has been fairly satisfactory, both in legislation and administration.)

There was a danger that rigidity might set in within the environmental movement itself. (But that has so far been avoided.) It could be expected that increasing numbers of concerned groups of citizens would arise to check the usurpations of bureaucracy and to create alliances and a new climate. (Progress here has been quite encouraging.) Finally, brief reference was made to the folly of obstructing family planning and encouraging further overburdening of the earth's carrying capacity. (Some progress has been made here, but it is still far too little and too late.)

At best there was a prospect of a Great Siege of Nature by mankind for something like a minimum of three centuries. I wrote:

> Functioning side by side with the biosphere on the same planet the technosphere leaks or deliberately injects or dumps within it so many, so vast, so pervasive and so deadly poisons and irritants as to threaten its capacity to continue functioning effectively, and its value as a source of support and a natural environment for mankind. The problem is no longer of nature threatened by man but of both man and nature in the same boat, both equally threatened by the temporarily uncontrolled workings of the technosphere.

It is a salutary exercise thus to have to review a forward-looking appraisal written more than a decade and a half ago, especially in the light of the not negligible list of advances during that period which has been included in earlier chapters. So many of the problems facing us remain much the same, and I personally see no reason materially to revise the diagnosis or to alter the targets for action.

How little, nevertheless, has been achieved in terms of grand strategy, and how many decades of further effort are going to be needed? Before becoming too discouraged, however, it is well to bear in mind that in regard to such fundamental changes in widely and deeply rooted idea-systems, history shows that the pace does accelerate, from a painfully and almost imperceptibly slow rate at the outset to a much more rapid adaptation and acceptance of innovation at later stages, which few of those who bore the brunt of the pioneering will live to see. One can have more confidence in what will happen, and even in how it will happen, than in when and how quickly it will happen.

Luckily the reckless race to despoil the earth, which so alarmed us in the 1960s, has already brought enough retribution in terms of economic depression to slow down substantially the rate of damage during the 1980s. Measures against pollution, waste and certain kinds of over-exploitation are measurably abating the scale of further damage in the developed world.

In the Third World, however, the continuing population explosion far outweighs any remedial measures that can be applied, with the equivalent of a whole new Nigeria every year and another India every decade. The biosphere shows increasing stress annually, but perhaps the increasing stress for man is even more conspicuous, in terms of famine, local wars, internal destabilisation, ill-health and ungovernability.

Quite apart from its catastrophic implications for the biosphere, one must wonder in human terms how much longer this folly can go on? Surely the manifest spread of misery and stress must impress enough people strongly enough to lead them to do something sensible about it, out of sheer self-preservation. What future for our children can any of us see, even forgetting about the environment?

The struggle in which environmentalists have been engaged for some three decades is evidently one which they cannot win single-handed, but which they will doggedly persist in, like Britain against Hitler, in the sureness that events will in time bring them the essential new allies. That could happen either through pressures from other quarters, such as those above mentioned, bringing others into line, or through environmentalists so broadening their appeal that enough other interests will be led to make common cause with them. The only other alternative, which is unthinkable, is that the default of all others to come to the rescue of our tottering civilisation in time will so discourage environmentalists that they will succumb to defeatism and give in.

Rejecting that possibility, and confident that environmentalists will not only maintain but improve upon their admirable recent track record, it remains to pull together the foregoing diagnosis and prescriptions so as to show as clearly as possible what are the assets and favourable factors that can be put to use, and what specific actions are called for in the foreseeable future.

We can take courage from the strong and conspicuous trend to reverse the build-up of state power and bureaucracy in many countries, to pare down the more selfish and obstructive exercises of national sovereignty, to reinforce international partnerships, and (with the aid of space exploration and astronomy) to intensify awareness of the littleness and ephemeral nature of man and the flimsiness of his disintegrating man-centred universe. Such influential and universal trends, with others such as growing impatience with the nonsense of modern armaments, are gradually doing much to create the right climate for the New Environmental Age, and to undermine continuing resistance to it.

They are especially valuable because they complement the successes of the environmental movement in pursuing both its positive tasks and the curbing of such direct and measurable threats as environmental pollution. They help with the more amorphous and elusive objectives of changing attitudes, policies, programs and practices, and the creation of new attitudes among the environmentally blind, or otherwise inaccessible adversaries. New natural allies are also emerging, for example, with the complementary growth of information and communications techniques, and in leisure activities, as well as through the strengthening of earlier like-minded interests such as health and safety, including the adoption of better diets.

It is often overlooked that, compared with a few decades ago, there have been immense advances in standards of management and professionalism among voluntary bodies, the best of which (and there are plenty) can deliver a wide range of essential services more cost-effectively and more acceptably than can the state or many big private enterprises. The great expansion of these voluntary bodies is now overdue and may lead to a better balanced and more satisfying pattern of society. In the United Kingdom there is an immediate need to match the strong National Trust, Royal Society for the Protection of Birds and Royal Society of Arts with a much strengthened Royal Society for Nature Conservation (this is in hand) and a powerful body for Urban Ecology, Conservation, and Livability of Cities.

The environmental movement, with its long perspectives and global concerns, is particularly affected by the prospective fundamental changes in the world economy and social system, but, like others, has no infallible crystal ball to predict what they will be. Any forecasts or expectations will need to be periodically reviewed to check how far they are consistent with developing trends, but, given readiness to go back to the drawing board, it is better to be equipped with some considered forecast than with none at all. Here, for what it may be worth, is mine.

The framers of the Constitution of the United States two centuries ago wisely placed it within the laws of nature. It makes a good starting point to assume that the world economy of next century will become adapted to conform to the limits of resources that can sustainably be provided from this planet, at least until that unlikely day when those of other planets can be adequately and economically tapped. That means setting budgets of energy use, primary production, and extraction of minerals on a new, realistic basis, and determining accordingly the carrying capacity of each continent at acceptable standards of living. In such an exercise environmentalists must evidently play a significant part, economists having done little to inspire confidence in their competence in such matters.

By a fortunate coincidence, trends in technology and industry show some convergence with the newly recognised environmental constraints. Methods of production and operation current until recently are now seen to be grossly inefficient and wasteful of fuel and materials, quite apart from their neglect of recycling and other sources of economy. It seems likely that availability of most material goods should at least be maintained, and in some expanded, by improved techniques operating within the new limits. At the same time automation and computerised controls will help to reduce rejects, to improve quality and durability, and to reverse the worst faults of the throw-away society by eliminating planned obsolescence and substituting longer-lasting articles of much improved design. At the same time monster factories and offices can often be superseded by decentralised more compact units, opening the way to a big reduction in wasteful rushhour traffic to and from work. For example, a greater variety of up-to-the-minute newspapers tailored to their readerships can be printed nearer to where they are to be read, allowing more resources for newsgathering and analysis, and

(a) Rubbish piling up in London streets during a refuse-collectors' strike in 1979.
(b) A polluted pond near Teynham, Kent, *c.*1984.

(a)

(b)

reducing the parasitic demands of their printers, which have for so long held readers to ransom and held up improved services.

National economies as a whole are part-way through a drastic transformation, employing far fewer unskilled and uneducated workers on tasks now being automated, but needing increased numbers of well-educated, trained staff with the new skills for which demand is tending to exceed supply. At the upper end, additional jobs must be created by increased requirements for education and training, including repeated in-service training, and by the potential to use and synthesise vastly increased data at much higher speeds, thus accelerating many processes and giving better rates of return on costly information investments. At the lower end, however, it must mean that more and more people will fail to qualify for conventional employment, and will present a challenge to make other uses of their services that will add to the community's welfare and give them the interest and self-respect that they are entitled to in their lives. Care of the environment is already proving helpful in this area. Given resourcefulness, it might directly and indirectly make a substantial contribution.

A ray of hope is thus visible in the relation of unemployment to the environment. Some of those most nearly identifiable as responsible for doing something for the unemployed have had the wit to perceive that the environmental movement has brought to light a large number of possible jobs, widely accepted as beneficial and easily created with the help of the movement's many practical organisations, which can form a supervisory and technical nucleus.

They observe quietly that, as the trade union movement has virtually failed to recognise that such a thing as environmental conservation exists (despite years of entreaty to it), the way to setting up these jobs is almost uniquely free of trade union obstruction. That has been proved by the success in this area of joint initiatives between environmental organisations and the Manpower Services Commission. It is an irony of fate that 'the environmental lobby', so often smeared as an obstacle to economic growth, has in fact proved to be an engine of faster than average growth, both in this way and in areas of conventional manufacturing and service employment.

So far, however, the surface has barely been scratched. Given more response to public opinion, and to the preferences of countless young people, environmental improvement could provide many times as many worthwhile jobs, which (allowing for savings in unemployment relief) could be developed at little or no extra cost in public expenditure, and with great spin-offs in tourism and leisure earnings, new impetus to inner-city redevelopment, reductions in crime and vandalism and in other directions. Who stand in the way of this? Conventional economists, and the politicians and civil servants who persist in following their discredited advice. It is to them that we owe this loss of opportunity and the human misery that accompanies it.

It is not a law of nature that able-bodied competent adults must normally spend their lives in full-time employment in order to earn their living. This custom is of relatively recent prevalence, and is already giving way to a more flexible pattern, allowing for increased part-time employment, and sabbatical years for further education, subsidised community work and early retirement. Such trends fit in with the need for increased care of the environment, and are indeed already assisting towards it.

The main obstacle is unreadiness to adapt more flexibly to new conditions, and to find acceptable patterns for putting to good use the many hours no longer required for the more routine forms of manufacturing and office work. Organisation of alternatives and finding means of paying for them are crunch points.

If the healthy trends towards reduction in state and local government and in factory and low-grade office employment are to continue without causing chronic unemployment, the obvious alternatives lie in expanding voluntary bodies, with the aid, for example, of much more generous tax concessions. A great new amenity realm embracing all kinds of conservation must be developed, including the arts, museums, libraries, broadcasting and provision for tourism, which might be funded by a special Amenities Levy, (or by sufficient tax-free donations and subscriptions) rather than out of conventional taxation, in order to minimise bureaucracy and to allow much more flexibility in changing patterns of development.

Given honest and serious efforts to reduce wasteful expenditure on armaments, and a corresponding relief to the cost of carrying unemployment, such a newly recognised and greatly expanded amenity realm might, with little if any increase in net public spending, reduce social tensions, improve the environment and promote a healthy shift away from outdated employment patterns.

In the case of opencast or strip mining of minerals near the surface, severe damage was done to the environment before it was learnt that this could be minimised, or even averted, by advance measures to remove and bank topsoil and to contour, shelter and drain affected areas in order to be able to restore landscape and fertility after extraction. In Great Britain, the National Coal Board and the ironstone miners and sand and gravel industry have been active and successful in this respect.

Comparable prescriptions are needed in many parts of the world for restoration of deforested and other biologically devastated areas, and for large-scale programs, if necessary with international aid, to restore appropriate vegetation, land-forms and soil fertility, and to conserve moisture and water supplies. Such programs to reverse as much as possible of twentieth-century environmental damage would have the three-fold merit of helping to restore life support systems, teaching and demonstrating methods of conservation, and providing valuable employment where it is most needed, including an element of international participation. Such projects should also be filmed and widely publicised to encourage and guide the initiation of similar work elsewhere, thus contributing toward realising a New Environmental Age.

Similarly comprehensive programs should be developed for the Greening of Cities, including not only laying out and planting a variety of open spaces, gardens, vegetable allotments, wayside shrubberies and spinneys of trees, and pools or streams of water, but also providing walls clad with climbing plants and roofs, wherever suitable, bearing attractive vegetation. Such an urban program would not be costly and would help to reduce tension and stress, vandalism and even crime by alleviating the hardness and inhumanity of urban environments and helping towndwellers to relax and enjoy them, as well as providing satisfying occupation. Above all it could reverse the mass desertion of cities by businesses and individuals, and salvage investments in them currently being written off.

It is indeed arguable that the rapid large-scale environmental transformation of cities is the key factor in progress towards a New Environmental Age. Our modern cities, so badly misdeveloped and misdesigned, are a main

Rio de Janeiro – greening of the city, showing trees and large areas of grass in the city centre.

source of the destabilisation and perversion of our civilisation as a whole. They do not need any more schools of architects and planners with trendy inhuman prescriptions for structures which people cannot afford, cannot keep in repair and do not want to be made to live in.

At a fraction of the cost every city could be freshly clad in what the great ecologist Tansley called a Green Mantle, bringing relaxation, better health, and less violence and crime. Resulting lessening of tension would reduce demands for relief, at best in mass exodus to ruin other places on holiday, and at worst in rioting, drug addiction and alienation from society.

Environmentalists should come out more strongly as holders of the key to decent urban renewal, in which process they have too long been elbowed aside by greedy, arrogant and wrong-headed rivals, whose blunders are plain for all to see, although the ongoing bills to be paid for them into the next century are discreetly concealed in complex public accounts. Nature, not tower blocks, should greet the city visitor. It is an absurd anomaly that the environmental movement, in Britain and most other advanced countries, still lacks any substantial body concentrating upon the environment of cities.

Having written twenty years ago a long book on *The System; the Misgovernment of Modern Britain*, making a case which has meanwhile been demonstrated by events to be wholly valid, I cannot attempt here to discuss the interactions of government with the environment in general. It must suffice to note that, as has been indicated earlier, environmental issues not only have had many specific impacts on the agenda of government, but also have begun to influence the style of government generally.

From an environmental standpoint, government should have five main functions:

> The first, and most neglected, is to monitor and to assist the successful long-term evolution of its nation in playing its optimum role in a changing world, both internally and externally.
>
> The second is to act as a good steward of the national heritage, both in natural and manmade resources, above all the land.
>
> The third is to promote and to ensure the best possible stable and well-balanced way of life for its current citizens of all ages and in all regions.
>
> The fourth is to translate these requirements into realistic and practicable strategies and programs, and to consult, and to secure participation of, the citizens to the fullest extent in carrying them out in concert and by agreement.

The fifth is to reform and reorganise the structure and techniques of
government and of recruitment and training for it, so as to
deliver the best possible performance in fulfilling the previous
four in practice.

The present British system of government does not even attempt the first,
and its political and administrative leaders misunderstand and assign low
priority to the fifth, on which they consequently fail, as they accordingly do
to a large extent on the fourth and the third. Oddly enough during the past
couple of decades, thanks to the environmental movement, government has
for the first time begun to make a serious effort to fulfil the second of these
functions, as a steward of the national heritage, which is now better
appreciated and better cared for than ever before, however many faults and
deficiencies can still be found with it.

That progress encourages the hope that, given firm pressure, the
environmental movement may soon play a part in stimulating and helping
government to do better in respect of the other main functions indicated
above.

A peculiar *idée fixe* of the period during which beating up the environment
has become a worldwide obsession has been the conviction that affluence for
all is readily attainable by the right mix of political and economic nostrums,
that it involves continuous rapid economic 'growth' (construed largely in
terms of unthinking consumption of materials), and that, regardless of more
and more labour-saving technology, it goes with full employment for
everyone who chooses to enter the labour market, with or without
appropriate training and skills or indeed with none at all.

As events prove that this whole ragbag of ideas is nonsense, as has been
shown years ago by the Club of Rome and other environmental spokesmen,
we do not find its champions withdrawing and apologising for having misled
us. They merely, as they would say, adopt a lower profile by ignoring such
inconvenient realities as chronic mass unemployment, decline in demand
for most manufactures, and actually declining standards of living in many
countries, especially in the Third World, which were led to believe that by
now they would be catching up with the most advanced.

This conspiracy of silence and concealment within the economic and
political establishment is not only dishonest and unworthy but forms a block
to fresh thinking designed to pave the way for a new type of society and
economy which really will be viable. If they will not come clean, the
environmental movement must find effective successors for the doughty
pioneers of the Club of Rome to come clean for them, and to leave them
thoroughly washed down. No less than this is owed to the suffering mass of
mankind.

What kind of picture emerges from the foregoing discussion? The biosphere has evolved over an immensely longer period than the human species, while man's evolution entirely within the constraints of his natural environment, and in response to its challenges, occupied in turn an immensely longer period than his evolution since beginning to be able to manage growing parts of it. Yet the rate of increase of his cranial capacity was extremely rapid, and reached its peak, many tens of thousands of years before the emergence of modern man and his involvement with a multiplicity of problems outside the realm of nature.

Is it not reasonable, then, to infer that man owes his superior powers and potential largely to his prolonged fruitful experience of adaptation to his natural environment, and that a conscious effort to renew something of that relationship in modern terms should prove rewarding and deeply reassuring, quite apart from its demonstrable value in assisting his survival on the planet?

During the relatively minute period since the emergence of an environmental movement with that objective, it has found such a widely sympathetic reception, and has been able to achieve so many practical adjustments, as to imply that it is working with, rather than against, the grain of profound human needs and motivations. Experience so far certainly gives no cause to suggest any need for fundamental changes either in its principles or in its practice, or to throw doubt on its capacity for further progress at its present rate, if not better.

Many of the worst obstacles to its progress now show signs of weakening, while the favourable tide of worldwide public opinion is becoming reflected in necessary expansions of resources, organisation and numbers of supporters, and in informal alliances outside its ranks. It is now well placed to profit by the rapid development of information services and communications, and by the nature of contemporary changes in life-styles. It is, however, faced by vast and formidable problems, and by still gravely deteriorating planetary resources.

At best it cannot hope to salvage what has been irretrievably lost, especially during recent decades, and what is destined to be lost at least in the near future. It can, however, on its track record, reasonably hope to stop the rot at some point short of a Doomsday catastrophe, and its performance entitles it to greatly increased support and confidence from now on, provided that its own members still prove as steadfast and true as so far they have done. All is not lost, although far too much has been.

To conclude, it seems desirable to set out in summary and logical form a number of guidelines that emerge from our present knowledge, and from the foregoing analysis. The implementation of the full implications of these appears best calculated gradually to resolve our present predicaments.

Guidelines emerging from our present knowledge

1. Our planet earth forms part of the universe, many of the mysteries of which will become clear to us at best gradually over a long time. Meanwhile, all that lies beyond earth's atmosphere should be treated with the utmost consideration; its exploration should be pursued with caution and care, and it should be exempt from human exploitation.

2. The earth, from its core to its stratosphere, is and remains the base and heritage of life, which mankind is learning to manage to a certain degree, but has yet to learn to manage in the interests of future generations. This should henceforth be paramount over any conflicting current interests. The necessary processes of so learning, and their careful application, should in future be held as central to public policy in all its aspects and sections.

3. The biosphere, comprising all life on earth and its complex and balanced functioning, is highly vulnerable to misguided exploitation and pressures by mankind. While it can and must be put to necessary use, its integrity and survival must come first, and must not be hazarded or damaged by human activities of whatever kind or purpose.

4. Within the biosphere, mankind has enjoyed a rapid and rich evolution, becoming endowed with faculties of the utmost significance, many of which have been neglected or abused, especially those concerning perception, foresight and the capacity to co-operate and to live in harmony with others and with other forms of life. The proper study of mankind is to advance understanding and fostering of the best use of human faculties for the furtherance of evolution and the wise care of the planet.

5. Within mankind, many diverse cultures have developed, combining valuable and proven benefits with serious faults, injustices, follies and failures of understanding. Modern analytical, interpretive and communications skills, already put to effective use by the environmental movement, need to be systematically brought to bear on the thorough but not revolutionary reform of civilisations on a basis of established knowledge, not dogma, and of social responsibilities, not alleged rights.

6. The supernatural, and religious beliefs, deserve to be treated with respect and tolerance, but should not be accorded any overriding role in human affairs generally, nor lead to any positive or negative rules of conduct being imposed on anyone, as distinct from being observed voluntarily, according to personal creed.

7. Population numbers, quality, health and demands on resource are fundamental to the survival, prosperity and happiness of mankind, and the urgent task of bringing them into harmony with these basic needs must henceforth be given priority in public policy, without more than essential interference with the liberties of the individual.

8. The wise stewardship of the earth shall be not only pursued throughout public policy, but shall be a principal object of study and development, and shall be fully and thoroughly monitored and its progress communicated to all.

9. The resources of modern communications need to be used fully to inform and educate people generally on adaptations urgently necessary for harmonious survival, on lines already successfully adopted by the environmental movement and in promoting healthy diet and living.

10. Civic design, landscaping, and environmental and traffic controls should be mobilised to reduce stress and promote happier and more secure living patterns, accompanied by economical and pollution-free use of resources and decentralised government and services.

11. All other appropriate ways should be pursued of integrating human living patterns with the enjoyment of the natural environment, and the appreciation of its working principles and values.

NOTES ON SOURCES

As this book seeks to review such a wide field in a realm of rapid change and of copious current literature, it would not be appropriate to accompany it by any usual sort of bibliography, which would indeed have to be almost as long as the book itself. Taking that into account, and also its relationship as a sequel to *The Environmental Revolution*, which had to face a similar problem, it has seemed best to follow the practice of providing the reader with a highly selective list of references, wherever possible in English and readily accessible, that amplify the various aspects of the subject, and frequently themselves include more detailed references to first-hand or specialist sources. Unless found necessary, sources already cited in *The Environmental Revolution* are not repeated here, and a number of references already cited in the text are also omitted from these Notes. The Index also should be helpful in pursuing further a number of the topics that are necessarily accorded no more than summary treatment.

Chapter 1

The environmental aspect of the Black Death has now been thoroughly treated by Professor Robert S. Gottfried in *The Black Death: Natural and Human Disaster in Medieval Europe* (Hale, London, 1983).

The poet quoted on p. 1 is Alexander Pope (1688–1744), *An Essay on Man*, Epistle ii.

The treatment of early human evolution is based on J.Z. Young's *An Introduction to the Study of Man* (Oxford University Press, 1971). A reliable and convenient review of the growth and spread of population is provided by C. McEvedy and R. Jones in their *Atlas of World Population History* (Penguin, 1978). *Climate, History and the Modern World* by H.H. Lamb (Methuen, London 1982) reviews the influence of climate on human fortunes from the earliest times. For example, it shows that the early development of a high civilisation in China was associated with a milder and warmer climate than to-day's, with such important plants as bamboo and rice growing much farther north, especially before 1100 BC. The impacts and economic and cultural significance of 'The hydraulic civilizations' are well reviewed under that title by Professor Karl A. Wittfogel in the Wenner-Gren Symposium, published in 1956 in Chicago, under the title *Man's Role in Changing the Face of the Earth*, edited by W.L. Thomas Jr.

The Environmental Revolution cited here and passim, was published for me in London by Hodder & Stoughton in 1970, in New York by McGraw-Hill, also in 1970, and in translation in Italian by Garzanti as *La Rivoluzione ambientale* (Milan, 1971), in German by Desch as *Umweltrevolution: Der Mensch als Spielball und als Herr der Erde* (Munich, 1972), and in French by Gallimard as *La revolution de l'environment* (Paris, 1973).

The Chinese attitude to nature is discussed briefly by John Passmore in *Man's Responsibility for Nature*, Chapter 1 (Duckworth, London, 1974); this book contains a valuable and well-documented discussion of the philosophical and ethical aspects underlying conservation, including the message of Plato's Critias.

A concise review of the evolution of conservation from early times to the present is given in my concluding chapter 'Economic society and environment' to *The Fontana Economic History of Europe – The Twentieth Century – 2*, edited by Carlo M. Cipolla (London, 1976).

Another important source is *The Times Atlas of World History*, edited by Geoffrey Barraclough (revised edition, London, 1986).

Chapter 2

In addition to sources already mentioned for Chapter 1, a most valuable global review with many excellent illustrations of human modifications of the land is contained in *The Landscape of Man* by Geoffrey and Susan Jellicoe, subtitled *Shaping the Environment from Prehistory to the Present Day* (Thames & Hudson, London, 1975). The concise accounts of each principal region of the earth in terms of environment, social history, philosophy, expression, architecture and landscape are especially illuminating concerning the many varied approaches and kinds of practice developed by different peoples. As in this chapter, the Jellicoe's approach is based on human efforts to make the best of humanly utilised or adapted land resources.

Relatively little work has hitherto been devoted to the reactive development of conservation in response to human impacts and resulting problems. The necessary material has to be gathered mainly from sources preoccupied with other approaches, such as the origins of agriculture and forestry, or the provision of energy from natural sources. A valuable conspectus of one important aspect is contained in *Plants in the Service of Man: 10,000 years of domestication* by Edward Hyams, Dent, London, 1971), which summarises the entire range of exploitation of plants for human uses of all kinds. Few countries have begun to assemble the facts about their total environmental history, except in relation to such special cases as the New Forest in southern England, reviewed under the title *New Forest: An Ecological History* by Colin Tubbs (David & Charles, Newton Abbot, 1969).

Chapter 3

The *United Nations List of National Parks and Equivalent Reserves* was prepared and published by the IUCN Commission on National Parks in its original version in 1961, in response to Resolution XXVII of the Economic and Social Council passed in April 1959. An expanded list on more critical criteria was prepared at the request of the Secretary-General of the United Nations on the basis of a General Assembly Resolution at its sixteenth session in 1962, and subsequent revisions added to, and updated, the work. It therefore combined unquestionable international status with thorough professional and scientific treatment, and had a profound influence on governments worldwide in developing their understanding both of the natural heritage of the planet and of their specific responsibilities in regard to it. This advance was reinforced by the holding of World Conferences on National Parks at Seattle in 1962, at Yellowstone in 1972 and on Bali in 1982, the Proceedings of which reflected the growing experience and confidence of the Parks profession internationally, and its success in transcending national boundaries and limitations of view.

References to accounts of the International Biological Programme are given in the text of the Chapter 5; they should be supplemented with citation of *The Ecological Century* by E.B. Worthington (Oxford University Press, 1983), including his personal appraisal, as the Programme's scientific director, with a number of other important chapters on nature conservation and related themes. The record of the Fauna Preservation Society (originally the Society for the Preservation of the Wild Fauna of the Empire) is outlined by Richard Fitter and Sir Peter Scott in *The Penitent Butchers; 75 Years of Wildlife Conservation* (Collins, London, 1978). A number of more detailed sources are cited in the text; a balanced and comprehensive review by some twenty contributors, including myself, is given in *Ecology, The Shaping Enquiry*, edited by Jonathan Benthall for the Institute of Contemporary Arts (London, 1972). Although it contains a valuable contribution from Barry Commoner reviewing origins of the environmental crisis and another from an American standpoint on 'Ecology and the Computer', this work mainly reflects British approaches, and should be read in conjunction with a specifically American review such as the earlier *Perspectives on Conservation; Essays on America's Natural Resources*, edited by Henry Jarrett (Resources for the Future, Washington DC, 1958). This work is particularly valuable in that it considered thematically the development of American thinking and action on conservation from the outset of the century, bringing together the political history, the philosophy, and the subjects tackled, as seen through the eyes of some twenty-two leading figures in the drama and in its analysis. There is much to be gained by comparison in depth between the very different American and European (especially British) approaches, priorities and conclusions on conservation. This would make an admirable subject for a carefully planned high-level seminar comparing the state of play on both sides of the Atlantic. A valuable basis on the British side is available in the two University College London collections of essays both edited by Andrew Warren and Barrie Goldsmith: *Conservation in Practice*, (1974) and *Conservation in Perspective* (1983).

A massive and important German contribution is G. Olschowy's *Natur und umweltschutz in der Bundesrepublik Deutschland* (Paul Parey, Hamburg, 1978).

Chapter 4

The background used for discussion here on mental processes is primarily that given by J.Z. Young in his *Introduction to the Study of Man* (see p. 66) and his *Programs of the Brain* (Oxford University Press, 1978). Two BBC books, one on the series *Men and Ideas: Some Creators of Contemporary Philosophy* by Bryan Magee (1978) and a second *States of Mind: Conversations with Psychological Investigators*, edited by Jonathan Miller, have proved stimulating for the background. *The Evolution of Intelligence: A General Theory and Some of its Implications* by David Stenhouse (Allen & Unwin, London, 1973) deals with relations between ethology and human intelligence and with barriers to acceptance of innovative ideas. *The Humanist Frame* (Allen & Unwin, London, 1961), edited by Julian Huxley, pursued a number of issues raised by the unpublished work of the Idea-Systems Group, described in this chapter.

My analysis of the contrast between polarisers and integrators among conservationists has been printed in the journal *Environmental Conservation*, vol. I (1974).

Chapter 5

Excellent accounts of the rise of natural history in Britain from its origins in the seventeenth century are contained in *The Naturalist in Britain;*

A Social History by David Elliston Allen (Allen Lane, London, 1976), and, more strictly for nature conservation, in *Nature in Trust: The History of Nature Conservation in Britain* by John Sheail (Blackie, Glasgow, 1976). Both these are thoroughly researched, well documented and attempt to explain as well as to describe the evolution of events. A similar service has been done for field ornithology by the British Trust for Ornithology's fiftieth anniversary review *Enjoying Ornithology*, edited by Ronald Hickling (Poyser, Calton, 1983), which also outlines the history of sister organisations such as the Royal Society for the Protection of Birds, and the Royal Society for Nature Conservation. A comparable service had been done for wildfowling by *The New Wildfowler*, produced in 1961 by the Wildfowlers' Association of Great Britain and Ireland (now the British Association for Shooting and Conservation). At the official level also excellent documentation has been provided by the Reports of the National Parks Committee (England and Wales) (Cmd 7121 July 1947) and the Wild Life Conservation Special Committee (England and Wales) (Cmd 7122 July 1947), with the parallel Scottish Reports. The background and basic documentation therein has been continuously updated in the official Annual Reports to Parliament by the Nature Conservancy (from 1953) and subsequently by the Nature Conservancy Council. In several of these, useful additional sources are listed; the whole story is on record for those who take the trouble to look it up, in as much detail as they require.

Until fairly recently the story of the National Parks in the United States and internationally was by no means so well covered. This deficiency has however, been largely remedied since the centennial celebrations at Yellowstone in 1972, notably in the work *World National Parks; Progress and Opportunities* produced for the International Commission on National Parks (Hayez Brussels, 1972), containing summaries of the situation both geographically and by subjects. At the same time the authoritative *The National Park Service* by William G. Everhart, a senior member of its staff, was issued in the Praeger Library of US Government Departments and Agencies (New York, 1973), complementing the mainly administrative and legislative standard work by John Ise on *Our National Park Policy: A Critical History* (Johns Hopkins, 1961) and the commentary on park policy and practice by F. Fraser Darling and N.D. Eichorn for the Conservation Foundation in *Man and Nature in the National Parks* (Washington DC, 1967). A more recent, comprehensive, documented critique from a modern ecological standpoint has been provided by Alfred Runte in *National Parks; the American Experience* University of Nebraska Press, 1979), which shows how embarrassment at commercialised maltreatment of superb scenery, with consequent adverse comment by European and other visitors, led to recognition that a counterpart to great cultural monuments elsewhere could be created by a series of National Parks in which Americans could take pride. To some extent a similar psychology has prevailed more lately in the Third World.

The story of the white man's effect on wildlife in North America has been thoroughly outlined in Peter Mathiessen's *Wildlife in America* (Viking Press, New York, 1964), which reviews both the role of the various interests and agencies and their effects upon different classes of wildlife. A comparable work for Europe is still needed. Legislative aspects, both for North America and internationally have been excellently covered in *International Environmental Policy: Emergence and Dimensions* (Duke University Press, 1984) by Lynton Keith Caldwell, Professor of Public and Environmental Affairs at Indiana University, which gives an exceptionally full range of references. His *Defense of Earth: International Protection of the Biosphere* (Indiana University Press, 1972) is also valuable not least for its excellent bibliography.

The earlier stages of American history in this field are compactly reviewed by David Cushman Coyle in *Conservation: An American Story of Conflict and Accomplishment* (Rutgers University Press, 1957). A more recent, documented, critical assessment is given in *International Environmental Action: A Global Survey* by Thomas W. Wilson Jr. for the Aspen Insitute (Cambridge, Mass., 1971). Despite its title, however, this helps little with matters beyond North America.

An intriguing individual picture, based on knowledge, was produced by Interior Secretary Stewart I. Udall, with departmental back-up in *The Quiet Crisis* (Holt, Rinehart & Winston, New York, 1963). Like Theodore Roosevelt, he combines a background of high office and the wide open spaces, but he also (as in Chapter 7 of the present work) tries to do justice to 'the concern of a few people for the rights of future generations', and (as William Vogt has written of it in *Natural History*, March 1964, p.446) 'It weaves conservation, an increasingly urgent human activity, into the tight living web that makes up our exploding interrelated world.'

The prehistory and beginnings of the International Union for Conservation of Nature are thoroughly documented in three scarce works – the *Report on the Conference for the International Protection of Nature* by Johann Büttikofer (Basle, 1946), the *Report of the Second Conference for the International Protection of Nature at Brunnen in July 1947* (Basle, 1947), also by J. Büttikofer, and the paperback *Report on the International Union for the Protection of Nature Established at Fontainebleau*, issued in Brussels in November 1948. An undated leaflet (?1955) entitled *What is IUPN?* is also informative.

Chapter 6

Ideally, those responsible for each major international movement would ensure that its progress in fulfilling its aims is continuously and fully recorded, monitored and appraised, within the context of current events and of other related movements. As the present book shows, the environmental movement is now able to make publicly available such a picture of itself. When, however, we seek to put it into perspective alongside other important international movements, it proves difficult to find comparable material, extending beyond piecemeal, highly subjective and unco-ordinated accounts from different, often controversial standpoints. Indeed, the very idea of comparing and evaluating various parallel world movements appears still to be strange and novel. Since I first attempted such a treatment under the title 'Towards world family housekeeping' in the *Journal of the Policy Studies Institute, London* (vol. 4, part 4, April 1984), I have sought in vain to trace any counterpart. Even comprehensive reviews of single movements, comparable to that available for environmental conservation, are hard to find. Yet, as we progress clumsily and painfully towards One World, such material becomes indispensable for sound decision-making.

Following the same order as in the main text, it is especially disappointing to find in the world of science that even the fitful initiatives of earlier decades such as Pugwash, the debates on the social responsibility of science, and the C.P. Snow discussion of the gulf between science and the arts have almost been allowed to die without any major serious current effort to promote thinking about the role of science in the emerging global society that it has helped to create. Science today seems to have lost much of the intellectual momentum which made its conquest such a prize for the military-industrial establishment, to which it seems to have become dangerously subject, even though that establishment is itself in rapid decay. Is this just a temporary lapse, or are we entering a period when maintaining the values, the independence and the hopes hitherto embodied in the sciences can no longer arouse interest or enlist the kind of leadership it did in the past? Where are the publications that would help us to judge?

While the learned professions were never accustomed to scrutinise themselves and their role in society as the more inquiring scientists did, they too show up disturbingly in their lack of interest or capacity to adapt to the modern world. Apart from the armed forces, which have not yet relapsed into their slumbers of decades before World War II, the leading professions such as medicine, the law, engineering and even accountancy have conspicuously failed to satisfy public opinion that they are pursuing the right aims with the vigour, the competence and even the integrity expected of them. I had a number of conversations on this, before the situation aroused such public disquiet, with the late Sir Alexander Carr-Saunders, one of the very few first-rate minds to be focussed on these problems in recent years. His work *The Professions* (with Norman Wilson, Oxford University Press, 1933) needs to be widely re-read and followed up.

The most important comprehensive treatment of development in relation to conservation and to international policy generally has been provided by the Brandt Commission's Report, published in paperback by Pan Books under the title *North–South: A Programme for Survival* (London, 1980). While largely preoccupied with more immediate development problems it does recognise briefly the key roles of family planning and of conservation. It states that the strain on the global environment 'threatens the survival and development opportunities of future generations. All nations have to co-operate more urgently in international management of the atmosphere and other global commons, and in the prevention of irreversible ecological damage.' Unfortunately, despite its prestigious membership and consultants, and the major effort devoted to its worldwide launch, international agencies and national governments have by no means revolutionised their policies and practice in accord with its wise prescriptions. Its intellectual impact, however, has been substantial, and it will stand as a landmark in a more balanced and comprehensive approach to the handling of world problems.

The pioneer towards this new model was, however, Barbara Ward's memorable Report, commissioned for the Stockholm Conference on the Human Environment, and prepared with the assistance of a 152-member committee of corresponding consultants from 58 countries (of whom I was one). Under the title *Only One Earth: The Care and Maintenance of a Small Planet*, by Barbara Ward and Rene Dubos (New York, 1972; and simultaneously in eight other languages in Europe, Asia, Africa and Central America), this was described as 'the first attempt to examine our environmental problems not only from a global perspective, but in their social, economic and political dimensions' including 'population, misuse of resources, the impact of technology, unbalanced development and the world-wide dilemma of urbanisation.' This well-written and persuasive work greatly reinforced the impact of Stockholm, and was followed in 1979 by Ward's sequel *Progress for a Small Planet* (Pelican, London, and Norton, New York), outlining in the light of seven years effort a 'planetary bargain between the world's nations that would guarantee every citizen the right to freedom from poverty, and keep our shared biosphere in good, working order.'

Dr Mostafa K. Tolba, Executive Director of the United Nations Environment Programme (UNEP) then invited her to write a book for the tenth anniversary of Stockholm, but sadly this was prevented by her illness and her death in May 1981, although she did manage to write a foreword to the work, which was taken on by Erik P. Eckholm and appeared as *Down to Earth: Environment and Human Needs* in 1982 (Pluto Press, London). It was complemented by UNEP's major review of the state of the environment, *The World Environment 1972–1982*, edited by Dr Martin Holdgate, Dr Mohammed Kassas and Dr Gilbert F. White (Tycooly, Dublin, 1982), which has set the scene for comprehensive monitoring of environmental trends.

An excellent introduction to the specific problems of industry in relation to the environment is provided by John Elkington's *The Ecology of To-Morrow's World: Industry's Environment* (Associated Business Press, London, 1980).

A thoroughly documented regular account of events and progress in the business world, primarily centred on the United Kingdom is given in the regular specialist publications ENDS (published by Environmental Data Services from Unit 24, Finsbury Business Centre, 40 Bowling Green Lane, London EC1R 0NE) and the *Newsletter* of the UK Centre for Economic and Environmental Development, published by CEED from 10 Belgrave Square, London SW1X 8PH. The best account of the systematic environmental quality improvements in American cities is to be found in *The Economics of Amenity: Community Futures and Quality of Life* (R.H. McNulty et al.; Partners for Livable Places, 1429 21st St NW, Washington DC 20036). *Proceedings* of the Duke of Edinburgh's three conferences on *The Countryside in 1970* were published in London in 1964, 1966 and 1970, respectively. The two American conferences mentioned are recorded in *Future Environments of North America: Transformation of a Continent*, edited by F. Fraser Darling and John Milton (The Natural History Press, New York, 1966: it gives an exceptional view of the thinking at that time of a group of outstanding conservationists and resource economists), and *Proceedings of the White House Conference on Natural Beauty* (Washington DC, 1965). These well-attended and well-planned conferences were instrumental in preparing influential circles on both sides of the Atlantic to respond favourably, as they did, to the public initiatives around the turn of the decade.

As already mentioned the series of Annual Reports to Parliament made by the Nature Conservancy from 1953 onwards included full and precise documentation of most of the events of the period, not only in Great Britain but internationally so far as the United Kingdom was concerned. Much relevant information concerning the thinking and action that went into the growth of the conservation movement will be found in their pages. A recent well-balanced review of the interaction in the United Kingdom of agriculture and forestry with conservation is given in Professor Timothy O'Riordan's report *Putting Trust in the Countryside*, published as no. 7 in *The Conservation and Development Programme for the UK* (Kogan Page, London, 1983)

Issues between afforestation and conservation have recently been worked over by the Nature Conservancy Council in *Nature Conservation and Afforestation in Britain* (Peterborough, 1986). Although there is a vast literature on marine resources and problems, including pollution and overfishing, the integrated conservation of seas and their coastlines has had much less attention. An attempt to fill this gap for British coasts and waters was made in Part 4, *Marine and Coastal*, of *The Conservation and Development Programme for the UK* in response to the world Conservation Strategy (?, London, 1983), which indicates a constructive approach, but gives few international references. An up-to-date review of global conditions will be found in Chapter 9, on 'Oceans and Coasts', of *World Resources 1986* and Chapter 4 on maintaining world fisheries in the *State of the World 1985*, (see p. 222).

International tourism in relation to the environment has been particularly poorly covered despite numerous international conferences about it. A shining exception, for those who read German, is the trenchant, well-informed, devastatingly illustrated work *Die Landschaftsfresser: Tourismus und Erholungslandschaft – Verderben oder Segen?* by Professor Jost Krippendorf of Bern (Hallwag, 1975). *Fresser* means a glutton, and the title may be freely translated as 'The gobbler-up of landscape'. The author's other post as Director of the Swiss Foreign Travel Association in no way inhibits him from making full use of the ample material at his disposal. Surveying the technical aspects in forthright and readily understandable terms he concludes that the fate of holiday landscapes can no longer be left mainly to amateurs, and that the 'management gap', grave in comparison with other industries, must be narrowed, since its raw material is irreplaceable and mistakes cannot be undone. It is almost incredible that the obvious and unanswerable case which he makes seems yet to lack a comparable source in English.

Environmental effects of aviation are richly documented in specific reports, but also seem to lack comprehensive critical treatment. The same cannot, however, be said of either the civil or military environmental aspects of nuclear energy, but here the trouble is that events, technical appraisals, practical developments and issues of public policy are in such a state of flux that it is almost impossible to select a work covering more than a part of the field which is not already out of date. Luckily, the most appropriate available literature is not difficult for the reader to track down according to his or her particular needs. On nuclear power, an excellent source is Ecoropa's information sheet series, obtainable from Crickhowell, Powys, Wales NP8

1TA. For the nuclear arms race a particularly valuable and penetrating review, including its implications for the environment is contained in Jonathan Schell's *The Fate of the Earth* (Pan Books, 1982). Otherwise, it must suffice here, then, simply to give the reference for the episode treated at length about the sinking of the vessel *en route* to demonstrate against French nuclear testing in the Pacific. This is *Rainbow Warrior: the French Attempt to sink Greenpeace* by The Sunday Times Insight Team (Century-Hutchinson, London, 1986)

Current population statistics, although so widely ignored, are readily available from many sources, including the *Atlas of World Population History* (see p. 209) and the *State of the World 1985* and *World Resources 1986*. Those who stubbornly persist in obstructing their unmistakeable message will be seen in an unenviable light by their children next century. The International Union for the Conservation of Nature, at the instigation of Common Ground International, has produced an excellent review of the interrelation of human population pressures and environmental conservation in *Population and Natural Resources: A supplement to the World Conservation Strategy*, revised edition (Commission on Ecology of IUCN and International Planned Parenthood Federation, 1984). Although no comparable appraisal of the relations between religions and conservation can yet be cited, an important attempt at a meeting of minds on this fundamental aspect is being undertaken, on the initiative of the World Wildlife Fund at its twenty-fifth anniversary celebrations in Assisi, and it is to be hoped that something worth while will emerge, perhaps even before this book is published.

Chapter 7

Until Assisi was chosen for the celebrations of the twenty-fifth anniversary of the World Wildlife Fund, few conservationists can have read the account in *The Little Flowers of Saint Francis*, (translated by T.W. Arnold, London, 1903). A brief extract seems worth including here, describing the event soon after his conversion when he received divine guidance to go throughout the world to preach, which he began to do at a little town called Savurniano. He first had to bid the twittering swallows to keep silence and later, going into a field, 'he began to preach unto the birds that were on the ground, and immediately those that were on the trees flew down to him 'and after listening would not depart unitl he had given them his blessing, and had gone among them touching them with his cloak. In his sermon he told them that they ought to praise God for the liberty to fly about everywhere:

> God feedeth you, and giveth you the streams and fountains for your drink; the mountains and the valleys for your refuge and the high

> trees whereon to make your nests. . . . And Saint Francis rejoiced with them, and was glad, and marvelled much at so great a company of birds and their beautiful diversity, and their good heed and sweet friendliness, for the which cause he devoutly praised their Creator in them.

It is this incident, at the outset of his mission, which entitles St Francis to be regarded as the patron saint of conservation.

The activities of the Emperor Frederic II in this field are described in *The Art of Falconry* by Frederic II of Hohenstaufen (Stanford University Press, 1943).

The story of John Evelyn is told by W.G. Hiscock in *John Evelyn and his Family Circle* (Routledge and Kegan Paul, London, 1955); his *Sylva* published in 1664 'had a tremendous effect . . . . Woods and avenues spring up everywhere to the great advantage of the nation.' Twelve years later he was regretting the great quantities of trees, oak, beech, and elm, felled earlier on his family estates, leaving only a poor remnant of beech, birch and holly.

An account of the life of John James Audubon is given in F.H. Herrick's two-volume biography *Audubon the Naturalist* (?, New York, 1938); that of the seminal American professional of the nineteenth century is authoritatively covered by Laura Wood Roper in *FLO; a Biography of Frederick Law Olmsted* (Johns Hopkins University Press, 1973)

The conservation aspects of Theodore Roosevelt's life have at last been carefully reviewed in *Theodore Roosevelt: The Making of a Conservationist* by P.R. Cutright (University of Illinois Press, 1985), who has already dealt with Roosevelt's activities as a naturalist. Roosevelt's *Autobiography* (Charles Scribners Sons, New York, 1926) makes fascinating reading; W.H. Harbaugh's *Power and Responsibility: The Life and Times of Theodore Roosevelt* is rated as the best full biography.

The contribution of W.H. Hudson is documented in a number of his works such as *Birds and Man*, quoted in the text, and more generally in his letters compiled in *Men, Books and Birds* (Eveleigh Nash and Grayson, London, 1925) by his friend Morley Roberts, who had just previously written an excellent biography *W.H. Hudson: A Portrait* (Eveleigh Nash and Grayson, London, 1924) in which, with prescience, he comments:

> the time is not come to measure Hudson among those to whom the world must own its indebtedness . . . . In the far future someone may truthfully declare that it was his books . . . which finally made justice possible . . . between man and bird and beast.
>
> If the time shall at last arrive when the beasts and birds he loved and would have protected shall cease to pass from the face of an emptied and desolate earth, he will have been the prophet and great cause of their salvation.

Sixty years after it was written this begins to make sense.

If Hudson was a prophet Arthur Tansley was a working pioneer, creating a rare blend of path-finding scientific theory and field observation, with statesmanlike and practical prescriptions for carrying through the vast tasks of conservation, and with the personal gifts to guide and lead the processes of putting theory into action. I think the second edition of his *Britain's Green Mantle*, revised by M.C. Proctor (George Allen & Unwin, London, 1968), best conveys the flavour and content of his outstanding contribution, setting the tone for all that has happened since. His work has been admirably reviewed in perspective in Sir Harry Godwin's Memorial Lecture 'Sir Arthur Tansley: The Man and the Subject' published in the *Journal of Ecology*, vol. 65, pp. 1–26 (1977).

The third of my selected British pioneers, Charles Rothschild, has been sympathetically but too briefly described in his daughter Miriam's distinguished family history *Dear Lord Rothschild* (Hutchinson, London, 1983). His activities in conservation are well reviewed in J. Sheail's *Nature in Trust* (see p. 213).

The fourth on my list, Julian Huxley, published a two-volume autobiography entitled *Memories* (George Allen & Unwin, London, 1970); unfortunately he relied too much on his then failing memory and it contains too many minor factual errors. More recently, his widow Juliette Huxley has written with great charm and candour an account of her married life entitled *Leaves of the Tulip Tree* (John Murray, London, 1986), which throws remarkable light on his unique personality, which in its curious way contributed so greatly to the environmental conservation movement. An extremely detailed bibliography is appended to UNESCO's Biographical Memoir, *Julian Huxley: Scientist and World Citizen 1887–1975* (Paris, 1978)

Among those included later in this chapter perhaps the most enigmatic was Frank Fraser Darling. His breadth and depth of thinking is well displayed in his 1969 Reith Lectures published by the BBC under the characteristically odd title *Wilderness and Plenty*. It won an attentive audience and was influential at a critical moment in helping to bridge the gap between environmentalists and more man-centred interests, for which its message is still relevant. A full and revealing account of his life and work is given in John Morton Boyd's *Fraser Darling's Islands* (Edinburgh University Press, 1986). As a person he is well described, alongside Charles Elton, in Anne Chisholm's *Philosophers of the Earth – Conversations with Ecologists* (Sidgwick and Jackson, London, 1972), which incidentally also contains a good chapter on Lewis Mumford, as well as other pioneers.

It becomes apparent in considering sources for this chapter that, apart from brief or ephemeral articles, some obituaries and a few autobiographies, there is still a virtual absence of serious accounts of the protagonists in the conservation movement and their respective contributions to it, apart from *Philosophers of the Earth*, above mentioned. Here is a gap which it is to be hoped will be properly filled without much more delay, and on an international basis.

Chapter 8

Emphasis is laid in this chapter on the key importance of detailed monitoring of progress. Fortunately, during the latest period under review, some excellent comprehensive reliable and up-to-date regular series to fulfil this requirement have been launched. They include the Worldwatch Institute's regular Reports on Progress towards a Sustainable Society under the title *State of The World, 1983, 1984, 1985* etc.; and the joint World Resources Institute and International Institute for Environment and Development publications beginning with *World Resources 1986: An Assessment of the Resource Base that Supports the Global Economy, With Data Tables for 146 Countries*. Although inevitably overlapping, these are largely complementary, since *State of the World* consists of a critical textual review with many Tables and Figures, edited by a leading authority, Lester H. Brown, while *World Resources 1986* gives well over a hundred pages of accurate and well-documented Data Tables on economic development, population and health, human settlements, land use and cover, food and agriculture, forests and rangelands, wildlife resources, energy and minerals, oceans and coasts, atmosphere and climate, and policy and institutions, preceded by over 200 pages of reviews on the same twelve aspects, themselves copiously illustrated by diagrams and Tables. These two global monitoring volumes, both produced by unofficial agencies, are formidable in their scale and significance. They vividly illustrate the state of play, but as solid reference volumes are scarcely suitable for normal consecutive reading. For decision-makers and followers of rates of progress they signal entry into a new, more sophisticated, world of global housekeeping. The international agency UNEP has shown the way in its Global Environmental Monitoring System (GEMS), and by the production of its special review *The World Environment 1972–82* (see p. 217).

Bernard Stonehouse's World Wildlife Fund Book of Conservation entitled *Saving the Animals* (London, 1981) gives a good factual account of the origins and varied activities of WWF, including CITES. Its activities are annually updated in detail by the *WWF Yearbook*, running now to nearly 500 pages, and reporting a truly vast range of worldwide projects and events. The most recent popular but informative summary of WWF's activities is given in its Anniversary View entitled *Protect our Planet* (London, 1986)

Chapter 9

In so far as this chapter is looking forward universally, it relates particularly to the *World Conservation Strategy*, published with the collaboration of the UNEP and the WWF by IUCN at Gland, Switzerland, in 1980, and updated by the progress report *Implementing the World Conservation Strategy: IUCN's Conservation Programme 1985–87* (Gland, 1985). Reference should also be made to *The Conservation and Development Programme for the UK* (see p. 115) prepared in response to the Strategy; among its detailed reports one of special relevance to the present chapter is that on *The Livable City*, which reviews modern urban development in Britain from an ecological standpoint. A handbook on the problems involved in the application of urban ecology is now available in *Promoting Nature in Cities and Towns* written by Malcolm Emery for the Ecological Parks Trust (now the Trust for Urban Ecology) (Croom Helm, London, 1986). Reference is made to my earlier book *The System: The Misgovernment of Modern Britain* (Hodder and Stoughton and McGraw Hill, London and New York, 1967), which deals not with the environment but with governmental defects that affect it and much else, and are not confined to the United Kingdom.

ACKNOWLEDGEMENTS

The author gratefully acknowledges photographs and figures supplied by many sources:

p.4 World Health Organization (WHO photo 10 883, E. Schwab)

p.6 From H. Lhote: *The story of prehistoric rock paintings of the Sahara* (Hutchinson, 1959), by permission of the Syndics of Cambridge University Library

p.7 Raymond Allchin

p.11 United Nations (UN photo 115 925, UNESCO/Blower Jr)

p.19 United Nations (UN photo 153 971, John Isaac)

p.23 United Nations (UN photo 167 616, John Isaac)

p.28 Satour

p.35 World Wildlife Fund (photo by G.F. de Witte)

p.37 © Wales Tourist Board Library

p.41 Royal Society for the Protection of Birds

p.45 (a) and (b) © Nature Conservancy

p.48 © Cambridge University Collection (photo by J.K. St Joseph)

p.53 © Greenpeace

p.59 Charles Tait

p.61 The Photo Source

p.77 Nature Conservancy Council

p.79 United Nations (UN photo 118 745, Nagata/JMcG)

p.80 Adrian Warren, BBC Bristol

p.88 John Rogers, Royal Botanic Gardens, Kew

p.91 British Trust for Ornithology

p.94 From a painting by L.J. Watson, courtesy of the Nature Conservancy Council

p.95 Brian Hawkes

p.97 From Nature Conservancy, *The first ten years*

p.109 World Wildlife Fund (photo by Zafar Futehally)

p.112–13 United Nations: (a) UN photo 115 912, FAO/Riney Jr; (b) UN photo 146 159, Q. Monsen

p.117 World Wildlife Fund (upper photo by Claude Berger)

p.122 School of Botany, University of Cambridge

p.123 Keystone Press Agency Ltd

p.127 A. France & Son (Holborn) Ltd, courtesy of Mrs Caroline Spires

224

p.130   Band Aid

p.133   Air Ministry Photographic Reproductions Branch, Crown copyright

p.137   © Forestry Commission

p.139   (Upper) Panos Pictures (photo by Mark Edwards); (lower) Seaphot Ltd (photo by Richard Matthews)

p.140   Icelandic Coastguard

p.143   (a) Brian Hawkes; (b) Seaphot Ltd (photo by Warren Williams)

p.145   United States Department of the Army, Washington DC

p.146   Evening Post, Reading

p.147   © Greenpeace (photo by Miller)

p.150   © United Society for the Propagation of the Gospel/MMS (photo by John Moss)

p.155   Courtesy of the Department of Library Services, American Museum of Natural History (neg. no. 335 470, photo by Logan)

p.157   The Mansell Collection

p.159   From Nature Conservancy Council, *The sea eagle* (1985)

p.162   From a painting by L.J. Watson, courtesy of the Nature Conservancy Council

p.165   Courtesy of Lady Huxley (photo by Karsh)

p.166   World Wildlife Fund (photo by Elizabeth Kempf)

p.169   The Hon. Mrs George Lane

p.170   International Council for Bird Protection

p.172   Douglas Stronach

p.186   United Nations (UN photo 146 269, Arild Vollan)

p.187   Vivamos Mejor (photo by A. Bret)

p.195   World Wildlife Fund (photo by Claude Berger)

p.200   (a) and (b) Brian Hawkes

p.203   Graficos Brunner Icad.

INDEX

Page references in **bold** type refer to illustrations in text.